MIDLOTHIAN PUBLIC LIBRARY

3 1514 00080 5961

W9-AXA-761

MIDLOTHIAN
PUBLIC LIBRARY

Midlothian
Public Library

14701 S. Kenton Ave.
Midlothian, IL 60445

DEMCO

THE WAY OF THE SAINTS

TOM COWAN

G. P. PUTNAM'S SONS

NEW YORK

THE

WAY

OF THE

SAINTS

Prayers, Practices,

and Meditations

G. P. Putnam's Sons
Publishers Since 1838
a member of
Penguin Putnam Inc.
375 Hudson Street
New York, NY 10014

Copyright © 1998 by Tom Cowan

All rights reserved. This book, or parts thereof, may not be
reproduced in any form without permission.
Published simultaneously in Canada

Library of Congress Cataloging-in-Publication Data

Cowan, Tom, date.
The way of the saints: prayers, practices, and meditations / by Tom Cowan.
p.   cm.
ISBN 0-399-14416-1 (alk. paper)
1. Christian saints—Biography.   2. Christian saints—
Prayer-books and devotions—English.   I. Title.
BX4655.2.C67   1998   98-14924 CIP
282'.092'2—dc21
[B]

Printed in the United States of America
1   3   5   7   9   10   8   6   4   2

This book is printed on acid-free paper. ∞

BOOK DESIGN BY JENNIFER ANN DADDIO

235.2

ACKNOWLEDGMENTS

Among the many people who gave support, encouragement, and ideas for this book, I especially want to thank Colleen Cannon, Diane Gibbons, Jack Maguire, Julie Merberg, and Dolores McMullan. There have also been many teachers, colleagues, and soul-friends over the years who provided valuable insights into the way of the saints through their own lives of service, love, and compassion. I am grateful to them all.

MIDLOTHIAN PUBLIC LIBRARY
14701 S. KENTON AVE.
MIDLOTHIAN, IL 60445

TO MY PARENTS

CONTENTS

THE WAY OF THE SAINTS

INTRODUCTION

The saints are men and women who have never disappeared. They look out at us from the stained-glass windows of great cathedrals, from murals, statuary, and other architectural features of chapels and churches, and in the more modest artwork found in our homes and prayerbooks. Their serene gaze observes the current generations who still struggle with the same human issues that they faced centuries before. More important, the saints have never disappeared from our consciousness. They haunt and hallow our thoughts about God, life, death, love, suffering, joy, companionship, and the meaning of human existence. The saints have gone before us in this life and into the next, but their lives continue to inspire us to seek answers to the age-old questions—questions that may never be completely resolved during anyone's lifetime, but without which life would be meaningless.

The saints were seekers of the sacred, men and women on fire with the idea of God and the ideal of perfection. As Christians they took seriously Jesus' challenge: "Be perfect as your heavenly Father is perfect." To this end, many saints radically transformed their lives to achieve holiness by means of superhuman efforts aided by divine grace. Others, however, did only common things, but they did them uncommonly well.

Yet when we look at the lives of individual saints, we find that they were far from perfect. They had faults, failings, human eccentricities, and quirks that made many of them hard to live with. But it is their striving for the lofty but impossible ideal of divine perfection that has made them unforgettable examples of the restless human spirit. They sought to transcend the earthly condition, and to some extent or other, they succeeded. Contemporaries who knew them recognized something special in their lives, and today, in the stories and legends that survive, their lives still reflect the sense of the sacred that made them saints.

We live in an age that is suspicious of perfection as a human goal. What we know about the shadow and dark areas of the human psyche tempers our belief that we can be perfect as the Creator is perfect. In our current culture, human imperfection has even become fashionable and rewarded. On talk shows and in self-promoting autobiographies, we flaunt the faults, mistakes, and imperfections that earlier ages were ashamed of. Many people today have no desire to be perfect and look upon those who worry too much about perfection as neurotic in their intolerance of human imperfections. Indeed, perfectionism—whether human or divine—can make it difficult to function happily and successfully in daily life.

But many of the saints were also neurotics, failures, and sinners, and at certain points in their lives, they even botched the basic requirements for successful living. Some, like St. Dominic of the Causeway, a twelfth-century Spanish hermit, were turned down for monastic life because they were unkempt, mentally slow, and lazy. Others, like St. Hyacintha Mariscotti, a Franciscan nun in the seventeenth century, acquired luxury items and flouted the spirit of their orders. Hyacintha was an embarrassment to her religious community. St. Marinus of Dalmatia and St. Illtud of Wales were two husbands who abandoned their wives to pursue a more devout spiritual life. In these two cases, both wives were clearly upset by their husbands' decisions. Some of the most famous saints abused their bodies to the point of illness, and some became hermits in part because they could not fit into respectable society. And yet their failings did not keep them from becoming saints.

One of the contradictions of our age is that in spite of our misgivings about trying to be perfect, there is a restless striving for personal improvement and transformation. We find this even among people who are outwardly irreligious and amoral. Our culture is obsessed with health, looks, possessions, pastimes, attitudes, clothes, and lifestyles that we hope will make us happier, more attractive, and more fulfilled. We take courses in self-improvement; read books on coping, surviving, and winning; and create personal regimens of exercise, diet, and meditation that promise to make us better human beings. And yet, ironically, we continue to believe that perfection is not a modern ideal to take seriously. We are too human for perfection.

The saints were not interested in physical health and beauty or popularity, as we are. They strived to find spiritual strength for the soul, and they cared little for the physical needs of the body. They sought eternity in time, heaven on earth, the sacred in the mundane rounds of existence. They hoped to infuse the nonordinary realities of the kingdom of heaven into the ordinary realities of daily life. Their methods may not be ours, but we can identify with their striving, and we can relate to the joys and sorrows they found in their efforts to enhance their lives. We can even understand their impatience to know and experience something of the otherworld right here in this one, for whether we are aware of it or not, even our contemporary mania for personal improvement and transformation is at heart a spiritual restlessness. Our hearts are restless until they rest in God.

Because the saints have never disappeared, they are still accessible. The idea of being a saint, after all, is to be reachable by prayer, meditation, and devotion. Saints have always been mentors, teachers, healers, and guides who help us through the struggles of life. Throughout the centuries, people have prayed to them, honored them with shrines and devotions, made pilgrimages to their graves and relics, named their children after them, and kept holy their feast days. We expect them to be silent partners in our lives, as well as active participants when we ask them to be.

People still pray to St. Anthony for help in finding lost objects, and they find them. Homeowners bury statues of St. Joseph in their yards when their houses go up for sale, and in a suspiciously short time, buyers appear. But sometimes the saints enter our reality unannounced and uninvited. Out of the blue, Joan of Arc (herself headed for sainthood) heard the voices of St. Catherine, St. Margaret, Michael the Archangel, and others, urging her to defy the gender traditions of her society and take up arms as a warrior and lead French troops against the English invaders. The saints are not just intercessors in some heavenly realm, sweetly taking petitions to God. They have always been active participants in their own right, reaching into our lives and bringing us otherworldly help when we need it, whether we like it or not.

In dreams, prayers, meditation, and ecstatic apparitions, the saints are with us. They are our spiritual ancestors, returning to be guides and teachers. Like the ancestors in many indigenous cultures, the saints are among the revered dead who continue to help us reach our goals, whether that entails acquiring divine perfection or simply making a good life for ourselves. The saints have known both goals. They are our ancestral past, the rich reservoir of wisdom we tap into to make sense of our lives and to find the spiritual consolation for which we hunger.

PEOPLE OF THEIR TIMES

Appreciating a Catholic saint of another era requires appreciating the age he or she lived in. In spite of the common humanity we all share, the saints had different worldviews from ours; the spirit of their times informed and shaped them just as the spirit of our times shapes us. We should not be alarmed that many of the saints believed and did things that we find abhorrent. Like their contemporaries, they often held values and prejudices that today we consider small-minded, intolerant, even bigoted.

Examples abound of saints who exhibited beliefs and attitudes that we would find distasteful today. Some saints, for example, were allied with the Inquisition which hunted down, imprisoned, and tortured lukewarm Catholics and even lapsed converts. Saints who were Christian missionaries, like St. Boniface, the patron of Germany, usually saw little redeeming value in the beliefs and spiritual practices of indigenous peoples and intentionally sought to undermine not only their spiritual traditions but their entire way of life. St. Josaphat, a seventeenth-century priest, worked to weaken local Eastern Orthodox traditions in what is now Ukraine by foisting Roman Catholic practices on devout Christians unwilling to give up their age-old customs. For many centuries, Church theologians denied that women had souls and argued that women healers who had not studied medicine at a university (and none were allowed to!) received their healing powers from an unholy alliance with the devil. The eighth-century saint John Damascene acquired an extensive education as a boy from an expensive slave that his father had bought to be his personal tutor. St. Ambrose, a fourth-century bishop of Milan, refused to raise money for a Jewish synagogue on the grounds that he could not support a building that would be used for "false worship."

We cannot expect the saints to live up to our current standards and ways of thinking. They lived before our time and predate our "more enlightened" attitudes. Many of them lived in societies that had very few options in thought, belief, and lifestyle. They had few or no books, no radio, television, newspapers, magazines, movies, videos, Internet, or easy airline travel to other countries. Their lives were very parochial, and they grew up with very limited choices; they could often do nothing other than what they did for the simple reason that they knew nothing else. Perhaps a century from now, our own values and practices will seem narrow-minded and wrongheaded to future generations. In reflecting on the lives of the saints, we must see them as creatures of their times, just as we are creatures of our own time.

Even some of the religious practices that appealed to the saints of another age may seem to us extreme, unnecessary, or even unhealthy and dangerous. Their methods of mortifying the body, fasting, depriving themselves of sleep, and in other ways inflicting physical pain upon themselves may fall into our category of masochism. St. Rose of Lima, for example, rubbed hot peppers into her skin to create blotches to counteract the beautiful complexion that she was born with, hoping to be less attractive to worldly eyes and to guard against vanity. Many saints held attitudes toward the human body that we might consider pathological. But their times are not ours, and attitudes about what is right and wrong, justifiable and unjustifiable, change over the years and from culture to culture.

Furthermore, most saints embodied the contradictions of their age, just as we do. They exhibited both the vices and virtues of their time and place in history. St. Magnus of Orkney, a Viking warrior, engaged in the bloodthirsty raids typical of his day, but he was also compassionate and, near the end of his life, stood up against indiscriminate killing. St. Thais, a famous Egyptian prostitute, impressed St. Paphnutius, a learned monk, with her spiritual insights and faith in God. In spite of being holy men and women, the saints did not lead lives of perfect consistency. Nor do we. Perhaps holiness does not require it.

We must accept the fact that in ways we may never fully understand, certain generations of Christians thought it was their God-given duty to wage crusades and massacre innocent people they thought of as "infidels." St. Louis—Louis IX of France—an enlightened and compassionate king, led such a crusade. Some saints saw nothing wrong in persecuting Jewish members of their own towns and communities in the belief that their ancestors were responsible for the death of Jesus. A European missionary would find it difficult, if not impossible, to understand native people in other parts of the world whose languages had no word for religion because their spiritual beliefs and practices were so intimately woven into the fabric of their daily lives they did not think of religion as a separate sphere of human activity. Hence the massive and tragic clash of cultures through mutual misunderstandings.

What today we consider prejudices, misjudgments, and atrocities were part of the lives of men and women who were sincere seekers of the sacred within the worldviews and values into which they were born. Accepting the saints as human beings with both virtues and vices, contradictions and inconsistencies, makes it easier for us to identify with them. While we seek to model our own lives on what is noblest and most praiseworthy in theirs, we can also see in them reflections of the vices and shortcomings we struggle to correct in ourselves.

MIRACLES AND THE MUNDANE

The biographies of the saints abound with miracles. St. Solange, a ninth-century French peasant girl, had a special star that shone on her during the day. Witnesses saw its light intensify when she prayed outdoors in the fields. The sixth-century saint Ia sailed from Ireland to Cornwall on a leaf that grew to the size of a boat. The Irish saint Kevin held his hand outstretched while a blackbird built its nest in it, laid eggs, hatched them, and nurtured its babies. Only when the young birds flew off did Kevin relax his hand. St. Benedict the Moor multiplied food in his sixteenth-century kitchen. Sts. Cosmas and Damian, twin physicians of the fourth century, raised the dead.

The miraculous was a normal feature of daily life for many of the men and women in the following pages. It is one of the hang-ups of our era that we don't know what to make of miracles. People living in earlier eras had fewer problems with them.

In modern times, we expect histories and biographies to be factual and therefore true. Our scientific worldview has shrunk the psychic world we live in, providing little, if any, room for miracles, so we tend to dismiss stories about the saints as untrue if they contain miraculous happenings that defy current physical laws. Are the stories true? Should we believe them?

Those questions themselves may be the wrong ones. Stories are just stories. The truth of someone's life does not depend on scientifically verifiable facts. There is more than one mode of belief, more than one way of knowing the truth. The men and women who became saints were genuinely loved for what they represented as much as for what they did. The stories about them, even if they strain our modern sensibilities about ordinary reality, nevertheless reveal something real, a reality that transcends the natural world and for which the saint is loved in the first place.

Men and women who were contemporaries of the saints told stories about them to express the spiritual truths that their lives embodied. These early storytellers lived in an age when fiction, nonfiction, biography, and the memoir were not as systematically distinguished and constructed as they are today. Both oral and written accounts of the saints' lives blended the natural and the supernatural. Writers and storytellers did not restrict their stories to what we today would call historical events.

Earlier generations recognized the reality of mythical events, incidents that play a critical role in understanding the truth about a given individual. Stories about a person are parts of a mosaic that depicts the human soul, not segments of a videotaped documentary that records only a person's physical words and acts. The greater truth of a saint's life depends on the events that take place in non-ordinary reality as much as it does on those that occur in ordinary reality.

The concept of ordinary and nonordinary reality is important in our thinking about the saints. Dreams, visions, healings, synchronicities, contacts with the deceased, the workings of subatomic particles, and what we call miracles take place in a reality that defies logical understanding. The saints lived in that nonordinary reality. In fact, otherworldly realities were actually more important and real to the saints than the merely physical world and its realities. The saints always lived in more than one world. They were "walkers between the worlds," crossing the betwixt-and-between realms where the unexplainable occurs, where miracles do happen. Saints are still walkers between the worlds. Miracles still happen.

Only in modern times have we lost the capacity to understand reality—and truth—with the intuitive, nonlogical, mythical powers of the mind. An exaggerated dependence on rational, linear thinking prevents many of us from even entertaining the idea of the miraculous. We forget that in an earlier age the best minds of their times—Galileo, Newton, Bacon, Shakespeare, Descartes—could understand creation with both astronomy and astrology, chemistry and alchemy, mathematics and mystical numbers, history and mythology, the evolving scientific method and old-fashioned prayer. Science and spirit always have been, and still are, partners in the maintenance of what we call reality. Science and spirit have always been necessary to understand the totality of existence.

So to ask if the stories are true, if the miracles really happened, if the supernatural can break through into the natural in the saints' lives—or in ours—misses the point. How could holy men and women who live in more than one reality *not* create around themselves the conditions in which the extraordinary and the miraculous occur?

BECOMING A SAINT

How did the men and women in this book become saints?

Since the time when Jesus walked upon the Earth, many of his followers have been honored with sainthood, but they have not all achieved that status through the same process. Over the centuries, there have been three distinct methods by which men and women were elevated to the position of saints.

In the earliest years, anyone who was put to death for witnessing to the teachings of Jesus was considered a saint. A martyr was thought to be automatically admitted into the heavenly kingdom and to be henceforth in the presence of God. The Greek word "martyr" means witness, and the greatest act of witnessing was to lose one's life for the faith. Laying down one's life for another was also, as Jesus himself taught, the greatest act of love. The first saints were people so in love with God and the new teachings of Jesus that they were willing to die for their beliefs.

As time went on, some individuals became saints through popular acclaim. They may not have been martyrs, but by their lives they witnessed to the same love and faith that the earlier saints witnessed to by their deaths. Recognized as holy women and men during their lifetimes, they were considered saints by their contemporaries both before and after their deaths. They were heroic spiritual members of their towns, regions, and communities. They were respected and loved for their holiness of life, the miracles they performed, their contributions to the poor and suffering, their preaching and advice, and their friendship and companionship on the spiritual path. At their deaths or shortly thereafter, they were acknowledged as saints. And even after death, their presence was felt among their survivors. They appeared in dreams and visions, spoke words of encouragement to those who prayed and meditated on their lives, and continued to perform miracles at their shrines and graves.

In 1170, the path to sainthood took a sharp turn. Determining saints became a prerogative of the Roman Catholic Church. Pope Alexander III declared that the only official saints were those recognized and approved by the Church. From then on, legates from the pope traveled across Europe to determine whether saintly men and women of a region or district far from Rome qualified for sainthood. In the fourteenth century, a legal procedure, called canonization, was instituted to determine who would or would not become a saint.

Canonization required petitions from the candidate's family, friends, or supporters; specific approval for the canonization process to begin; the collecting of evidence from the candidate's life; officially recognized miracles attributed to the saint; written treatises; formal presentations before a tribunal; and a sort of trial in which a cleric known as the devil's advocate argued against granting sainthood to each individual. Only when the legal process had fulfilled all the current requirements would the Church honor a man or woman as a saint. The entire process could take years or centuries after the saint's death.

The Roman Catholic Church has always been concerned with the moral lives of its members, and under the process of canonization, the candidates for sainthood needed to be shining examples of virtue and moral rectitude in order to serve as models for others. Saints had always been larger than life in some sacred way, but as we have been noting, many had their faults and failings. Seekers of the sacred could and did have human imperfections. But since the Church's selection of candidates for canonization was dominated by priests, monks, and nuns, it seemed to imply that a particular lifestyle was the sine qua non for the saintly life. The vows of poverty, chastity, and obedience were virtually requirements for seekers of the sacred who were heroic enough to become saints.

Although the Church never said that laypeople could not seek and find the sacred in their lives, it implied that it would be difficult for them to become canonized saints by doing so. A far better candidate for canonization was the person with a commitment to the priestly or religious life. The commitment itself constituted the heroism the Church expected in saints. The lifestyle of the lay Christian, which did not include that commitment, seldom seemed to nurture saints, judging by the few lay saints and the vast majority of canonized saints who were clergymen, monastics, or members of religious orders.

SELECTING SAINTS FOR OUR TIMES

In selecting the men and women for this book, I followed certain guidelines. My selection was a personal one, determined by criteria that I believed would create a useful and enjoyable book.

In general, I chose saints who are interesting in some way for modern readers and can inspire readers to deepen their own spiritual lives. Paradoxically, the reasons for including them, and the features of their lives emphasized in these short biographical essays, may not be the reasons for which they became saints in the first place or reflect the areas and concerns for which they are the traditional patrons. It seemed to me more important to take a fresh look at these men and women in order to see them as realistic models for a modern spiritual life rather than to repeat the standard and official accounts of their lives, which can focus on aspects that do not inspire or that seem irrelevant to contemporary spiritual needs. For example, St. Joseph of Cupertino is best known for his ability to levitate, or fly, but my entry on him, while acknowledging that characteristic, emphasizes his more ordinary, human quality of laziness. St. Patrick is best known as the patron saint of Ireland, but my essay focuses on the intimate relationship he had with a spirit companion he called Victor.

Here are the four criteria that shaped my selection:

First, I wanted to include as many of the major saints as possible, because they are the most popular and the ones that many readers would expect to find in a book such as this. Nevertheless, some of the most famous saints are not in the following pages, in order to allow room for others whose lives would appeal more easily to modern readers. I also omitted major saints if the circumstances of their lives tended to replicate the lives of other saints whom I did include.

Second, I chose saints who fulfilled my general guidelines of being interesting examples of the spiritual issues that concern modern men and women, even if many readers might find them obscure and unfamiliar. I also tended to favor a more obscure saint over a better-known one if his or her life exhibited unique circumstances that would give the book variety and make for more interesting reading. As I went along, I actually developed a curious "mission" to retrieve these "lost" saints, who seldom get included in current literature.

Third, I tried to include a good number of saints who lived in the modern age—that is, since the Renaissance—in order to balance those who lived in the first centuries after Jesus and in the Middle Ages, eras that are so remote from our own that we are less able to identify with them. For some readers, even saints who lived in the seventeenth or eighteenth century will seem remote, but at least they are living under conditions that we can recognize as similar to our own: a scientific worldview; a growing secularization of society; increasing urbanization with its problems for the poor; the rise of hospitals, schools, and other civic institutions that the Church complemented with its own; the horrors of modern warfare.

Fourth, I tried to include as many laypeople as possible to balance the overwhelming majority of saints who are priests, bishops, nuns, monks, and brothers. Laypeople have always found it difficult to accept as effective models for holiness the saints whose lives were circumscribed by vows of poverty, chastity, and obedience and whose daily activities followed the rules of a religious community. While the religious life was the ideal of the Church, it is seen as unattainable for many laypeople and for that reason a good excuse for not trying to live up to it. In many cases, my essays emphasize the years that some saints lived in the world as laypeople before becoming members of religious orders for the same reason.

THE ROLE OF THE CHURCH IN EARLIER CENTURIES

Perhaps a word about the importance of the institutional Church in European society is in order to give a perspective on the men and women who joined it in an official capacity. We tend to forget that next to the castle, the Church was the major social, economic, cultural, and political force in Europe up to modern times. Church officials were the movers and shakers of the centuries that spanned the end of the Roman Empire down to the emergence of the modern state and secular institutions. The bishops, archbishops, abbots, and abbesses who ran the major ecclesiastical institutions were, for all practical purposes, the major landowners next to the noble classes. In some places, Church property and wealth exceeded that of the nobility.

Ecclesiastical institutions were the major economic developers of their day. A well-run monastery plowed fields, grew important crops, raised domestic livestock, brewed beer, made wine, harvested healing herbs, provided medical help to the sick, and produced medicine and pharmacological products, as well as the major foodstuffs on which the population of the surrounding area depended. Monasteries also sent monks to distant areas to begin the process of settlement by clearing fields and bringing new land under cultivation. Monasteries were involved in nonagricultural pursuits as well. For example, the monastery of St. Peter in Salzburg, Austria, gave financial assistance to the salt mines in Hallein. In many ways that we no longer remember, the institutional Church was involved in the major economic activities of the day.

The Church's monasteries and abbeys also served as centers of learning, collecting books that became the only libraries for miles around. Scholars, writers, and researchers flocked to monasteries as today people flock to the best colleges and universities. The monastery was an important research center for agriculture, medicine, metalwork, and other scientific pursuits. Some monasteries gained a reputation as patrons of the arts, enticing painters, sculptors, architects, glassblowers, weavers, and other artists and craftspeople who wanted to learn and perfect their skill. A boy or girl who wanted the rudiments of education studied at a monastery school. Drama, music, song, and theatrical performances of many kinds were sponsored by the Church.

Last, many monasteries were veritable towns, rivaling the smaller villages that grew up around the base of the mountain or hill on which they were built. A large monastic complex included churches, chapels, administrative buildings, overnight lodging for pilgrims and travelers, dining rooms, kitchens, hospital facilities, stables, storehouses, and many types of workshops. Joining the religious life was a means of plugging oneself into the most dynamic enterprise of the day.

Which brings us to the reasons that many men and women—the saints in this book—became monks, nuns, canons, clergy, and administrative officials in the Roman Catholic Church. Obviously we like to think of their decisions as pure "vocations" as that term is traditionally defined by the Church: a calling from God to lead a more devout and nonworldly life. Certainly many individuals felt that call and responded primarily out of spiritual motives. But we must not overlook the more "secular" motives for becoming a religious, nor forget that the Creator works through and with Creation, and has always used average, human motivation to call people to certain ways of life, including the religious life. Secular motives and spiritual motives for becoming a nun or priest can dwell in the same human heart.

The medieval Church actually offered something for everyone. For many women, life as a nun was the only alternative to an arranged marriage or a life greatly circumscribed by the opportunities of one's family. Throughout most of Western history, a woman was forced to live her entire life under the protection and responsibility of a man, whether that be a husband, father, brother, uncle, or son. Independent living for a woman was not an option until the twentieth century. An important convent in the region, perhaps even at an exciting crossroads of European commercial and intellectual life, was an attractive outlet for women of independent thought and with creative and adventurous life goals.

Because the Church was so influential in all areas of European society, it offered logical careers for many men and women of the upper classes, who by law could often not inherit or command their family estates if they had older siblings or if their parents were still alive. As executives and administrators of powerful ecclesiastical offices, they found a niche for which their education and upbringing prepared them and for which they felt entitled.

Ironically, the Church could also provide an outlet for the upper- or middle-class person who wanted to drop out of society. Francis of Assisi is perhaps the best-known example of this desire, refusing to live as the son of a prosperous town merchant and choosing instead the life of an essentially homeless beggar. From the earliest days of Christianity, many men and women have made the choice to live as hermits who in time might become the administrators of small monastic communities living simply, poorly, and isolated from the world's turmoil.

The Church also offered advancement in society for the sons and daughters of lower working-class families. Many saints came from farming and working-class environments where career prospects were bleak. They knew they would most probably live and die in the same condition as their parents and grandparents before them. Joining the priesthood or a religious community was a way to move up in the world. Sometimes these individuals rose rapidly in the Church because of their innate talents and practical skills, which were required to run Church institutions.

Every age has its misfits, its bohemian dropouts who will never be part of society. Some of these people lack the intelligence, personal qualities, or emotional stability to live as respectable and useful members of society. Others, for various reasons, refuse to do so. The Church was an outlet for them as well, some living as obscure and humble members of religious orders, others choosing the isolated life of a solitary hermit. Some of the hermits were never recognized by the Church as official monastics, while others received approval for their communities and rules of order. So, ironically, the most important institution in its day, the Roman Catholic Church, was a haven for people who might be classified by others as the "cream of the crop" as well as the "dregs of society." God calls his saints from all conditions of human life.

Lastly, the monastic communities offered retirement options for many people, especially women. When husbands died, children moved on, and old age set in, some women chose the all-female world of the convent as a place to find peace and quiet to live their final years (which in earlier centuries might begin somewhere in their mid- to late thirties). Life in many monasteries was quite pleasant, with food, medical care, companionship, and the knowledge that one was living a holy lifestyle in his or her last years. It was a chance to make up for previous sins and failings and an opportunity to live the loftiest ideals as defined by the Church.

PRAYERS AND DEVOTIONAL PRACTICES

Their great love for God lured the saints into lives of prayer and spiritual devotions, practices that expressed and nourished their faith. Prayer and devotional practices also gave their lives structure, so that the ordinary rounds of the day were imbued with spiritual significance and moments of intense awareness and mindfulness of God. Their devotions, both private and public, spilled over into the services they performed for their communities, friends, families, and the less fortunate members of society. Each entry in this book is accompanied by a prayer and a devotional practice, which are intended to express and nurture your own spiritual life and enrich your own community of family, friends, and acquaintances.

Some of the prayers and practices reflect traditional Catholic activities, but I have tried to present them in terms that non-Catholic readers will find meaningful as well. Many prayers and practices are neutral in terms of specific religious orthodoxy but are based on the time-honored spiritual activities found the world over in many cultures and spiritual traditions. Using core, universal practices makes it possible to accommodate a wider variety of beliefs and values than the more narrowly Catholic ones, which may not be part of the spiritual lives of some readers. The neutrality in wording will allow each reader to add the gloss of his or her specific religious traditions and sentiments.

I have tried to focus on modern and universal spiritual practices and aspirations but to present them in the style of the saint for which they are written. In this way, readers can incorporate the saint as a model or pattern of the sacred without feeling that they must imitate a given saint or even approve of everything the saint stood for. Unless the saints-as-models-of-the-sacred are flexible and adaptable, they will not speak to our age. They will remain lifeless icons that seem as frozen and silent as artists' renditions of them in statues and stained-glass windows. Instead, we hope that they will be intimate and ever-present companions from the spirit world, accompanying us on our journeys through life.

Some of the devotional practices make use of traditional objects such as candles, incense, statues, holy pictures, and shrines, and they incorporate traditional activities such as fasting, pilgrimages, night vigils, spiritual reading, examination of conscience, and the recitation of prayers. Other practices are similar to the many techniques for self-development and personal improvement that have become popular in recent years. Some are intended to expand the readers' awareness of the world, society, nature, and the possibility of finding the divine presence in Creation. All the practices, whether they seem to be traditional religious activities or not, should be done in a devotional spirit that creates a moment or two of reflection and awareness in the course of a busy life.

Aristotle tells us that image is the language of the soul. Through imagery our souls communicate with us, and allow us to communicate with other spiritual beings. The Catholic tradition has always honored this need for the human soul to be nurtured by imagery that represents spiritual realities. The interiors of churches and the lavish ceremonies and liturgies of traditional Catholicism are rich with symbol and image. Many of the devotional practices in this book use physical objects such as stones, water, incense, photographs, flowers, and clothing because as images, they speak to our souls. They stimulate and reveal the workings of the interior life. When we use objects from the natural and cultural worlds we live in, we make them "sacred," which is the root meaning of the word "sacrifice"—to make sacred. To paraphrase the sentiments of Antoine de St. Exupéry's Little Prince, they are natural objects like a million others, but we have blessed them, and now they are unique in all the world.

The use of a shrine or sacred place is also a traditional Catholic practice. Many of the devotional practices in this book assume that you have such a place. If not, find or create one. It can be as simple as a corner of a dresser or desk, a small table by a window, or an outdoor nook in a garden or grotto. You can designate the place with the traditional religious crucifix, statue, and candle, or develop a place that reflects the beauty of nature: a stone, seashell, vase of flowers, bowl of rainwater. It can be a place that you change in no recognizable way except by your intention, so that it is known only to you. When we use the same place regularly in our spiritual practice, it gathers power, and simply by going to it and being in its presence, we create that reflective state of consciousness conducive to meditation and spiritual awakening.

HOW TO USE THIS BOOK

I have not tried to find a saint for every day of the year. Many of the saints share the same feast day, and it would require choosing one and rejecting the others. Also, the official saint for a given day may not fulfill my guidelines—that he or she be interesting and inspirational for the modern reader.

Here are some suggestions for using the book:

As a practice of spiritual reading, read one saint a day to discover the great diversity of personalities and styles of spiritual seeking. Mark the ones that particularly inspire you, and come back to them for meditation or reflection. Since the essays are short, you may want to find and read longer biographies of the saints that appeal to you.

My sources for the biographical essays were Alban Butler's *Lives of the Saints,* John J. Delaney's *Pocket Dictionary of Saints,* Clemens Jockle's *Encyclopedia of Saints,* Woodeene Koenig-Brocker's *365 Saints,* and Victor Hoagland's *The Book of Saints,* as well as articles and essays from other books on the saints. Most biographies of the saints rely on Butler's massive volumes, which have been updated regularly since they were originally published over two hundred years ago. There are also many recent, modern publications dealing with the lives of the saints that are suitable for further study and reflection.

You can consult the calendar in the back of this book, which lists the saints according to the month in which their feastdays occur, and then read those entries for the current month.

Obviously, you cannot do all the devotional practices in the book, nor will you want to. Even a hermit or a monastic would probably go crazy trying to attempt them all. But by reading them you will get a sense of how to incorporate activities like them into your life. You may discover ones that attract you even though the saints that accompany them do not particularly inspire you. Feel free to adapt them to your own spiritual needs. Consider them models and create similar ones that better fit your own spiritual life.

Some saints are associated with certain seasons and times of the year. Often their feast days coincide with that time. You can check the calendar to see whether the saints who are honored around those times offer inspiration, and, if so, you can incorporate them into your rituals or ceremonies.

On important days in your life—such as birthdays, death days, anniversaries, or any other special event or milestone—look to see if the saint for that day (or near that day) has some relevance. Often there are synchronicities between the saints for a given day and the high points of our own lives.

Similarly, a saint with the same name as someone important to you may provide insights into that person or your relationship. Sometimes knowing the life pattern of the saint can enhance your appreciation of the person who has the same name.

The idea of a saint is quite remarkable—that a human being so lived that the power and goodness of God was seen in that individual while alive, and that after death the person still connects the human community to God in mysterious ways. Intelligent and thoughtful people throughout the centuries have valued the saints as examples and models for living a spiritual life. Not every saint has appealed, or will appeal, to every person's sense of sainthood, for everyone has personal standards of holiness that an individual saint might not attain. But taken as a whole, the company of Christian saints offers a rich panoply of inspiration for people who seek the sacred in their own lives.

All cultures have some concept similar to the saints. It is most likely part of the human psyche and imagination to recognize in certain people some special quality that singles them out from others, some blessing of divine power and grace that connects them to the realm of spirit. People everywhere have created ritual and ceremony to honor the memory of those special human beings in the belief that they have not faded into oblivion. The ancestral past is still alive in the present age. The ancestors are still with us.

The Christian saints are our ancestors in several ways. Many lived in the same regions that our families are from, so there conceivably could be, unbeknownst to us, actual bloodlines with some of them. As members of a culture heavily influenced by Christianity, we can recognize and appreciate the saints' efforts to put into practice the values, beliefs, and attitudes that Jesus taught two thousand years ago and that have continued to make sense over the years, even as the times changed and continue to change. Our heritage, whether familial or cultural, includes these men and women.

The saints are important links in the great chain of humanity that stretches from the beginning of human life far into the future, when all of Creation will pass into the divine presence at the end of time. As links in this chain, we share the responsibility to keep alive the memories of those who have gone before us and to pass on their beliefs and practices to the coming generations. In this way, we, along with the saints, strengthen the continuity of human history.

In the accounts of the saints, we find men and women whose lives shone with their love for God, whose sense of the sacred was found in the life and teachings of Jesus, whose noblest desire was to do more with their lives than was required or expected according to the standards of their times. When we find inspiration for our own spiritual practice in the prayers and practices of the saints, we too can do more with our lives than is expected by our society. We can leave our stamp upon the world and make it a better place in which to live. We can create in our own lives a sense of the sacred that may inspire others to anticipate the joy and happiness that the Creator has prepared for us.

In ways that may seem improbable to us, we are the next generation of saints, the next generation of men and women who will never disappear.

ST. ABRAHAM KIDUNAIA

"A homeless man famous for holiness and bad odor."

SIXTH CENTURY

MARCH 16

On the last day of the seven-day marriage ceremony arranged by his wealthy parents (who also selected his bride), Abraham Kidunaia fled into the desert and hid. Obviously upset, his parents organized a search party, which eventually found the wayward groom lost in prayer. The young Mesopotamian clearly did not want to get married. In fact, he had always felt called to a celibate life and had only gone along with his parents' wishes to please them. Now that was over. They soon gave up trying to get him to come home.

Abraham stayed in the desert, built a cell, and lived as a hermit. When his parents died, he had his inheritance distributed to the poor. His own possessions were extremely sparse: a cloak, a bowl for food and drink, a woven mat to sleep on, and a goatskin garment that would become famous, and smelly. Over the next fifty years, Abraham never changed the goatskin that he wore as his primary article of clothing.

According to a biographer, Abraham was never seen to smile, and he considered each day to be his last. The local bishop, recognizing a saintly though eccentric man, ordained him a priest, and Abraham began a career of preaching to unbelievers, somewhat against his will. His sermonizing was intense. He preached with great excitement, harangued his listeners, destroyed their sacred places, and acted crazy. He was frequently kicked, stoned, dragged away, and beaten unconscious. Many considered him to be a dangerous, homeless man who smelled bad and kept coming back for more abusive treatment.

In time, Abraham mellowed, and he softened his presentations, and some people began to accept him as one of "God's fools." He made some conversions.

Eventually, however, he left the community and found his refuge in the desert, where he could spend his time in prayer. When he was about to die, at age seventy, he had the reputation of being a holy man, and many people rushed out to hear his final words and be blessed. They also tried to take scraps of his clothing back home with them as relics.

PRAYER

Abraham, if you were alive today on the streets of our cities, we would treat you like a dirty, homeless man. Most of us would shun you. Many would fear you. Give me the insight to look at the homeless as human beings like myself. Let me see in them the same potential for prayer, devotion, and gentleness that is in all of us. Help me to help them.

DEVOTIONAL PRACTICE

The beggar's bowl is both a physical reality among the poor and a spiritual symbol of our neediness. Fasting is a method for experiencing that neediness in a physical way. Select a small cereal bowl before you go to bed and place a flower and some water in it. Begin your fast in the morning by making the intention that your hunger will be a form of prayer for the homeless in your area. Eat nothing all day. In the evening, remove the flower and water, and limit your dinner to the amount of food that will fit in the bowl.

ST. ADAMNAN

"Visualize peace."

C. 624–704

SEPTEMBER 23

Up until the seventh century, the Celtic peoples had a strong tradition of women warriors. Some of the best martial-arts instructors in Celtic history were women, and many of the great male heroes and warriors studied with them. Women even led armies into battle, such as Boudicca, the Celtic leader who fought the Romans in Britain. But traditions were changing, and the Western world was moving away from the notion of women taking active part in warfare. Adamnan, the ninth abbot of Iona, was instrumental in bringing about this shift.

Adamnan was born in Donegal and eventually settled on Iona, at the monastery founded by Columba. He visited Aldfrith, king of Northumbria, to arrange the release of Irish prisoners. While he was there, churchmen who were more Romanized convinced him of the need to get the Celtic monasteries in line with the Roman Catholic Church on a number of issues, an important one being the method for determining the date of Easter each year. Adamnan returned to Iona to reform the community, but Columba's Celtic practices were too entrenched and the monks there were too independent and Celtic at heart to kowtow to the Roman calendar and other practices. Adamnan realized his failure, and returned to Ireland.

Back home, Adamnan continued his mission to eliminate older, more traditional Celtic customs. He attended the Council of Birr, where the question of women warriors was discussed. Under his leadership the council adopted a strong statement attempting to create "rules of warfare," which included the provision that women should not fight in war and that women and children should not be killed or taken prisoner by enemy forces. The rule was called "Adamnan's Law."

Adamnan returned to Iona and wrote a biography of its founder, Columba, which is one of the most extensive early-medieval documents to survive. He also recorded the reminiscences of a Frankish bishop, named Arculf, who traveled extensively in the Holy Land. Adamnan died on Iona in 704.

PRAYER

Help me to work toward peace, Adamnan, in whatever ways I can. I pray for the men, women, and children suffering in war-torn countries today, especially those taken prisoner by their enemies.

DEVOTIONAL PRACTICE

The slogan "Visualize world peace" makes a lot of sense when we consider how influential thoughts and feelings are in producing the world we live in. Obviously, the move to protect mothers and children from the horrors of war began in the minds and hearts of men and women before it became an accepted (if not always practiced) rule of modern warfare.

Occasionally, use your meditation time to visualize world peace. Try to see families and communities working together peacefully. Don't just think about this in your head, but also feel in your heart the joys and blessings that come when you are with friends and amicable acquaintances and there is no strife, competition, or enmity. Have great faith that these moments of visualizing world peace are productive.

STS. AGAPE, CHIONIA, AND IRENE

"Possessors of subversive books."

D. 304

APRIL 3

As part of the emperor Diocletian's persecution of Christians, a decree went out making it a crime punishable by death to have or read the sacred literature that was becoming standard scriptures for the new faith. Three sisters—Agape, Chionia, and Irene—had the forbidden texts. So they hid them and read them in secret. The young women became experts in deception. No one, it seems, knew about their clandestine and subversive activities.

But the sisters were arrested for another charge that was also part of the crackdown on Christians. It was a custom in the empire to sacrifice meat to the gods and then consume the meat in a ritual meal. When the girls refused to eat the ritual meal, they were arrested. At that point, their house was searched, and the forbidden scriptures were discovered.

At their trial Agape and Chionia answered the attacks upon them with clever rebuttals that infuriated the authorities. When asked if they had "books, papers, or writings relating to the religion of the impious Christians," they replied, "We have none. The emperor has taken them from us." The two women were condemned and burned at the stake.

Then Irene was questioned. She too kept great composure under the ordeal. When asked, "Who persuaded you to hide these books?" she answered, "God." Then she was asked who knew about these hidden books. "God," she replied. Then she was asked about their flight into the mountains, where the three hid out during the persecution. "Who fed you up there?" her inquisitor asked. "God," she replied. "He provides food for all creatures." Then she was asked if anyone in her neighborhood knew about the hidden books. "Inquire in the neighborhood and make your search," she suggested.

Clearly, Irene's answers were not calculated to please her enemies. The governor decided that her punishment should be more torturing than her sisters'. First, she was sent to a house of prostitution to humiliate her, and then she was shot through the throat with an arrow.

PRAYER

Agape, Chionia, and Irene, you showed great courage in the face of horrible deaths. Had you lived in other times, your sacred scriptures would not have gotten you in trouble with the authorities. I am grateful that I live in an open society where I am free to read and believe what I want. Help those today who live under governments that restrict the freedom to read, write, speak, and believe according to one's conscience.

DEVOTIONAL PRACTICE

It is good to remind ourselves of the freedoms we so often take for granted. For the next book you read, get a postcard or photograph to use as a bookmark that will remind you of the freedom you have to read whatever you wish. It might be an illustration that depicts something related to your own country's defense of freedom or an illustration that depicts a repressive society where human freedoms are not respected or protected. Either way, each time you open this book to read, offer a prayer of thanks for your life and a prayer of courage for those who must read under the threat of punishment.

ST. AGNES

"Lamb of God."

D. C. 304

JANUARY 21

The culture of the Roman Empire was based on strong family ties. Loyal wives and mothers, civic-minded fathers, healthy children, and the conservative family values that cemented these relationships all worked toward producing a dynamic society. In its youthful years, Roman society put its stamp on the entire Mediterranean world. Much of its power and success was due to the large Roman population produced by the commitment to and glorification of family life. But life expectancy at birth during these years was only twenty-five. This meant that for women, there was stong pressure to marry early and have, on the average, five children. The Empire required it.

Some women, however, had other plans.

When Christianity spread through Roman societies, it promoted the celibate life, an option that appealed to many young girls and women. They vowed not to marry. Agnes, the daughter of a wealthy Roman family, chose this route. A spectacularly beautiful girl, she took a vow of celibacy at thirteen, the age when parents began to find suitable husbands for their daughters. When word got out that she had vowed not to marry, it became public knowledge that she was a Christian.

During the persecution under the emperor Diocletian, citizens would denounce one another for Christian sentiments. Agnes was so denounced by the suitors whom she refused to marry. Eventually she was taken before the authorities, where she was shown the instruments of torture. Unflinching, she remained steadfast in her faith. Since she could not be intimidated by physical pain, the governor decided to inflict her with another sort of pain. She was sent to a house of prostitution.

Remarkably, Agnes preserved her virginity while living with the community of prostitutes, and when word of this got back to the governor, he summoned her before him again. Accounts differ as to how she met her death. She was either beheaded or stabbed through the throat.

Agnes was buried on the Via Nomentana, where a church dedicated to her still stands. Since her name means "lamb," the thirteen-year-old Agnes is frequently depicted in artwork with a lamb, a symbol of virginal innocence.

PRAYER

Agnes, bless the children today who are confused about the right decisions to make for themselves. There are so many options and temptations, and so much conflicting advice, that young people are understandably frustrated and uncertain about what they should do. May your spirit encourage at least one child today and put him or her on the right path.

DEVOTIONAL PRACTICE

Say the prayer above whenever you see a school bus go by, or schoolchildren walking along the street. You might also look at the children as they pass, and let your inner sight show you a specific child who is having trouble either at home, at school, or with friends, and then offer the prayer for her or him.

ST. AIDAN

"The wandering gift-giver."

D. 651

AUGUST 31

The Northumbrian king Oswald wanted Irish missionaries to convert the non-Christian people living in his realm. So the Irish monk Aidan was consecrated a bishop and arrived in the kingdom in 635. He founded his monastery on Lindisfarne, and from there he traveled to meet people and tell them about the Christian faith.

Located off the eastern English coast, Lindisfarne becomes an island twice a day when the tide is in. At other times it is connected to the mainland. Aidan seems to have been following the Celtic love of places that are betwixt and between, locations that are neither this nor that—places that have always held a special spiritual fascination for the Celtic imagination as being between the worlds.

Aidan is remembered for many virtues and strong, powerful teaching, but one of his most endearing traits was his love of strangers and his generosity. Like many early monastics, he cared little for riches, comfort, or possessions. In fact, he was known to give away gifts almost as soon as he had received them. On one occasion, King Oswin gave Aidan one of the best horses in his stable. Although Aidan usually walked, he rode now and then when he was in a hurry. On the first trip out with the horse, Aidan met a beggar asking for alms. He dismounted and gave the horse to the poor man.

Later Oswin questioned Aidan about the reasonableness of that gesture. "We have lots of horses that are not as well bred or expensive as the one I gave you. Couldn't you have given the man a less valuable horse?" he asked. Aidan reminded the king that the horse was not more valuable than the poor man who received it. When the king recalled these words that night at dinner after he had come back from hunting, he took off his sword and gave it to one of his retainers for having helped him during the day. He went over to Aidan and said that from now on he would never question the price or worth of any gift that Aidan wanted to give to the poor, even if the gift came fom the king's own store.

Usually Aidan did not ride horses. He preferred to travel on foot as he traversed the land far and wide to preach the Gospel. One reason for this was that he wanted to be able to meet strangers face-to-face and on their own terms. He could go up to people on the road, whether they were rich or poor, and talk to them without having to dismount and make a stiffer, more formal introduction. Aidan saw himself like other walkers and wanderers, traveling simply and steadily through life.

When Aidan died, he was, as usual, outdoors on a mission. He had been living in a tent near an estate where he was preaching. Probably feeling that the end was near, he leaned against the outside buttress of the church and expired.

PRAYER

Aidan, help me to be less greedy about receiving gifts. In fact, inspire me to give away gifts that I don't really need as you did.

DEVOTIONAL PRACTICE

We often get more gifts than we need and feel compelled to keep them out of some sense of honor to the people who give them to us. But if a gift is given freely with no strings attached, it should be yours to do with as you want. On your next birthday, anniversary, or Christmas, promise yourself that you will give at least one gift away within the week before you use it. You can give it to some friend or acquaintance who would enjoy having it. And you don't have to tell the giver what you have done with it.

ST. ALBERT CHMIELOWSKI

"A disabled freedom fighter and artist."

1845–1916

JUNE 17

Adam Chmielowski joined the uprising against the Russian occupation of Poland in 1863. He was captured and spent time in a Russian prison, where he had to have his leg amputated. After the revolt failed, the disabled freedom fighter returned home. His former interests of agricultural studies and engineering gave way to art, and he became a well-known artist, exhibiting his work for the first time in 1870.

But Chmielowski's life was missing something important, and in 1880, he entered the Society of Jesus. Within six months, he had a nervous breakdown and left the order. He found a more congenial life as a Franciscan tertiary, working with the poor. As his commitment to a life of service increased, he found less and less time for his painting, and eventually gave it up.

When he was forty-three, Chmielowski donned the religious habit to live a more fully religious life, and took the name Albert. Like his fellow freedom fighter, Rafal Kalinowski, who had joined the Carmelites, Chmielowski embarked on a life more committed to the service of others.

To carry out this mission, Chmielowski founded the Albertine Order, with separate congregations for men and women. The Albertine brothers and sisters continue to work among the poor and homeless in Poland.

When he died, Chmielowski's fame as a public servant and deeply religious man drew great crowds to his funeral, where he was honored by both the mayor and bishop of Cracow. His reputation continued after him. In 1938 he was posthumously awarded Poland's highest honor, the Grand Ribbon of the Order of Poland Restituta. Later, a fellow Pole, Pope John Paul II, wrote a play about the former freedom fighter, artist, founder of a religious order, and servant of the poor. It was entitled *Our God's Brother*. The same pope would also canonize Chmielowski in 1989.

PRAYER

Albert, you lost a leg in fighting for the freedom of your nation. Remind me that any worthy cause has its price, and sometimes the price can be high. Give me the strength and commitment to fight for freedom wherever I see the need, especially where it will help the poor and the powerless, who may not be able to fight for themselves.

DEVOTIONAL PRACTICE

Every day people die fighting for freedom. Create a "freedom altar" in your home, a simple nook where you can place a candle. Whenever you see an article in a newspaper or magazine about the struggle for freedom anywhere in the world, cut it out and place it in front of the candle, and light the candle with the intention that God view your action as a sign of your solidarity with the oppressed and suffering people of the world. Replace each article whenever you find a new one.

ST. ALBERT THE GREAT

"A rigorous mind lost in Alzheimer's disease."

C. 1206–1280

NOVEMBER 15

By the time he died, Albert the Great had written the equivalent of thirty-eight books on the following topics: biology, chemistry, physics, astronomy, botany, mineralogy, geography (with proof that the world was round), alchemy, logic, metaphysics, mathematics, theology, human and animal physiology, and the Bible. He was also a student of Arabic culture. But for all the knowledge that filled his mind and thoughts throughout his long life, he spent his last two years sinking deeper and deeper into what may have been Alzheimer's disease.

Albert was the eldest son of the Count of Bollstadt in Germany. He studied at the University of Padua and became a Dominican monk. Over the course of his academic life, he taught in Cologne, Hildesheim, Freiburg im Breisgau, Regensburg, and Strasbourg. Among his students was Thomas Aquinas, the great scholasticist of the Middle Ages, who greatly influenced Catholic philosophy and theology up into our own time. The two men were also close friends.

Albert's great contribution to Western learning was to weld Aristotelian logic to Catholic theology, giving the latter the same intellectual rigor as science. In the process he created the scholastic method that would come to dominate Catholic education. It was this methodology that Thomas Aquinas would perfect and bequeath to the Church.

Because so many of the natural sciences in Albert's day were still rooted in spiritual understanding, he acquired the reputation of being a great magician as well as a great scholar. For example, astrology and alchemy were still reputable disciplines in the Middle Ages and would be for several centuries, until the scientific revolution, with its narrow focus on only physical realities, would lure scholars away from the spiritual dimension of these disciplines. But Albert is a great example of how magic, science, and religion are interwoven, and his understanding in all three perspectives enhanced his brilliance.

In 1278 while in Paris defending the teachings of his student and friend, Aquinas, Albert suffered a memory lapse during a lecture. It was the first rumbling of the quake that would shake and shatter his great body of knowledge from active recall. Over the next two years, his loss of memory became severe. He died calmly sitting among his brethren in Cologne.

PRAYER

Albert, grant me the patience to deal compassionately with my own lapses of memory, as well as those I see in people around me. Keep me mindful that memory loss is not a sign of ignorance, and should not be the occasion for anger or hostility. Rather, encountering forgetfulness, particularly in others, is a call to compassion, patience, and greater understanding.

DEVOTIONAL PRACTICE

Our ability to remember is a great gift. Exercise and strengthen it by pausing at the end of each day to recall moments of love, grace, or tenderness that you personally experienced or witnessed in others. If you cannot recall any, tell yourself that your memory is faulty, for surely you did not make it through the day without any loving encounters. Resolve to be more attentive tomorrow.

ST. AMBROSE

"Churches under siege."

C. 340–397

DECEMBER 7

Ambrose lived through a tumultuous and violent era during which the institutional Church became a militant power itself. Survival mandated it.

Ambrose had been appointed a governor in northern Italy by the emperor Valentinian. When the bishop of Milan died, the city was thrown into turmoil, with Arian Christians and orthodox Christians insulting and battling each other over who should succeed him. Ambrose himself appeared at an assembly to keep the peace, and he so impressed the crowd with a speech that they began shouting for him to be the next bishop. Ambrose was surprised and befuddled by the cheering. He was not even a baptized Christian!

Ambrose tried to hide in a friend's home, but the emperor heard of the incident and threw his support behind Ambrose as both bishop and governor. Realizing the tide was against him, Ambrose surrendered, was baptized, and was made a bishop—all within a week.

Ambrose's reign was chaotic. The two Roman emperors of the eastern and western empire vied for influence. The Arian controversy continued to rage. Gothic tribes from the north attacked Roman settlements. There were massacres, battles, and assassinations. The empress Justina sided with the Arian contingent, had laws passed to outlaw Catholic gatherings, and tried to force Ambrose to turn over orthodox churches to the Arians. He refused. On one Palm Sunday, armies surrounded the church where he was preaching. The people, including Ambrose, barricaded themselves inside and stayed until Easter. During the week they sang psalms, hymns, and songs that Ambrose had written. Ambrose's position was clearly stated: "The emperor is in the Church, not over it."

At another time, imperial troops surrounded a circus where thousands of people were attending. The soldiers massacred almost everyone in retaliation for a governor who had been killed. Ambrose put pressure on the emperor, who eventually did public penance for the massacre. But Ambrose himself was not always above the bigotry of the times. When Christians destroyed a synagogue, the emperor ordered Ambrose to rebuild it. Ambrose refused, saying that he could not pay for a building where there would be "false worship."

Ambrose lived through the apocalyptic years when the old Roman Empire was crumbling. During his time as bishop, he wrote many essays on theology, asceticism, spirituality, and the problems of the day. One of his last works was titled "The Goodness of Death." He died on Good Friday at the age of fifty-seven.

PRAYER

Ambrose, I pray that my soul can stay calm and peaceful amid the atrocities committed around me every day. May I find the kind of strength you found to weather the storms of politics, war, and bigotry and to keep faith in the Creator, who is above us all and loves us all.

DEVOTIONAL PRACTICE

When crime, violence, cheating, bigotry, and other abusive atrocities depress you, do this ritual to clear your soul and to make symbolic amends for the problems caused by human beings:

From one or two newspapers, cut out the headlines that disgust or upset you. Collect a half dozen or more. Then go out into a wooded area and bury each strip of paper at the base of a tree. Place a pinch of some sweet-smelling herb on top of the spot. Make a prayerful blessing to each tree, and offer apologies for the misery that humans create. Consider each piece of paper a giving-back to the trees the gift of themselves that they share with us, and which, unfortunately, we use to print stories about our atrocities.

ST. ANASTASIUS THE FULLER

"Honor the work of the hands and the mind."

D. 304

SEPTEMBER 7

Anastasius was born at Aquileia in Italy into a prosperous family and could have lived a comfortable life without engaging in manual work. But when he heard St. Paul's advice in the Letter to the Thessalonians to "do your own business and work with your own hands," he took the admonition to heart. He learned the trade of a fuller, which was to shrink and thicken wool by moistening and pressing it so it would be appropriate for clothing. He practiced his trade in Dalmatia (later Yugoslavia), where he seems to have become successful as a skilled and respected worker.

During the persecution of Christians under the emperor Diocletian, Anastasius painted a cross on his door to witness to the faith and show his solidarity with others who were being arrested, tried, and martyred. Soon Anastasius was apprehended and taken before the governor, where he was expected to renounce his faith and demonstrate his devotion to the religion of the empire, thus proving his loyalty. He refused. The governor ordered that he be drowned in the sea with a stone tied around his neck. And so he ended his life witnessing to his belief in Jesus and the tenets of the Christian religion.

But the story of Anastasius continues. Asclepia, a wealthy woman of the city, announced that she would grant freedom to any of her slaves who could recover his body. Some of her slaves searched throughout the city and found a group of Africans who had pulled the body from the shallows of the water. The Africans were reluctant to give it up, but the slaves threatened to turn them over to the authorities and claim that they had murdered Anastasius. The body was surrendered, and the slaves took it home and received their freedom. Asclepia buried

Anastasius in her garden. Later the garden developed into a Christian cemetery, with a basilica that became a famous pilgrimage site.

PRAYER

Anastasius, help me to value all honest work even though I live in a culture that gives manual labor a very low status. I pray that I will always appreciate working with the hands and remember that it is just as valuable in God's eyes as working with the mind.

DEVOTIONAL PRACTICE

As more and more people make their living by computers, other forms of high technology, and white-collar services, it is important to maintain respect for manual work and the physical tasks that our ancestors performed. Whether it be sweeping the floor with a broom rather than a vacuum cleaner, washing the car with a hose rather than at a drive-through carwash, or writing a letter by hand rather than sending an e-mail, try to upgrade these activities in your own mind to where they command the respect they deserve. Occasionally, as a devotional practice, choose to do something the "old-fashioned way," even though it may take a little longer or involve a little sweat and muscle power. We are still creatures of the God who wanted us to have both bodies and minds, and to find the meaning of life by using both.

ST. ANDREW THE APOSTLE

"A practical optimist."

FIRST CENTURY

NOVEMBER 30

Andrew was a Galilean fisherman and the son of a fisherman. There are differing accounts of how he met Jesus and became one of the first disciples. One is that he was fishing with his brother Peter when Jesus approached them and said to put down their nets and follow him. Jesus' offer to show them how to catch men, instead of fish, was irresistible to the two brothers. From that day on, they followed Jesus and learned how to win the hearts and minds of men and women to the new spiritual message that would become the Gospel.

In St. John's account, Andrew was a follower of John the Baptist and was present at Jesus' baptism. He and another of the Baptist's disciples asked Jesus where he was staying, to which Jesus replied, "Come and find out." Andrew and his companion did so and stayed with Jesus the rest of the day. Then Andrew went to Peter, his brother, and said, "We have found the messiah."

It was Andrew who responded to the need to feed a large crowd that had assembled to hear Jesus teach. When the question came up as to how to feed so many people, Andrew mentioned that a boy in the crowd had five loaves of bread and a couple of fish, but he doubted that so little food would really help. Jesus told him to get the boy, and the small amount fed the entire crowd with twelve baskets of leftovers.

Legends tell that Andrew preached in Scythia and Greece, and was eventually crucified on an X-shaped cross. He became the patron of Russia because of an unsubstantiated tradition that he preached there as well. He also became the patron of Scotland, from the tradition that tells how St. Rule, the custodian of Andrew's relics, had a dream that he should take the relics there. An angel guided Rule to Scotland where he preached the Gospels to the Scots.

PRAYER

Help me to see the divine potential of ordinary situations as you did when Jesus said to follow him and when you brought the boy with five loaves and a couple of fish to provide a meal for hundreds of people. Give me the insight to trust that miracles can occur in the most ordinary of everyday situations.

DEVOTIONAL PRACTICE

When preparing food or collecting leftovers, place some outdoors to honor the spirit of the land that gives us food. Leaving food offerings outdoors is a worldwide custom, found in many cultures. As a practice in honor of St. Andrew, your intention is to return to the earth a portion of the blessings that it multiples in your own life every day.

ST. ANNE LINE
"Breaking the law for the sake of religious freedom."

D. 1601

FEBRUARY 27

At Anne Line's trial, one witness testified that he had seen a man in her house dressed in white. The other incriminating evidence was the altar set up for a Catholic Mass. The jury did not think these two pieces of evidence were substantial enough to convict Line and sentence her to death. The judge, however, did. He instructed the jury, and they came forth with the guilty verdict. Anne Line was convicted of harboring a foreign priest in her home and sentenced to the gallows.

Actually Line was guilty. She was a notorious figure in the underground network that hid and protected priests and other Catholics hunted by the English authorities. Line had dedicated her life to this work.

Born to a prominent Protestant family, Anne and her brother converted to Catholicism, which infuriated their father, who disinherited them. Anne then married Roger Line, a Catholic convert, who was exiled to Flanders after being found guilty of violating the anti-Catholic laws in England. When he died in 1594, Anne decided to use her connections to help priests and Catholics elude the English authorities.

A Jesuit priest set up a "safe house" for clergy in London and put Line in charge. Soon she came under suspicion, and the authorities began to close in. She terminated the house and moved to another, where she routinely hid priests and allowed them to say Mass for Catholics. In 1601, on the feast of Candlemas, when a large number of Catholics showed up for Mass, neighbors became suspicious and alerted the authorities. The priest had already vested for Mass, but enough time elapsed from when the priest hunters arrived until they broke through the door that the priest escaped. When they did force entry, however, it was rather clear what the gathering was all about. Line was arrested.

At her trial, Line defiantly acknowledged her complicity in breaking the law. She declared, "My lords, nothing grieves me more but that I could not receive a thousand more priests." She was executed on the gallows, along with a Jesuit priest who had been her friend and confessor.

PRAYER

Anne, you took great risks in breaking the law of the land in order to follow your conscience and obey a higher law as you saw it. May I, too, find such courage, even though I may not be confronted with as dangerous a situation as you were. In countless ways each day, I find myself tempted to do things the "accepted" way, when I know in my heart that they are not right for me. Help me to follow my conscience.

DEVOTIONAL PRACTICE

Meditate on one of the great moral controversies that concerns you, such as racism, sexism, capital punishment, abortion, or assisted dying. Do this meditation in two scenarios on two different days.

First Scenario: Spend ten to fifteen minutes "creating" a drama in your imagination in which you are a participant in this issue *on the side you do not approve of.* Try to think and feel as the person would, even though the arguments and reasons are not your own.

Second Scenario: Repeat the meditation seeing yourself *play a role comparable to your own position.*

When you have finished the two exercises, pray for the real-life people you have imagined in your meditations so that each will be able to understand his or her opponent's position and be able to deal with the other civilly and compassionately.

ST. ANSELM OF CANTERBURY

"A believer in the beauty of perfection."

C. 1033–1109

APRIL 21

In 1060 at age twenty-seven, Anselm finally became a monk at Bec in Normandy. He had hoped to begin the monastic life twelve years earlier, but his father was so upset with the idea that the monks in an abbey in the Piedmont region where he was born would not accept the fifteen-year-old boy. Anselm pursued his studies, bided his time, and realized his dream when the time was ripe.

Thirty-two years later, in 1092, when he was appointed archbishop of Canterbury, Anselm was tossed into the religious and political fracas in England that followed the Norman invasion of 1066. The Norman kings struggled with the Church over many issues, the major one being their desire to influence the selection of bishops. Bishoprics were lucrative positions, involving land, money, and people. Until Anselm died in 1109, he expended much time and energy on the dispute.

Nevertheless, he found time to teach, write, preach, and prove himself one of the most creative thinkers of his age. He wrote powerful treatments on truth, free will, the origin of evil, the ability to reason, and the Incarnation. In his *Proslogian,* he argued for the existence of God based on our human understanding that a perfect being could exist. In this notion of a perfect being, every man and woman has the seed for great faith in the existence of God as the source of perfection and our ideas of perfection. This reasoning influenced many thinkers after him, including Descartes and Hegel, right down to our own day.

In 1102 Anselm called a council to meet at Westminster to resolve political and ecclesiastical matters in the never-ending dispute between the pope and the king, but out of the meetings came a far-reaching and remarkable resolution denouncing the slave trade. Anselm is one of the first high-ranking individuals to stand up for human freedom and dignity, and to denounce the buying and selling of human beings. The rest of the Western world, however, was slow to catch up with him.

Anselm died at Canterbury, a compassionate, sincere, loving man who seemed to have gotten along well with all types of individuals from all ranks and classes of society.

PRAYER

Anselm, give me the wisdom to hold on to the idea of human perfection even when I see so little evidence of it around me. May I keep a strong belief in God's own perfection, and a belief that each of us, who are made in his image, contains at least a nugget of that perfection and probably much more. Help me to bring forth the best in my companions and neighbors, so that they, too, can make strides toward living a more perfect life.

DEVOTIONAL PRACTICE

Perfection is a human goal, although it is probably not attainable while we are called to live with the imperfections of this reality, this world, this life. Nevertheless, perfection exists in the eternal realms, and we long for it. Go outside on a clear starry night, some place where the lights of civilization do not dim the stars, and look up into the heavens. Allow yourself to be calmed and transformed by the beauty and majesty of the night sky, and recognize in it a kind of perfection, not totally unlike that which you seek or that which exists in the Creator of such a beautiful sky. Give thanks for such beauty.

ST. ANTHONY OF EGYPT

"The founder of desert monasticism."

250–356

JANUARY 17

Anthony of Egypt was born near Memphis into a wealthy Christian family. His parents died when he was eighteen, leaving him and his sister orphaned. Six months after their deaths, he was in church and heard Jesus' advice: "If you want to be perfect, go sell all you have, and give to the poor; and come, follow me and you will have treasure in heaven." Anthony took the scripture seriously, sold the estate he had inherited, gave the proceeds to the poor, and arranged for his sister to live in a convent. Shortly thereafter, he himself took up residence in a tomb in a nearby cemetery.

Anthony lived as a hermit for fifteen years, enduring incredible temptations and periods of agonizing self-doubt. He suffered from boredom and loneliness. In his visions, an angel advised him to counteract these sufferings with work and prayer. He lived a life of great austerity, eating only bread and water once a day.

In 285 Anthony sought even greater solitude, so he moved to an abandoned fort atop Mt. Pispir, where he ate only what people threw over the walls to him. Over the next twenty-five years he continued his life of solitude, prayer, and austerity. Slowly a community of ascetics, inspired by his example, formed around the base of the mountain. In 305 he organized them into what is considered the first Christian monastery. The monks lived alone and came together only for worship services.

When the Roman emperor Maximin increased his persecutions of Christians in 311, Anthony came down from the mountain, went to Alexandria, and encouraged Christian communities to resist the political oppression. When the persecutions abated, he returned to the desert with his disciple and companion, Macarius, and took up residence on Mt. Kolzim near the Red Sea.

Anthony's final years brought him a celebrity-like status, as thousands of people from all walks of life came to visit, seek spiritual advice, and, in many cases, join the monastic life that he had developed. These years also tested one of his many visions, that of the world snarled by loops and hoops that threatened to entangle and smother it. A voice in the vision explained to him that the practice of humility is the only way to escape the world's entanglements.

PRAYER

Anthony, give me the same courage you found to withstand the bouts of loneliness, self-doubt, and boredom that can threaten my spiritual practice. Help me find the proper work, prayer, and humility that will pull me through these troubling times so that I may escape the entangling loops of the world.

DEVOTIONAL PRACTICE

Find a photograph of the planet looking like a blue marble, and with paint or colored pencils draw a series of interlocking loops around it, signifying the entanglements of the secular world. Place the photo somewhere that you will see it as a reminder to pursue your spiritual life with great commitment in spite of the world's distractions.

ST. ANTHONY OF PADUA
"Finder of lost objects."

1195–1231

JUNE 13

Anthony of Padua was born to young parents, members of the Portuguese nobility. They named him Ferdinand. He studied in Lisbon and joined the canons of St. Augustine at age fifteen. Because of distractions from visits by his friends, he asked to be transferred to the priory at Coimbra where he continued his studies. Young Ferdinand was known for his quick and agile memory, which allowed him to recall extensive passages from the Bible. As a saint he would become the patron of finding lost articles.

In 1220 when the Portuguese king brought the relics of Franciscans who had been martyred in Morocco to Coimbra, Ferdinand was inspired to join that order and dedicate his life to Christ. The following year he became a Franciscan and took the name Anthony. That same year he attended the general chapter of Franciscans at Assisi, attended by St. Francis himself, although he was no longer the vicar general of the order he had founded.

Anthony was hailed as a magnetic preacher who was able to speak spontaneously, allowing the Holy Spirit to put the appropriate words in his mouth for the occasion. He was eloquent and easily persuaded many listeners to reform their ways and live more devoutly. He also worked to abolish debtor's prisons and to alleviate the sufferings of the poor.

On one occasion, a visitor saw Anthony holding the infant Jesus in his arms. The two seemed to be surrounded by a heavenly mist. The report of this vision inspired many depictions of the saint after his death.

In 1231 Anthony succumbed to overwork and dropsy. He retired with two friars to a wooded hermitage at Camposanpiero where he realized that his death was imminent. He headed back to Padua, and died at age thirty-six in a Poor Clare convent just outside the city.

PRAYER

Anthony, help me to remember what is most important in life. When I forget or lose sight of spiritual realities, let me find them, just as you have helped many people over the centuries find lost objects. Give me the grace and humility to accept my forgetfulness.

DEVOTIONAL PRACTICE

When you misplace your keys, leave something important behind, or can't find something, pause for a moment and realize that your loss is probably minor compared with the losses of many people around the world. Offer a prayer for others, those who are deprived of the very necessities of life.

ST. ANTONINO OF FLORENCE

"Pawnshops for the poor."

1389–1459

MAY 10

Antonino became bishop of Florence when he was in his mid-fifties. He spent most of his life, after entering the Dominican order at age sixteen (one year after he applied and was turned down), as prior at a series of monasteries all across Italy. When he became bishop of Florence, however, his concern for the evils of capitalism had a waiting outlet.

Florence was developing the mercantile and banking practices of the capitalist economy that would come to dominate the Western world. Investing money in order to make money, lending money for interest payments (called usury in Antonino's day), the increasingly lavish lifestyles of those who struck it rich, and the competitive drive and disregard for the less fortunate were becoming typical of the new economy. He preached against dishonesty, cheating, overcharging for poor-quality goods, and so forth, but Antonino's criticism went deeper than the usual crimes. He argued that the very nature of a capitalist society caused the most suffering.

By Antonino's reading of scripture, money should not be invested for profit. Whatever profit was made honestly through goods and services should be used to provide a comfortable living for those who made it, but surplus profit should be returned to society in relief for the poor and the upkeep of state institutions that would work for the common good. He also felt that the government or the bishop should fix prices so the poor would not be hurt. "Poverty must be ruled out of the State. . . . God has established the rich . . . not to provide for their own private ends, but for the common good," he argued. He even suggested that monopolists should have their goods confiscated and be exiled perpetually from the city.

When Antonino became bishop, he put his ideas into practice. He dismissed the bloated household staff and turned part of his formal gardens over to the poor to grow vegetables, which they could keep or sell. He walked the streets with his mule laden with food and drink to give away to those in need, and he also walked through his entire diocese once a year to see firsthand the conditions of the poor. He set up pawnshops so the poor could get money without having to pay interest to the moneylenders and fall further into debt.

Eventually Antonino gave away his own clothes and furniture. In his will he decreed that all his possessions that remained after he died were to go to the poor. After his death, his staff searched his quarters to make an inventory. They found only four coins.

PRAYER

Antonino, I pray that I may understand how riches are not an end in themselves but a means to an end. Help us to use our wealth wisely and compassionately and not succumb to the avarice that makes us want to always have more.

DEVOTIONAL PRACTICE

If you are not chronically strapped for money each month, consider adopting the practice of tithing—that is, giving one-tenth of your income to a worthy cause. Compute what one-tenth of your monthly income is and seriously consider whether you could live without it. If you find that you could live without it, then ask yourself, "What could I do with this money that would help people in greater need than I am?"

ST. APOLLONIA

"Healer of head injuries."

D. 249

FEBRUARY 7

In the first centuries after Jesus' death and resurrection, there arose strong Christian communities in Alexandria, Egypt. Apollonia was one of those early Alexandrian Christians, the daughter of a local ruler. She enjoyed considerable wealth and a luxurious lifestyle, but inspired by Christian teachings of poverty and communal living, she gave away her jewels, including some that were gifts from her favorite brother.

Apollonia's response to Christian teachings did not endear her to her family. She refused an arranged marriage and was led by an angel into the desert to visit a hermit, who baptized her into the new faith. The angel encouraged Apollonia to return to the city and preach. The details of her life as a Christian preacher are not known. But her presence and prestige alienated her from the old guard in the city, and she seems to have been criticized and attacked for her preaching repeatedly throughout her life.

Near the end, Apollonia incurred the wrath of local magicians and healers, probably with the support of the political powers. Mobs were incited against her and others in her community, and they were chased through the streets and eventually caught and tortured. Legends of Apollonia's torture vary: she had her eyes gouged out, molten lead poured in her ears, her skin flayed with a knife, and her jaw shattered to knock out her teeth. When a fire was prepared to finally end the ordeal, she voluntarily leaped into the flames rather than give her torturers the pleasure of throwing her into it.

Devotional practices connected with teeth arose over the centuries following her death. In Germany, rinsing your mouth with water from St. Apollonia's well on the Kapellenberg protects you from toothache. In Germany's Black Forest, laying a spoon at the feet of Apollonia's statue eases tooth pain, and mothers whose children are teething hang their little shirts on the statue to bring relief.

PRAYER

Apollonia, help me endure the afflictions of (eyestrain, hearing loss, toothache, etc.) with a greater acceptance. Let me find in my pain the strength to call upon higher powers to rise above the discomfort of the flesh.

DEVOTIONAL PRACTICE

When you take medicine or remedies for any head-related ailment, use a special spoon that you bless especially for that purpose. Each time you use it, let it remind you that others suffer greater pain, and offer up your suffering for them.

ST. ARDALION

"Every soul is a stage."

D. C. 300

APRIL 14

One day Ardalion, an actor, strutted out onto the stage to begin his scene. It was one he had performed many times, and it was always a crowd pleaser. He burlesqued a Christian who was so dedicated to his faith that he would undergo extreme torture rather than relent and take part in the traditional religious practices of the Roman Empire. Just what scenes, dialogue, and banter Ardalion portrayed on this day, we do not know. But he was convincing and funny. The crowd was in stitches at the antics Ardalion had perfected in making fools of the Christian martyrs. The audience was roused to its feet, and Ardalion took his bows.

But on this fateful day, Ardalion's portrayal of a condemned Christian moved something deep in his soul. As he listened to the applause, he may have heard a heavenly audience clapping, not for him but for the martyrs he portrayed as buffoons. At the moment when he received his greatest adulation, he realized the truth of the characters he had portrayed, and realized equally how much that truth made sense to him. When the applause died down, Ardalion spoke his last line as an actor: "I, too, am a Christian!"

The authorities seized Ardalion and took him before a local judge who insisted that he recant his confession of faith. He refused and was burnt alive in an eastern city of the Roman Empire, the exact site now lost in the past.

Ardalion, the ability to understand and appreciate human emotions is a great gift. Teach me how to identify with others by being aware of our common humanity whenever I see strong emotions in real life, in movies, or on the stage.

DEVOTIONAL PRACTICE

It is not uncommon for actors to identify with the characters they portray as they come to understand the goals and motivations of human behavior. Even people who are nothing like us share our common humanity, and if we can get inside their minds and hearts, we come to understand better how they can do what they do.

Choose a saint who seems extreme or very different from you, someone who does not appear to have much in common with your own character and way of life. Imagine one or two statements that this saint might use in his or her conversation, statements that reflect the commitment and dedication of that saint. Rehearse these lines either silently or out loud, and impress them upon your memory. Then, remaining mindful of them during the day, look for a moment when you can work them into your conversation with others. You need not call attention to this; just slip them in. In this way you will come to understand more fully the truths and insights of the saints, and perhaps appreciate your common humanity.

ST. ATHANASIUS OF ATHOS

"The fugitive saint."

C. 920–C. 1000

JULY 5

The monk who called himself Dorotheos while hiding in a primitive cell on Mt. Athos was an imposter. In reality, the disguised holy man was Athanasius, monk of the monastery at Kymia, in Bithynia, friend and protégé of the recently deceased abbot and next in line to assume abbotship of the monastery. But Athanasius wanted nothing to do with the abbotship and fled to Mt. Athos in Greece where hermits lived isolated lives far removed from civilization.

Athanasius thought he was safe from the responsibilities of running a monastery, but he was tracked down by Nicephorus Phocas, the former abbot's nephew and future emperor. Phocas asked if the holy man would return with him to Crete to bless his troops and send them off to wage war against the Saracens. Athanasius realized his ruse was up, and he went with Phocas.

The war was successful. When Athanasius asked to return to Mt. Athos, Phocas gave him money to build an actual monastery. In 961 Athanasius constructed the first building of a community that would become the center for Eastern Orthodox monasticism.

When Phocas became emperor, Athanasius headed for the hills once again, this time to Cyprus, fearing that his friend would summon him to be part of the imperial court. And again the crafty Phocas snooped him out, convinced him to return to Mt. Athos, and gave him even more money to build a harbor. He agreed, and the monastic settlement was on its way to becoming an even more important institution in the Eastern Church.

Ironically, the hermits who had lived on the mountain for generations did not appreciate Athanasius's efforts. They were quite content to live in isolation, poverty, and peace. They wanted nothing of institutions, ecclesiastical regulations, imperial rules, money, and harbors. Most of all they did not want Athanasius (or anyone) to tell them what to do. Twice they tried to murder Athanasius, but failed. Finally, they resigned themselves to the fact that with the emperor's support and Athanasius's determination, their mountain would never be as isolated from the world as it had once been.

Meanwhile, Athanasius proceeded to create a community based on the desert traditions of Egypt and Syria in which monks lived in individual cells loosely clustered around a central church building for common prayers and services. Unlike the Benedictine reforms in the West, the monastic tradition of Mt. Athos would be, and still is, an example of a more ancient way of retreating from the world and living in religious community.

Around the year 1000, Athanasius and five monks were killed when the keystone for a vault of one of the churches fell on them while they were working on it. The once-reluctant abbot died, having become the superior general of fifty-eight communities of monks and hermits, and the "Father of Mt. Athos."

PRAYER

Athanasius, when I feel like running away from my duties, help me to understand that if God wants me to do something, he will find me. Pray that I find the grace to live up to the commitments and responsibilities of my life. And may I perform them with enthusiasm, humor, and goodwill.

DEVOTIONAL PRACTICE

Whenever you feel like running away to hide rather than face up to your responsibilities, try this: Take a small stone to represent you, put it up to your lips, and breathe into it the "part of you" that wants to run and hide. Then hide the stone somewhere outside. It will do your hiding for you. Then ask for the grace and courage to face your responsibility. When you have finished your obligations, retrieve the stone, place it next to your heart, and let the "part of you" that was in hiding return to you.

ST. ATTRACTA

"A whiz at Irish cursing."

FIFTH OR SIXTH CENTURY

AUGUST 11

Attracta came from a family that was politically powerful in the network of Irish tribes and communities. Like many women and men in those days, Attracta found the religious life to be an admirable alternative to secular Irish society. She asked her father for permission to leave, but he refused, so she struck out on her own without her father's blessing and became a nun. She then settled at Lough Gara, where she built a hospice for travelers at a place where seven roads came together. The hospice survived for over a thousand years, until 1539, when it was destroyed during the Protestant Reformation.

Attracta was a fiercely independent Irishwoman who did what she wanted even though she made enemies. Once she wanted to establish a hermitage for herself in Roscommon near the monastic community of her half brother, St. Conal. He and another religious leader, St. Dachonna, refused her permission to build a hermitage in their district. So she cursed them! Irish cursing is an age-old tradition, and Attracta was evidently good at it. She wished that the two men's churches would be reduced to insignificance by the rise of a grander church nearby. (She also put other curses on them, which were not recorded by her biographers because the curses were so "disagreeable.") Centuries later the great Cistercian abbey of Boyle was built, and it completely overshadowed the smaller churches. Even before the Boyle abbey, however, rival churches undermined the power of Conal's and Dachonna's institutions.

On another occasion Attracta helped a raiding party escape the king of Connacht. The legends relate that she mysteriously parted the waters of the loch for the raiders to pass through. There are still two natural weirs on the lake named after her. The king of Connacht retaliated against her for helping his enemies (who may have been connected with her father's folk) by demanding that she help construct a fort for him. With strands of her own hair, she harnessed a deer to pull logs for the fort.

Attracta, I pray that I might be able to control my thoughts and wishes when they concern harm befalling someone I don't like. Pray for me that I might realize my common humanity with people who anger me and not wish on them some harmful condition that I would not want for myself.

In the Irish tradition there are categories of curses, including curses by priests, saints, widows, and poets. Basically a curse is a formal wish that misfortune occur to someone else. In some cases, the misfortune wished upon another is so bizarre, extreme, and complex that it is clear from the details that the curse will never come true. But it is a good way of getting the anger out of your system. On some occasions, however, a curse can come true.

As a spiritual practice, whenever anger causes you to wish something harmful to happen to another, stop for a moment and consider the power of cursing. Ask yourself two questions: If your wish came true, would you be able to live with the psychological consequences of knowing the harm you caused? Would you want someone to put a similar curse on you? The answer to both questions is probably no. So block that curse even as it forms in your mind by remembering that you should not do to someone else the very thing you would not want someone to do to you. It is simply the obverse of the golden rule, and it should apply to our thoughts, whether they be just wishful thinking or outright curses.

ST. AUGUSTINE OF HIPPO

"Casting words and stones at others."

354–430

AUGUST 28

It has been said that Augustine's *Confessions* was the first autobiography in the West and that it expresses Augustine's deep psychological need to justify himself. Certainly Augustine is one of the few early saints whose personal views on their inner life have survived. In addition, his opinions on such topics as human nature, the relationships between men and women, sex, sin, and guilt have influenced Catholic thinking for generations. Many people today find his positions strange and unappealing for a healthy spiritual life, but one issue that was very important to him is still extremely relevant: the use of language to influence thinking and behavior.

Augustine was given the best education of his day, and he became a superior student of rhetoric and philosophy. He left the Christian upbringing he received from his mother, St. Monica, and explored Manichaeanism and other spiritual movements that were popular at the time. He was especially drawn toward those that offered explanations for an issue that intrigued him all his life: the problem of evil.

In 383 Augustine went to Rome and set up a school of rhetoric, an important discipline for young men who hoped to make a career in government or politics—fields where the ability to persuade others was paramount. But he was disappointed in Rome, and the following year he moved to Milan where he came under the influence of St. Ambrose, bishop of that city. Ambrose's rhetorical skills in preaching impressed Augustine, but it was the bishop's commitment to truth that changed Augustine's life.

Augustine found Ambrose refreshing compared with most orators of the day who used half-truths, flattery, and outright lies to gain power for themselves or others. He realized that oratory was a tool used by many to dehumanize opponents, to enhance one's own standing at the expense of others, and to deny justice to certain classes of people. For most public figures, he realized, language was a self-serving instrument of propaganda.

In 386 Augustine somewhat callously sent the woman he had lived with for fifteen years and who was the mother of his son back to Africa. The next year he was baptized, and in 388 he himself returned to Africa and set up a religious community at Tagaste. He was ordained a priest and became an assistant to the bishop of Hippo, whom he succeeded in 395. He used his position to write and speak on behalf of the downtrodden, less fortunate, and despised members of society.

In addition to his *Confessions*, Augustine wrote *The City of God*, a book that placed the dissolute society of the dying Roman Empire within the Christian view of history. Later, in his *Retractions*, he updated his voluminous writings, corrected his mistakes, and again displayed the need to publicly announce the truth about his life.

Augustine died in 430, during the fourteen months when the Vandals laid siege to Hippo.

PRAYER

Augustine, help me find the appropriate words when speaking about myself or others. Let me be ever mindful of the ability of words to distort the truth and misrepresent the facts. I pray that my speech will always be shaped by a strong commitment to the truth, to a fair treatment of others, and by a humility born of the realization that I might be wrong.

DEVOTIONAL PRACTICE

It is easy to criticize politicians who use language to cover up mistakes, put a better spin on their faults, and deceive the public. But don't we do the same thing?

One of Augustine's favorite lessons was the story of Jesus asking that the person without sin cast the first stone at the woman caught in adultery. As a spiritual practice, carry a small stone in your pocket or purse and call it the First Stone or the Hypocrite Stone. When you find yourself criticizing others for lying or misrepresenting the truth, reach into your pocket and turn the stone three times, recalling that no matter how reprehensible the speaker is, you are not worthy to cast it.

ST. AYBERT

"Sing it!"

1060–1140

APRIL 7

Aybert's father was a French knight, but the young boy knew early on that he was not going to follow in his father's footsteps. Young Aybert was a seeker of the spirit, fond of praying, genuflecting, and performing other religious practices. He would often get up at night, slip outside, and go to the sheepfold where he would pray and genuflect until he fell asleep exhausted. In the morning members of his household would find him there.

One day in his youth Aybert heard a wandering minstrel singing a long and sorrowful song about a heroic hermit who had recently died. The many verses recounted the hermit's entire life. Aybert was transfixed by the beauty of the song and the inspiration of the hermit's remarkable life. From then on Aybert was not able to think about anything except that he too wanted to live the way that hermit did.

Finally, Aybert found a monk named John, who had been given permission to live as a solitary, and asked if he could join him. John accepted the young man as a companion and began to train him in the spiritual practices of prayer and asceticism. Together the two hermits led a happy life apart from society. Later they were invited to accompany a Benedictine envoy to Rome, and on their return Aybert had a dream that he should join that religious community. He joined the order and worked as provost and cellarer for twenty-five years. The life suited him, and he was content and happy.

But at some point, his former solitary way of life began to haunt him. Or perhaps once again the minstrel's song echoed in his head, stirring up the enthusiasm he had known so many years before. He sought and received permission to leave the community and build a hermitage to be alone with God. There he lived as a solitary for another twenty-two years, gaining such a reputation for wisdom and holiness that people from all walks of life came to visit him and ask his advice.

PRAYER

Aybert, help me realize that any song lyrics about love, happiness, joy, or the excitement of living are really about the emotions that God has given us to carry us through life. Teach me to hear these melodies and words with my inner heart, which longs for gladness of the spirit, and teach me not to be afraid to sing these songs as expressions of my gratitude to God for the goodness of my life.

DEVOTIONAL PRACTICE

God can inspire us as much through popular music as through religious hymns and chants. In Aybert's day, minstrels were popular entertainers, singing about love, sex, war, and the current heroes. Occasionally, their songs touched on the lives of holy people such as the hermit who inspired Aybert. That song changed his life.

We all remember songs that inspired us at different times in our lives, even though they may not have led us to be hermits. In fact, any song that you associate with an earlier period of your life and that fills you with strong positive feelings can serve a spiritual purpose in your present life. Recall the song or the melody, play it if you can, or sing and hum it intentionally to recapture the enthusiasm or love of life that you had in that earlier period.

We should value enthusiasm, for the word comes from the Greek "en-theos" which means "in God." We are meant to have enthusiasm and strong positive feelings about the goodness of life. God wants us to respond to life with courage, hope, and great joy. If a popular song helps you to live in this way, then sing it!

ST. BASIL THE GREAT

"Seeking God through the five senses."

329–379

JANUARY 2

Basil was one of ten children born into a Christian family in Caesarea, in Asia Minor. He studied in Constantinople and Athens, and became a teacher of rhetoric in Caesarea. In 358 he was baptized and began the life of a hermit on the Iris River in Pontus, where he wrote a rule for monks and nuns that is still the basis for monastic life in the Eastern Church today. He attracted many followers, and was ordained a priest in 363. Seven years later, on the death of the current archbishop, Basil was elected to succeed him.

Basil was a powerful speaker and writer, and was caught up in the Arian controversies of the day, arguing against the Arians, who viewed Jesus as human but not divine. The emperor Valens was an Arian and opposed Basil both theologically and spiritually. Valens split the region into two dioceses in order to weaken Basil's authority.

But Basil continued to lead an active life to improve social conditions. He founded a large hospice to care for the ill, organized relief programs for the poor, worked against the ravages of famine, opposed those involved in the widespread prostitution traffic, and tightened up the discipline of the clergy and church officials.

Many of Basil's writings are still available today. He wrote that human beings are not capable of knowing God's supreme essence, but that through physical reality we can experience God's power and energies. Even though our senses are subjective, Basil argued, they can teach us much about the Creator. His advice for leading a more perfect life was "Recognize yourself, and watch yourself."

Like other neo-Platonists of the day, Basil placed great faith in human reason and free will.

Help me to trust the beauties and powers of nature that are doorways to understanding the power of God. When I have doubts and feel distant from God because I cannot know him directly, let me find encouragement in his creation. Help me also to recognize myself and watch myself so I might lead a more perfect life.

DEVOTIONAL PRACTICE

Place a small sign on your mirror that says "Recognize yourself," and when you look at your reflection each morning, form an intention that you will spend the day observing your words and actions so that you might eliminate those that are harmful to yourself or others, and focus on those that nurture health and happiness. Also when you see yourself in the mirror, know that you are seeing a reflection of God's energies as they manifest in you.

ST. BEDE THE VENERABLE

"The father of English history."

C. 672–735

MAY 25

When Bede died, he was in his sixties. All but the first seven years of his life had been spent in a monastery. And yet, in spite of what might appear as extreme isolation from the world, Bede was one of the most influential people of his day in almost every area of human culture.

Bede entered the monastery of St. Peter and St. Paul, near Wearmouth-Jarrow in England, when he was seven. He began as an oblate in the Benedictine order and later became a monk. He was ordained a priest at age thirty. Except for a few visits to other places, he spent most of his life behind the cloistered walls, living the life of a devout monk. What places Bede in the mainstream of Western culture, however, is the fact that during these centuries, monasteries were about the only places where the great intellectual traditions were preserved, and Bede quickly discovered that he had the mind, aptitude, and interest to become a major figure in the Western intellectual tradition.

Bede was one of the most learned men of his day. He wrote about all fields of human knowledge, including math, meteorology, natural science, grammar, prosody, rhetoric, astronomy, music, poetry, and history. In fact, his *Historia Ecclesiastica,* or history of the Church in England, is about more than just the Church. It is about the English people as well. Bede is one of the most important sources for English life and customs during these early centuries, and that's why he is considered the "father of English history." He is also the first person to date events *anno domini,* which means "in the year of the Lord"—or, as we say today, A.D.

A story told about Bede is that when he was blind, a friend accompanied him to an outdoor area where he was to preach. As a prank, the friend took him to an empty field and told him that a great crowd had assembled to hear his sermon. Bede proceeded to preach to the empty countryside, but when he had finished, the stones responded with a great cry of "Amen!" In a sense, the Western world continues to resound with "Amen!" to the legacy that Bede has left us.

PRAYER

Bede, help me to remember that when my life seems narrow and uneventful, I need not be alone or cut off from the world. Show me how to get interested in as many areas of human life as I can, to study them, and take part in their activities. Every aspect of life is an invitation to find God.

DEVOTIONAL PRACTICE

In the great tradition of being a "fool for God," go out alone into an empty field or meadow where there are clusters of stones. "Preach" to them about your love of God and how you strive to find God in all your daily activities. When you have finished, spend a few quiet moments, listening to what the stones might have to say to you.

ST. BENEDICT THE MOOR

"They also fast who only nibble."

1526–1589

APRIL 4

The twenty-one-year-old Benedict was working in the fields with some oxen he had bought when less prosperous and envious neighbors began to make fun of him because of his dark skin and his previous status as a slave. (Benedict was not a Moor; the term was used at this time to refer to someone of African descent.) Just at that moment, Lanzi, a hermit, came by and rebuked Benedict's attackers. "You make fun of this poor African now," he said. "I can tell you that before long you will hear great things about him." Moved by Lanzi's defense, Benedict asked to join the hermit (who had once been a nobleman) and his small group of companions who lived near Palermo in the simple lifestyle inspired by Francis of Assisi.

Years earlier Benedict's father, also a slave, had won the admiration of his master, a wealthy Sicilian landowner, for his organizational work as foreman of the household's servants. In appreciation, the landowner promised that Benedict would be released from servitude. Although not able to read or write, Benedict must have had innate managerial skills—or picked them up from his father—because over the course of his life, he was twice chosen by his brothers to supervise the religious community. Once he also served as novice master.

But Benedict's favorite office was that of cook. A mysterious light sometimes shone in the kitchen when he worked there, and it was reported that angels helped him prepare meals and run the kitchen.

Benedict's wisdom and innate understanding of scriptural passages won him a wide following among religious and laypeople. He was known for his sanctity, sound spiritual advice, and miracles, among which was his ability to multiply food when he was a cook. He was also reputed to read people's minds. In spite of the celebrity status that eventually accrued to him, Benedict preferred to be a humble cook, far removed from the public and involved with simple tasks where he could commune with the angels while performing one of the most important jobs in any community.

When asked about fasting, Benedict answered that to deprive oneself of food was not the most difficult penance. Far more severe, he said, was to take a bite or two, and then eat no more. He also encouraged his brothers not to hesitate in eating food that was given out of charity or hospitality, because doing so expressed gratitude—and it made the donors feel good to see the monks eating so well!

After a short illness at age sixty-three, Benedict passed peacefully into the next world.

PRAYER

Benedict, I pray that I might be able to accept people as they are today and not place great stock on their previous lives, whether they come from lowly backgrounds or from the world of the rich and powerful. May the friendship between you, a former slave, and Lanzi, a former nobleman, inspire me to overlook past differences and focus on the present bonds of love and affection.

DEVOTIONAL PRACTICE

On days when you are not able to fast but want to practice some form of asceticism, try Benedict's approach of eating just one bite or swallow and then refraining. Do this with food that you really like and find hard to resist, such as snacks or dessert. For example, eat just half of your favorite cookie, take only one spoonful of ice cream, nibble just one peanut (or maybe two), take one swallow of soda, eat only one piece of candy.

Similarly, when you are a guest, eat heartily and with great enthusiasm, knowing that you are giving your host great pleasure. Give thanks for the goodness of food.

ST. BENEN

"Flowers and song."

D. 467

NOVEMBER 9

When St. Patrick was preaching in Ireland, the population was divided into traditional, tribal-like communities headed by chieftains. The powerful families
that dominated Irish life provided the political and spiritual leaders, as they had
since pagan times. Whatever success Patrick had in Ireland depended on having
allies among these strong families.

On one occasion, Patrick was staying with Sechnan, a chieftain in Meath.
Sechnan's entire family took to Patrick and his new religion, and they were
all baptized. Sechnan's son, Benen, was particularly drawn to the charismatic
teacher. At night the young boy scattered flowers over Patrick while he slept.
When it was time for Patrick to move on, Benen clung to his feet to hold him
back. His father allowed him to go with Patrick, in the old Celtic tradition of
fosterage.

Benen accompanied Patrick and his men on their travels throughout Ireland.
Because of his good voice and love of singing, he was known as Patrick's
psalmodist. In time, he became Patrick's primary associate and successor. The
evangelization of Clare, Kerry, and Connaught is attributed to his preaching in
those districts. Patrick founded a church at Drumlease and turned it over to
Benen, who administered it for twenty years. When Patrick died, Benen became
the chief bishop in Ireland.

A story relates that when Benen grew tired of administration, he resigned
and went to Glastonbury in England, where he met Patrick, who encouraged him
to be a hermit. When Benen asked where he should go to create his hermitage,
Patrick replied that he would know the spot because his staff would burst into

leaves and flowers. Benen headed out, and his staff flowered in a swampy area known as Feringmere, where he stayed until he died.

PRAYER

Benen, share with me your love for flowers and song. Help me bring more beauty into my life through these two gifts that the Creator has given us.

DEVOTIONAL PRACTICE

It is an ancient custom to put flowers in sacred places. If you have an altar or shrine, keep a vase there with at least one flower in it. If you do not, decide on some place in your home or at work where you can keep a vase for flowers. Even in winter, a single flower from a florist or a dried wildflower is enough. When the flower dies, return it to the earth rather than throwing it in the trash.

ST. BERNADETTE

"The Virgin's broom."

1844–1879

APRIL 16

On February 11, 1858, fourteen-year-old Bernadette Soubirous was gathering firewood on the banks of the River Gave, near Lourdes. She looked up and saw a radiant woman standing in the rocks of a grotto by the river. Further visions (there would be eighteen in all) continued, and people began accompanying her. On March 4, twenty thousand visitors came to see Bernadette and, they hoped, the lady herself. On March 25, the lady announced, "I am the Immaculate Conception." Bernadette continued to have visions until July 16, when the final one occurred.

Bernadette was the oldest of six children. Their parents were neither thrifty nor lucky financially. Her father was a miller by trade, but when the visions began, the family was destitute and living in the basement of a crumbling building. Bernadette herself suffered from asthma and other illnesses. She was also a victim of the cholera epidemic in 1854. Naturally, the notoriety that came from Bernadette's visions of the Virgin changed their lives. People found work for her father, and their financial situation improved. But the family was pestered by visitors and curiosity seekers even after the visions ceased.

Eventually Bernadette decided to enter the convent, but her ill health forced her to leave four months later. She had been near death and had received the last sacraments.

Two years later in 1866, however, she recovered sufficiently to try again, and she was received into the order of Notre Dame de Nevers. Although she had never been particularly bright or intelligent and was a slow learner, she served as infirmarian and sacristan in the order. About herself she said, "Don't I realize that the Blessed Virgin chose me because I was the most ignorant? If she had found anyone more ignorant than me, she would have chosen her. The Blessed Virgin used me like a broom. What do you do with a broom when you have finished sweeping? You put it back in its place, behind the door."

But the Virgin's "sweeping" changed that area of France forever. During one vision, she asked Bernadette to dig in the ground beneath a rock. Water from an underground spring flowed up, and the Virgin requested that a chapel be built there. The water continues to flow, and thousands of visitors come yearly to bathe, drink, and take the water home. Its curative powers have healed people with all types of illnesses and afflictions. The spring near Lourdes is today one of the world's major pilgrimage destinations.

PRAYER

Bernadette, I hope I can understand that God does not choose only the smart and learned people to accomplish his will. Even the slow, unlearned, and dull are called to lead a life of holiness. Help me believe this when others put me down or criticize my ideas or call me stupid. Teach me that even if I am only a broom, I am still useful, and that my humble life is part of the divine plan.

DEVOTIONAL PRACTICE

Tie a ribbon around the handle of a broom, or carve some sacred symbol in its handle. When you use the broom, recall Bernadette's statement that the Virgin used her becaused she was nothing special. Sweeping the floor is also neither special nor exciting, but practice prayerful mindfulness while you sweep and try to find spiritual meaning even in the most humble task.

ST. BERNARD OF CLAIRVAUX

"A great medieval celebrity."

1090–1153

AUGUST 20

Bernard, the twenty-two-year-old son of a wealthy Burgundian noble, collected thirty-one companions, including four brothers and an uncle, went to the Cistercian monastery at Cîteaux, and asked to join. The monastery had not had any new recruits for several years, and the abbot, Stephen Harding, was delighted. Within two years, he appointed Bernard abbot of a daughter house at Clairvaux. In five years the number of monks at Clairvaux swelled to one hundred and thirty. Bernard was only twenty-seven. It would seem that the young man, who just a few weeks before he asked to become a monk was uncertain what to do with his life, had gone about as far as he could go in the monastic life. But Bernard's fame had only begun. He became one of the most influential and well-known men of his age.

In 1130 Bernard took to the roads in France, Germany, and Italy to campaign in the disputed papal election in favor of Innocent II, who was eventually accepted as pope. From then on, princes, bishops, and popes sought his advice. He began public preaching in 1140 to students in Paris, and was caught up in the intellectual and religious disputes of the day. He fought against the Albigensian movement in southern France, helped to stop pogroms against Jews in the Rhineland, called for a second Crusade against the Turks after they captured Edessa, and was instrumental in discrediting the popular teacher Abelard over his notion of the role of human reason in knowing the truth. Using shrewd diplomatic understanding, he drew up a treaty that resolved a political crisis arising from the Duke of Lorraine's attack on the town of Metz.

Bernard also found time for writing mystical works, over three hundred sermons, voluminous letters, and reflections on the scriptures. Under Bernard's influence, sixty-eight Cistercian monasteries sprang from the monks at Clairvaux. In the last forty years of his life, there was hardly a political, religious, or intellectual event in which he was not involved. Bernard of Clairvaux was one of the most influential individuals in his century. He died at age sixty-three.

PRAYER

Bernard, show me ways to stay involved in the historical events that occur in my life. Your life was an example of how spiritual perspectives can be brought to social, intellectual, and political movements. Help me to view the great and not-so-great events of the day through my faith, my religious values, and the spiritual goals of my personal life. Whenever possible, teach me how to make positive contributions to the important issues of the day.

DEVOTIONAL PRACTICE

Prayer helps in mysterious ways that we may never comprehend. Deepen your faith in the power of prayer with this practice. For one week (or longer), take the morning newspaper and open it randomly to any page with your eyes closed. Lay your finger on the page and open your eyes. Read whatever article you have selected, and find a way to offer a prayer for the people, circumstances, or suffering contained in the article. Pause for a moment at noon and in the evening and repeat your prayer.

ST. BERTILLA BOSCARDIN

"Be a goose."

1888–1922

OCTOBER 20

"I'm a poor thing, a goose. Teach me. I want to become a saint," the sixteen-year-old Annetta Boscardin pleaded with her novice mistress after she had been formally accepted into the Sisters of St. Dorothy and given the name Bertilla. Her superiors, however, decided that the goose image fit, and sent Bertilla to wash dishes in the kitchen, help out in the bakery, and work in the laundry room. She threw herself into these duties, remembering that she had been turned down already in another convent and that one of the local priests had said she was good for nothing but peeling potatoes.

Bertilla had peeled a lot of potatoes. She had been born into a poor peasant family in northern Italy, and had suffered under the abusive treatment of a violent, hard-drinking father. Bertilla attended school only now and then, spending most of her time helping at home and working as a domestic servant for neighbors. When she told her novice mistress, "I can't do anything," she meant anything beyond the humblest of jobs. And yet in time the young nun was trained in nursing and assigned to the order's hospital in Treviso. Unfortunately, her reputation of being inept had preceded her, and her new superior put her to work, once again, in the kitchen.

In 1907 Bertilla took her vows and began working in the children's diphtheria ward. She herself fell sick, and her infirmity stayed with her until she died. During World War I, when Italian troops suffered setbacks, the hospital was on the front line and subject to air raids. Many patients were taken to the basement for safety, but some could not be moved. Bertilla heroically continued to care for those on the vulnerable upper floors. Eventually the hospital was evacuated, and the nuns were moved to a military hospital.

Bertilla's superiors thought she was too attached to her patients and that she overworked herself unnecessarily. In reality, Bertilla had found her calling in the self-sacrificing dedication of a nurse and nun. Again, as a kind of reprimand for foolish behavior, she was sent to work in the laundry! She did not complain. Finally, the mother general of the order discovered her wasted talents and assigned her to an administrative post in the Treviso hospital, where she managed the children's isolation ward.

In 1922 at age thirty-four, Bertilla succumbed to the illness that had plagued her most of her adult life. She died three days after an unsuccessful surgery.

PRAYER

Bertilla, help me find the good qualities in myself even when I am not able to see them very clearly. Show me how to keep faith in myself when others think I am inept or good for nothing. I will try to recall at all times that any task done well for the love of God is pleasing to him.

DEVOTIONAL PRACTICE

Bertilla thought of herself as a goose, a not very flattering image for someone who had great dedication to her work and her desire to be a nun. Actually, the female goose is a dedicated mother, capable of defending her brood with great ferocity. Later in life, Bertilla demonstrated just that aspect of the goose, as she protected both infirm adults and children under her wing.

If you had to think of yourself as an animal or bird, what would it be? What animal or bird have you been called by others? You may be able to think of more than one, both flattering and not flattering. No matter what animal or bird you associate with yourself, think of it as a teacher who can help you live a full life and be of great service to others. Read up on its habits, and use the animal as a kind of spiritual totem or reference for living more fully and, like St. Bertilla, becoming a saint in spite of being a goose.

ST. BLAISE

"Everything can use healing."

C. 316

FEBRUARY 3

Blaise was the son of well-to-do parents who gave him the education befitting a young Christian boy of the fourth century. Growing up he was attracted to the priestly life and became a bishop at a rather young age, stationed at Sebastea in Armenia. The times he lived in were susceptible to outbreaks of persecution, since Christianity was a relatively new religion and had not been fully accepted yet by many people in the Roman world.

When Agricolaus, the local Roman governor, launched a persecution, Blaise received a vision that told him to leave the city and retreat to the wilderness. He was directed to a cave in the mountains where he lived for a while alone, having only wild animals as his companions. Surprisingly, the animals recognized in Blaise a remarkable human being, blessed with divine grace, for they approached him when they were ill or injured and the holy man healed them.

People also came to Blaise for healing. A woman brought her little boy who was choking on a fish bone, unable to catch his breath, and almost at the point of death. Blaise healed him, and the boy lived.

When imperial hunters scoured the countryside for wild animals to capture and take back to the city for use in the amphitheaters and colosseums as part of the gladiatorial games, they found Blaise calmly talking and interacting with wild beasts. They were amazed, and they captured him along with the animals and took him back to Agricolaus.

On the way a woman came up to Blaise to tell him that her pig had been carried off by a wolf. Blaise called the wolf out of the forest and commanded it to return the pig to the woman unhurt. It did as it was commanded.

In a dark prison Blaise was scourged and given no food to eat. But the woman whose pig he had returned came secretly, bringing him meals, and candles so that he would not have to sit in darkness. When it became apparent that the torture was not breaking Blaise or convincing him to renounce his faith, the authorities ordered his flesh to be ripped and his head cut off.

Today Blaise is the patron of sore throats.

PRAYER

Blaise, give me the insight to recognize the places where healing is needed. It is easy to see the need in physical ailments, but often the feelings, the heart, and the emotions also need healing. Sometimes the land, plants, animals, and water need purifying and restoration. Help me to be mindful of these situations and bring to them my prayers, good wishes, and blessings and any practical service of mine that will hasten recovery.

DEVOTIONAL PRACTICE

The liturgical custom of blessing throats on February 3 is to place two crossed candles (unlit) on either side of the neck of the person being blessed, along with the priest's official prayer for health. As a healing ritual, get two new candles and dedicate them for healing purposes. Whenever you know of someone or some condition that needs healing, hold the candles in one hand, crossed to form a kind of V, and visualize between the two candles the person or situation that needs healing. Hold that image while you offer prayers to St. Blaise, God, Mary, or any saint who could help. The ritual activity of holding the candles will help to focus your attention and keep your intention strong while you pray.

ST. BONAVENTURE

"Finding God in dirty dishes."

1221–1274

JULY 15

According to legend, when Bonaventure was seven years old he was cured of an illness by Francis of Assisi. The result of this auspicious meeting was that the boy decided to become a Franciscan. He studied theology and philosophy at the University of Paris, and in 1243 he joined the Franciscan order. He became a renowned teacher and established himself as one of the best minds of the Middle Ages. He wrote many essays, over five hundred sermons, and the official biography of St. Francis.

Bonaventure became enmeshed in a controversy over whether the new order of mendicant friars, such as himself, should teach along side the lay professors. The lay teachers saw the mendicants as intruders who threatened their tight control over the teaching profession. Bonaventure argued vigorously against the lay professors, and in 1256, the pope ordered that the professors cease their attacks against the new teachers.

Later, when Bonaventure was appointed cardinal-archbishop of Albano, he received the news of his appointment while washing dishes in the kitchen. His motto was "Do common things well and be constantly faithful to small matters," so he asked the delegation to hang the cardinal's hat, a symbol of the office, on a tree until he had finished cleaning up the kitchen's clutter.

Bonaventure seems to have valued the ordinary tasks of daily life as much as the great theological and philosophical issues that concerned him as a teacher and writer. He said that "joy is the great sign of God's grace within the soul." He wrote that creation was a means to discover the image and likeness of God, and that human beings are capable of finding God in the shadows, traces, and appearances of the physical world—even in dirty dishes.

Bonaventure died while attending the Council at Lyons that achieved the successful, although short-lived, reunion between the eastern and western Churches.

PRAYER

Bonaventure, show me how to find God in daily tasks. Help me to do ordinary things in extraordinary ways and to be faithful to the small tasks that make up my day. Show me the way to find joy in these common activities and to radiate that joy to others.

DEVOTIONAL PRACTICE

Bless the ordinary tasks of daily life, such as washing dishes, before you begin them. Look for and cultivate the joy that can come from being mindful of what you are doing at the moment, rather than from some anticipated activity. Remind yourself: Joy exists only in the present. Past joys have ended. Future joys do not yet exist. If I miss the joy right now, I will have missed God.

ST. BONIFACE OF GERMANY

"Chopping down trees but not the roots."

C. 680-754

JUNE 5

When the English monk Boniface cut down the sacred oak tree in what is now Germany to impress the tribal people with his power as a Christian, he miscalculated the results. Legends tell us that the people were indeed impressed that nothing harmful befell the missionary for desecrating a holy tree, and they were converted to Christianity.

But like so many Christian missionaries before and after him, Boniface supposed that in accepting Jesus' teachings, his converts were rejecting the older spiritual traditions that were part of their way of life. Boniface was aghast later in his career to discover that his converts had "lapsed" into pagan ways and needed "reconverting." In his last years, he resigned his bishopric at Mainz to bring back the fallen German tribes into the Christian fold.

Originally Boniface was sent by the pope to preach to the German tribes in 722. With the Gaulish emperor Charles Martel's support, he had tremendous success making inroads into the Germany territory. After Martel's death in 741, Boniface reformed the Christian communities in Gaul through a series of councils in the 740s. In 747 the pope appointed him bishop over all of Germany, and when Martel's son Pepin, who succeeded his brother Carolman, united Gaul into what would become France, Boniface continued to enjoy royal protection and support for his work. He imagined that Christianity was becoming the only religion of central Europe.

But in his later years, Boniface realized what countless missionaries to native people would discover again and again: indigenous cultures are remarkably tolerant of various deities and spiritual beings, a far cry from the monotheistic and monolithic attitudes of the Church. To missionaries like Boniface, the Germans were "lapsing." From the tribal point of view, they had never given up all their traditional beliefs and practices when they accepted new ones.

In his early seventies, Boniface once more hit the roads and rivers to preach to the Germans. He reconverted some, and went on to new tribes. He met his death on a day when he was quietly reading in his tent and his camp was attacked by hostile warriors. He refused to let younger men defend him, and he willingly died for his faith.

PRAYER

Boniface, help me to understand what you learned in your life as a missionary among people who held different spiritual views from your own—namely, that for many people it is possible to entertain various ideas and concepts about the Creator and the meaning of creation. While I seek the courage to speak boldly about my own beliefs, let me be tolerant and understanding of others who believe differently.

DEVOTIONAL PRACTICE

Many cultures have honored sacred trees, including Christians who honor the Tree of the Cross. St. Columba would not allow a sacred grove of oak trees to be cut down to build a church, and St. Brigid named her monastery Kildare, which means Church of the Oak. Find an oak or other majestic tree, and honor it and its Creator in some special way. You might tie a prayer ribbon to it; bless a cup of water and pour it slowly around the roots; leave a cookie, bread, or piece of cake for the animals and birds who live near the tree; or simply sit with your back against the trunk, and feel and appreciate the sacred life that flows through it.

ST. BONIFACE OF TARSUS

"Gigolo and martyr."

D. C. 306

MAY 14

Boniface was probably a kept man, what today we would call a gigolo. Officially he was the head steward for a wealthy Roman woman named Aglae, but it was also well known that he was her lover. Descriptions of him as being morally loose, a heavy drinker, and exceedingly free with Aglae's wealth might raise doubts about how efficiently or ethically he supervised her household. To his credit, however, Boniface gave generously to the poor and showed great hospitality in entertaining visitors. He and Aglae seemed to have had a mutually supportive relationship.

Aglae enjoyed her reputation of being a powerful woman in Roman society. She liked the attention that her wealth and public charities brought her. On several occasions, she sponsored lavish entertainments for the entire city. The city loved her. It may have been to heighten her image even more that Aglae sent Boniface on a mission to the eastern empire to buy relics of martyrs. "I have heard," she told him, "that they who honor martyrs will have a share in their glory." Boniface promised not to fail in bringing back relics, but then, having a premonition, he asked her, "But what if my own body comes back to you as one of them?"

Boniface went to Tarsus in Cilicia, where a brutal persecution of Christians was then taking place (the western empire at that time had tempered its harassment of Christians). Boniface sent his servants and horses to an inn, but he himself went directly to the sadistic governor, Simplicius, who was having, at that very moment, twenty Christians tortured before him. Boniface, however, was now a changed man, for during his journey he had given up drink and he now spent much of the time praying and fasting. He bounded up to the governor and shouted, "Great is the God of the Christians! Great is the martyrs' God!"

The governor ordered Boniface to be arrested and tortured in various ways, but he remained unharmed. Finally, a soldier cut off his head. His servants bought his body for five hundred pieces of gold, embalmed it, and took it back to Italy.

Aglae received word that her lover was returning as he had predicted: a martyr. Boniface had become the relics she had sent him to buy. She buried him at the place where she met his body outside Rome, and later she had a church built there as a shrine for his relics. Aglae reformed her own life, lived simply and prayerfully, and died fifteen years later. Her final request was that her body be buried beside that of her one-time lover.

PRAYER

Boniface, your life went from luxurious comfort to a painful, horrible death. Help me to be mindful that nothing lasts forever, and that all things have their season, which must come to an end. Keep me from being so attached to the material aspects of my life that I cannot accept the time when they too must pass.

DEVOTIONAL PRACTICE

The lives of the rich and famous are held up as ideals to aspire to, even though many celebrities are plagued with money problems, addictions, unhappy marriages, rebellious children, illness, depression, and scandals. Many saints in the early years of Christianity were the "rich and famous" of their day. Aglae and Boniface were two of them.

Buy one of the tabloids in the supermarket (or page through one if the checkout line is slow), and find two pictures of celebrities that immediately grab your attention: one picture that you find disgusting, and one that appeals to you because of its glamour. Regardless of what you personally feel about these two celebrities or the actual details of their lives, use the photographs for meditating upon the notion that everything contains its opposite, that even in the most glamorous lives there are moments of drabness, and in the most squalid events there are rays of hope.

You might also consider the situations depicted in the photographs in light of Jesus' promise that "the first shall be last, and the last shall be first."

Or consider what the photos say about the Old Testament wisdom, "For everything there is a season, and everything has a purpose under heaven."

ST. BRENDAN

"Seeker of paradise."

486–579

MAY 16

Brendan is best remembered as the Irish monk who together with his twelve companions pushed off from the coast of Ireland in a small boat, trusting that the winds of God would take them to the Island of Paradise. Brendan, the risk taker and adventurer, had a yearning for otherworldly experiences, and when Barinthus, a holy man, told him about the Island of Paradise that he and his son had visited, Brendan's curiosity was aroused. He knew that he too must see this marvelous place. Tradition relates that Brendan's two voyages, taking about seven years, did bring them to an island where they saw the glories of the life that awaits us after death.

Other Celtic voyagers also discovered marvelous islands, sometimes called the "Isles of Wonder" or the "Blessed Isles," but it is Brendan who inspires us to look for glimpses of heaven here on earth: a place without fear, misery, sickness, or strife, where flowers and fruit trees are in perpetual bloom, and people are youthful, healthy, and beautiful. Sometimes this otherworldly place is called the "Land of Truth" or the "Land of Wisdom."

Having grown up in monastic communities, Brendan founded several himself, including the great monastery at Clonfert, which he began around 559. His main center of activity was in the Dingle Peninsula in western Ireland, where the ocean views draw the eye far out to sea and where on the right days the horizon seems to contain islands that appear and disappear.

In later life, Brendan had another unusual glimpse of heavenly realms. One day a bird flew threw the chapel window and landed on the altar. The light coming from the bird was bright and glorious. Brendan asked who it was and why it had come. "Michael, the angel," it replied, "and I have come to play for you." Then the bird drew its beak across its wing, like a bow across a violin, and the most beautiful music Brendan had ever heard came from that wing. After this, the saint was never satisfied with the ordinary music of the local harpers.

Brendan died while he was visiting his sister. He asked that his body be taken back to Clonfert, for that was to be his "place of resurrection."

PRAYER

Brendan, put into me the same spirit of adventure that you had sailing across uncharted seas, wandering the roads and pathways of Ireland, and founding monastic communities to satisfy the longings of men and women looking for their place of resurrection. Most of all, teach me to look for signs of heaven here on earth, and to believe that God has placed them here if we but knew how to recognize them.

DEVOTIONAL PRACTICE

We should not deny ourselves the pleasure of dreaming about the glories of the heavenly realms just because they are in another realm most people never enter until they die. Often we imagine that the wonders of heaven have no counterpart to the physical wonders of this world, but Jesus himself referred to heaven as having many mansions and to the kingdom of heaven being within us.

In the spirit of St. Brendan, create a meditative practice that uses both music and landscape. Find photos of landscapes that match your "physical" image of a heavenly realm, and select some recorded music that suggests otherworldly melodies. (A good harper can often create this kind of music.) Then, whenever you want to relax and forget about the cares of the day, put on the music and dream about the landscape, actually imagining yourself wandering through it as a spiritual adventurer, enjoying the beauty and pleasure that God put there for you to find.

ST. BRIDGET OF SWEDEN

"A flaky dreamer of practical visions."

1303–1373

JULY 23

Bridget's father was a wealthy landowner and the governor of Upland, Sweden, and her mother was the daughter of the governor of East Gothland. Growing up in a powerful feudal family, Bridget married Ulf Gudmarsson when they were fourteen and eighteen years old, respectively. Their marriage lasted for twenty-eight happy years and produced eight children, including St. Catherine of Sweden. While living on their estate at Ulfasa, Bridget displayed considerable independence for a woman of her time by having a large number of male friends, most of them sharing her own scholarly interests.

Around 1335 Bridget became lady-in-waiting for the somewhat spoiled and weak-willed Queen Blanche, married to the scoundrel King Magnus II. The visions that Bridget began having as a child continued during this time. They covered such diverse topics as hygiene (the need for washing to prevent disease), peace between England and France, the improprieties of the current pope, Urban V, and the need for pilgrimages. She developed a somewhat flaky reputation at court, as people gossiped about the outlandish dreams she must be having each night.

On the return from their pilgrimage to Santiago de Compostela, Spain, in the early 1340s, Ulf became ill, and the two vowed to enter religious life if he recovered. He did improve, but relapsed and died shortly thereafter. Following her vow, Bridget lived at the Cistercian monastery at Alvastra where her revelations continued. Fearing she was deluding herself or being duped by the devil, she sought advice from the prior who assured her that her visions were from God. He recorded them for her, and they are still available today.

Bridget founded a monastery at Vadstena on Lake Vättern that attracted both men and women. The coed community of nuns and monks totaled about eighty-five individuals, gave money generously to the poor, and collected an impressive library that made it the intellectual center of medieval Sweden.

Heedless of the Black Plague, in 1350 Bridget traveled to Rome, where she continued to do good works, reform monastic life, criticize the pope for dissolute living, and in general generate gossip and persecution around herself. In 1371 she made a pilgrimage to the Holy Land with her favorite children—Catherine, Birger, and Charles, who died in her arms of a severe fever. In the Holy Land she had strong visions of the sacred history that had occurred there. On her return to Rome, her health failing, she died at age seventy-three.

PRAYER

Bridget, support me in dreams and visions of a better life and in the revelations that come to me in prayer. Let me seek counsel when I am uncertain, and have the courage to stand up for my views when I truly believe they are from on high. Give me strength also to speak out for what is right, no matter who disagrees.

DEVOTIONAL PRACTICE

Spend ten to fifteen minutes at least once a week, or more often, relaxing, clearing your mind, and meditating on one difficulty you are facing, asking God's light to shine on the problem and show you how it can be resolved. Evaluate the solutions that occur to you during these times, but take them seriously, no matter how outlandish they might seem. They just might be the beginnings of the end of your problems.

ST. BRIGID

"Fiery sunbeam of love."

C. 452–524

FEBRUARY 1

Brigid was born and grew up in a druid's household, where her mother was a slave. She was given the name of an ancient Celtic fire goddess who was the patron of poetry, healing, and metalwork. In her own life the holy woman Brigid displayed the same flaming power that the Irish have associated with the older goddess. A hymn to St. Brigid reads, "Brigid, golden sparkling flame, lead us to eternal day, the fiery radiant sun."

Brigid founded the monastery at Kildare, meaning Church of the Oak, and established there an eternal flame tended solely by women. The flame lasted for centuries, until political strife violated the sanctuary and the flame went out. But it is hard to put out Brigid's flame completely, for her role as a firekeeper continues in households that honor her patronage over health, cooking, and the domestic arts. The traditional Brigid cross, woven of dried grasses on her feast day and hung near the hearth or stove, is in the pattern of an ancient sun wheel, a design found the world over.

Two stories about Brigid illuminate her role as the bringer of warmth and life. On one occasion, she arrived at a chapel for services just as a rainstorm was ending. Her cloak was dripping wet, and not wanting to bring it indoors, she hung it on a sunbeam that was just breaking through the clouds. At another time, she asked a local chieftain for land for her monastery and he said he would give her as much as her cloak could cover. So she removed her cloak and flung it across the land. It covered as far as the eye could see.

So many stories about Brigid associate her with fire or the sun that it is hard not to see her power and presence as being that very element itself. A classic

Celtic phrase to address the Creator is "God of the Elements," and it seems that the divine element that manifests most dramatically in Brigid is the power of the sun.

Brigid is honored on the First of February, the beginning of spring in the old Celtic calendar. The pregnant ewes are once again lactating, reminding rural people of the coming supplies of milk and butter that are associated with Brigid. An old saying confirms the importance of this time: "Brigid breathes life into the mouth of dead winter."

PRAYER

Brigid, help me breathe life into whatever is dead around me. Let your radiance shine in my life so that my activities and conversations may sparkle with the heavenly light that the Creator of the Elements showers upon us.

DEVOTIONAL PRACTICE

It is important to recognize signs and omens that God gives us through the natural world. Rainbows and sunbeams have been honored in many places as indications of the divine presence in our lives. Brigid's cloak is made of heavenly sunlight; it can hang on sunbeams; it can be cast over the entire land. Get in the habit of watching for sunbeams and greeting them with a short prayer or affirmation, such as "Brigid, you have cast your cloak upon us once again. You are the sunbeam of our love."

ST. CAMILLUS DE LELLIS

"Addictive gambler, soldier, health-care provider."

1550–1614

JULY 14

With a height of six foot six, Camillus de Lellis was an imposing soldier in the war against the Turks. Nevertheless, in spite of his size and strength, he was severely wounded in the leg and the wound became infected. At the youthful age of seventeen, de Lellis found himself in Rome in the San Giacomo Hospital for incurables. Although a patient, he also helped to care for others. After nine months, however, the staff could no longer endure his quarrelsome nature, and de Lellis was asked to leave. Still suffering pain in his leg, he returned to the Turkish war.

This time it wasn't battle that did de Lellis in but his addiction to gambling. In 1574 he lost all his money and his military equipment and found himself a hungry, homeless man on the streets of Naples. As he "bottomed out," he recalled a vow he had made years earlier to become a monk, so he found work in a construction project for the Capuchin monks. The following year, at age twenty-five, he wanted to join the friars but was rejected because of his leg wound. So he returned to Rome, now a reformed sinner, and asked the hospital that had once thrown him out to let him return, this time as a nurse.

Hospital care in de Lellis's day was far from professional. Hired servants cared for the sick, but usually without much commitment since they were basically just earning their wages. De Lellis organized health-care workers who had a desire to serve out of charity and compassion. De Lellis so impressed the hospital administrators that they appointed him superintendent. Eventually he was ordained a priest, established his own order under the name "Ministers of the Sick," and founded fifteen houses of brothers and eight hospitals. In 1596 and 1601, his men went to Hungary and Croatia to serve wounded soldiers on the battlefields. This is the first recorded incident of what would become "military field ambulances."

De Lellis continued to serve the sick, particularly on the plague-infected ships that arrived in Naples and Rome. Throughout his life, he himself was among the sick and suffering. He endured pain from his leg wound for forty-six years. He also had a severe rupture for thirty-eight years and two persistent sores on the sole of his foot. Near the end of his life, a stomach disorder prevented him from enjoying or retaining his food. De Lellis is the patron of the sick and of health-care providers.

PRAYER

Give me the self-knowledge I need to spot the addictions in my life, as you, Camillus, realized your own addiction to gambling. Help me put an end to the ways I waste time and energy that could be used in serving others. If my addiction is too strong for me to handle alone, ask God to lead me to the people or organizations that will offer support.

DEVOTIONAL PRACTICE

Even if you do not consider yourself addicted to some activity, consider the ways you waste time in behavior that might be self-destructive or a problem for others in your life. The addictive activity might involve alcohol, nicotine, drugs, food or some specific food, television, shopping, gambling. Even beneficial activities such as athletics or reading can become problems if used as escapes from important responsibilities.

If you engage in some harmful activity or devote too much time to any activity, create a ritual in which you destroy the symbol of that activity, such as liquor, cigarettes, pills, the *TV Guide,* cards, or food. You might burn the symbolic object in a fireplace, bury it, put it outdoors where the elements will remove it, or just slowly and mindfully tear the symbol apart and throw it away. Offer prayers and resolve to eliminate or reduce the activity in your life. Repeat this regularly if necessary, and seek professional help as well.

ST. CANAIRE

"Worlds of men, worlds of women."

SIXTH CENTURY

JANUARY 28

Not much is known about Canaire except her confrontation with an abbot named Senan, and it is this story that has inspired followers through the ages.

Canaire lived near Bantry Bay in Ireland, and like many Irish men and women inspired by the Gospel message, she retired to a hermitage to live a life of prayer, hard work, and asceticism. At some point, she sought her "place of resurrection," the term used by Celtic monastics to mean the place where they would like to die and enter the heavenly realms. Canaire decided it would be on the Island of Cathaig.

Inis Cathaig, as it is called, was located at the mouth of the Shannon River, and on that island was a venerable men's community led by Senan. Like some religious communities, this one practiced absolute separatism for men and women. So strict were the monks on Inis Cathaig that no woman was even allowed on the island, much less into the monastic grounds. Not all Irish communities were so strict; in fact, some were double monasteries, having communities of both men and women.

Canaire approached the island, the legend saying that she walked across the Shannon. Senan went out to meet her and denied her an approach, citing the all-male character of the monastery. He told her to go to a women's island. Canaire replied that she was seeking hospitality with Senan, no one else. Hospitality was one of the cardinal Celtic virtues and a mainstay of monastic life. Canaire demanded to be admitted.

Her arguments were hard-hitting. "Christ is no worse than you," she told Senan. "Christ came to redeem women, no less than to redeem men. Women gave service and tending to Christ and his apostles. No less than men, women enter into the heavenly kingdom." Why, then, she asked, could she not be admitted to Inis Cathaig?

Senan realized he was dealing with a formidable adversary, and that he had been bested by her reasoning. He allowed Canaire to come on ashore. There she received the sacrament, and apparently died at that moment. She had found the place of resurrection that she had desired.

PRAYER

Canaire, help me to evaluate the needs that men and women have to be separate and to be together. There are valid reasons for both, and true wisdom is in understanding individual circumstances when and where they arise. May God grant that I can fight separatism where it is not justified and accept it where it is truly needed.

DEVOTIONAL PRACTICE

Canaire had her own hermitage but desired a different place for her resurrection. Sometimes we too need the inspiration of a holy place different from our customary church, grotto, or chapel, or wherever it is we find God. Consider a place near you that is a "holy place," even if it is part of a religious tradition different from your own. Visit it, make a pilgrimage, or attend services there if possible. Do this in the spirit of expanding your spiritual experiences, not as a rejection of your own tradition.

ST. CATHERINE DE RICCI

"Visions, ecstasies, and out-of-body-experiences."

1522–1590

FEBRUARY 2

Saint Philip Neri, a popular preacher and confessor living in Rome, was visited by a woman who had been corresponding with him from the town of Prato, many miles away. She was Alexandria de Ricci, who was born into an important Florentine family, joined the Dominican order when she was thirteen, and took the name Catherine when she professed her vows as a nun. The remarkable feature of her visit to Neri is that she never left her convent in Prato. She journeyed to him in what today we would probably call an out-of-body experience. Neri attested to her presence, as did five witnesses.

Catherine de Ricci had other mystical experiences as well. When she joined the Dominicans, almost immediately she began to suffer severe diseases that lasted for two years and that medications only seemed to complicate. During these years she found strength and solace by meditating on the Passion of Jesus. When she was twenty, she began to have visions of the Passion and ecstatic experiences in which she would feel the pain and suffering of Jesus. Eventually she began to act out the scenes that led up to Jesus' Crucifixion in a kind of visionary drama for others to witness. These ecstasies occurred weekly for twelve years.

Catherine's visions gained much notoriety for her and her community. Pilgrims and curiosity seekers flocked to the convent to see what was going on. In 1552 when she was elected prioress, her visionary life and ecstatic experiences became troublesome for her and her sisters. Community life was disrupted. The nuns, including Catherine, decided to pray that the visions cease. Two years later, they stopped. Catherine lived for another thirty-six years and died at the age of sixty-eight.

PRAYER

Catherine, help me to believe in mystical and supernatural occurrences. Our age scoffs at many paranormal experiences, and while not all of them are necessarily valid, many are. And it is through mystical experiences, such as visions and powerful dreams, that God touches our lives. Pray also that I might be able to discern the true visions from the false.

DEVOTIONAL PRACTICE

Out-of-body experiences, remote viewing, and shamanic journeying are three somewhat similar techniques for "seeing" or "being" in distant places without leaving the physical place where your body is. All three can occur spontaneously, but they can also be practiced intentionally. We will use the idea behind these methods of "distant seeing" to develop a simple meditation technique, which can be done when you feel the need for spiritual renewal from a particular place but cannot go there physically.

Choose some spiritual or sacred place that is important to you, such as a church, chapel, the grounds of a retreat center, or a cemetery. Close your eyes and get comfortable as you would to meditate. When you feel relaxed, allow your imagination to bring up a picture of the place you chose. "Zoom in" on it, and experience yourself standing there. Use all your senses: see the colors, smell the scents, hear sounds, touch objects, feel the air, taste food or water if they are there. Then slowly move around the place as if you were strolling leisurely, observing and taking in all that is going on. When you have made the circuit or begin to feel tired, let the scene fade, and bring your awareness back to the place where you are sitting. Recall the feelings of peace and tenderness of this place whenever you need a spiritual boost during the day.

ST. CATHERINE LABOURÉ

"Worldwide fame and anonymity."

1806–1876

NOVEMBER 28

At 11:30 at night on July 18, 1830, in the French convent of the Sisters of Charity of St. Vincent de Paul at Châtillon-sur-Seine, Sister Catherine Labouré woke from her sleep and saw what she described as a "shining child" standing in her room. The child led her down the hall to the nun's chapel where a brilliant lady appeared to her. Recognizing the vision as the Virgin Mary, Labouré spoke with the Mother of God for over two hours, and then went back to bed. About four months later, Mary appeared again to Labouré in the chapel, this time in the form of a picture that was to become world-famous.

The visionary picture showed Mary standing on a globe of the world with streams of light coming from her hands. Encircling her were the words "O Mary, conceived without sin, pray for us who have recourse to you." The picture revolved so that Catherine could see the back of it. Here was the letter "M" with a cross and two hearts. One of the hearts was crowned with thorns; the other was pierced by a sword. Catherine Labouré heard instructions that she should take this image and have it made into a medal and that anyone who wore this medal would be blessed and filled with grace through the protection of the Virgin Mary.

Similar visions recurred for about a year. Labouré told only her confessor about them, but he took the bold step of turning her visionary picture into the kind of medal she described. In 1832, fifteen hundred medals were struck. Eventually millions would be produced and distributed worldwide. It was known as the "miraculous medal," and wearing it became one of the most popular spiritual practices in the modern Church.

Catherine herself, however, received absolutely no recognition. At her own request, she demanded complete anonymity and secrecy. Throughout the official investigation into her visions (which declared them authentic) and the popular enthusiasm that resulted, Catherine remained uninvolved publicly. For the next forty-five years, she worked as the convent's portress, tended chickens, and cared for the elderly in the convent's hospice. Members of her community knew her as somewhat aloof, matter-of-fact, even distant and unimportant. Only eight months before her death did she reveal to her superior that it was she who had received the visions that began the now-famous practice of wearing the "miraculous medal."

PRAYER

Catherine, you lived for forty-five years with a great secret, seeking no publicity or honor for yourself. May I be inspired by your example to deny my ego now and then, and not always be so eager to step forward for praise and recognition, even when it would not be inappropriate to do so. By forgoing the world's praises, may I learn to value the secret, hidden, deeper worth of knowing that I am simply and quietly living a good and decent life.

DEVOTIONAL PRACTICE

The most obvious practice in the spirit of Catherine Labouré would be to wear the miraculous medal that came from her visions. But to enter even deeper into her remarkable humility, you might get a medal and tell no one that you have it. Carry it secretly in a purse or pocket so that only you and God know about it. In this way, you will not receive any public praise for the practice or be considered devout because you wear a medal around your neck.

ST. CATHERINE OF GENOA

"A wife at wit's end."

1447–1510

SEPTEMBER 15

In 1473, depressed and trapped in a horrible marriage, Catherine Adorno prayed to St. Benedict that he would ask God to strike her with an illness that would force her to stay in bed for three months. But God had other plans. Two days later, and still in good health, she was filled with a great spiritual consolation, went to Communion, and began to live an intensely mystical life that would continue until she died. Her husband also shaped up, and their marriage took a startling new turn.

Catherine had been a pawn in a contrived marriage between the powerful Guelf and Ghibelline families of northern Italy. Her husband, Julian Adorno, whose family was declining financially and politically, hoped that his marriage to the sixteen-year-old daughter of a prosperous Guelf family would bolster his own family's status. Catherine was not interested in marrying. Nevertheless, the marriage took place, and for the next ten years, she was depressed and miserable.

Julian was hardly ever home. He squandered their money, pursued a wild reckless life, and failed to control his hot temper. He was also unfaithful to Catherine. For the first five years she led a lonely miserable life at home. During the next five years, she threw herself into the social whirl of the time, hoping that would make her feel better, but it, too, left her miserable.

But then there occurred Catherine's almost miraculous transformation and recommitment to a spiritual life. Soon thereafter, Julian finished squandering practically all their resources, and he was forced to come to terms with their lives. They moved out of their palazzo and into a small house and decided to live together celibately. They also began to do volunteer work at the Pammatone hospital in Genoa. In 1479 they actually moved in and lived at the hospital, and eleven years later Catherine was appointed hospital director.

The couple worked heroically during the plague year of 1493, when four-fifths of the city died. Catherine herself caught the plague and recovered, but her health was never the same. In three years, she resigned as director, but she continued to live and work in the hospital. The following year Julian died.

Catherine was a remarkable hospital administrator, balancing budgets, mangaging property, directing staff, caring for the sick, and all the while leading a deeply mystical life of prayer and spiritual devotions. She is proof that a mystic can be a sensible, practical, hard-nosed administrator. Her two works—*Dialogue Between the Soul and the Body* and *Treatise on Purgatory*—are still classics in mystical literature.

In 1507 Catherine's health was broken, and she suffered greatly during her last years. On September 15, 1510, delirious from a high fever, she died.

PRAYER

Catherine, teach me how to make the best of my marriage (or relationship), even when times are rough. May I acquire the same kind of wisdom that you developed living with someone who was unable to create and share a good life with you. Help me and my partner to make the changes that will bring us happiness together and allow us as a couple to be of use to others.

DEVOTIONAL PRACTICE

Here is a ritual to put the problems you may be having with your partner into a spiritual context. Light a candle for clarity. Burn a stick of incense to sweeten your mood. For ten to fifteen minutes sit quietly in a chair and visualize or imagine your partner's higher self or guardian angel standing before you. Clear your mind and heart, and think about nothing in particular, except how peaceful it can be to sit within the companionship of your partner's higher spirit. When a thought arises, let it go, and bring your attention back to the spiritual energy that comes from this image of your partner. Do this every day, or as often as you can. Try to recall this feeling, especially when you are together and not getting along with each other.

ST. CATHERINE OF SIENA

"The world is lost through silence."

1347–1380

APRIL 29

Catherine of Siena believed firmly when she wrote these words that the world would be lost if average men and women did not speak up for the truth. Catherine's life was one of speaking up—by her actions, her speeches, and the letters she wrote to the highest levels of the Church, accusing abbots, bishops, cardinals, and popes of not living up to the Gospel.

At age fifteen Catherine cut off her hair to protest her parents' wishes that she marry. She lived in a cell on the top floor of her parents' house as a recluse, ascetic, and visionary. Next to their home was a Dominican church, and in time she became a tertiary of the order while continuing to live at home for the next three years. Then a vision of Jesus inspired her to step out into the world and speak about God, religion, and the need to reform. At times her preaching and organizing caused her to forget to eat. Her activism caused some people to see her as a charlatan. But soon Catherine built up a following of like-minded people who were equally concerned about the conditions of their times.

These were the years when the scandals in the Church ruined people's lives. The popes lived in France, Church discipline was lax, money influenced appointments, and decisions were based on personal and political reasons rather than the good of the people. War and the Black Plague wreaked havoc on men, women, and children of all ages and social classes. Catherine engaged in the social services and political activism that the poor and the sick always require. She was bold and forthright, even to the point of looking people in the eye when she spoke—something women were not supposed to do in that era.

Catherine even "meddled" in local politics, arguing that the towns of Pisa and Lucca should not support antipapal forces and fight other Christians but embark on a crusade. In an early letter she called the Moslems "infidel dogs who possess our Holy Place," but later she referred to them as "our brothers, redeemed by the blood of Christ, just as we are." Her words could scorch, offend, and make the guilty feel uncomfortable.

In 1376 Catherine went to Avignon and convinced the pope to give up his French residency there and return to Rome. The election of his successor, Urban VI, however, was disputed within the Church and launched the Great Schism when rival popes and political factions warred against each other and divided the Church. She wrote the Italian cardinals, "You are not sweet-smelling flowers but corruptions that cause the whole world to stink."

Urban VI called Catherine to Rome to ask her advice and assist him in his papacy. She arrived with her followers, took up residency, and encouraged others to support Urban as the rightfully elected pope, even though she was personally disgusted by the corruption around him. Probably because of her ceaseless activities and ascetic practices and the strain of Roman politics, Catherine suffered a stroke from which she never recovered. She died at the age of thirty-three.

PRAYER

Catherine, help me find the words to speak up when I see scandals, corruption, and mistreatment of others. Lend me the courage you enjoyed not to worry about what others will think of me but to say what needs to be said to uphold the truth.

DEVOTIONAL PRACTICE

In silence the world is lost, but in another kind of silence we find God. Sometimes the silence in which we find God can bestow on us the courage to break the other silence, in which goodness and the world are lost.

Search for times and places where you can find the silence of God: in a chapel, in your home late at night, on a country road, on a walk through the woods or a field, at a beach, anytime or place you are alone. Listen to the silence, feel it, imagine it wrapping its love around you and filling you with strength. Praise God who gives you these moments. Then when you find yourself in situations where you know you must speak up, feel that encouraging presence of silence around you, and do not be afraid to say what you know is the truth.

ST. CECILIA

"Singer of inner songs."

DATES UNKNOWN

NOVEMBER 22

Cecilia came from a wealthy Roman family, and like the marriages of many young girls, hers was arranged by her parents. The husband chosen for her was a young man named Valerian. During their wedding (it is said), Cecilia did not hear the nuptial music, for she was singing silently in her heart to God. On their wedding night she asked her husband not to have sexual relations with her, for if he did, the angel that watched over her would be angry. Valerian asked to see the angel. Cecilia told him that he would have to become a Christian first. So he went to the bishop, was baptized, and returned to find Cecilia and the angel standing together.

Valerian's brother, Tiburtius, was also baptized, and the two dedicated themselves to good works, which included burying the bodies of Christian martyrs. To do so, however, was a public offense at the time, and the brothers were arrested and brought before the authorities, where they were asked to renounce their faith and to sacrifice to Roman gods. They refused and were subsequently scourged and beheaded. Cecilia, then, was arrested for burying their bodies.

Cecilia's execution was to be suffocation in her own bathroom. The furnace was heated up to an intense degree above its normal capacity to make the bathroom unbearably hot and reduce the air supply. Cecilia, however, was unharmed, and she was then condemned to death by beheading. The executioner bungled the attempt, leaving her still alive after three strokes. She lingered in agony for three days before she finally expired.

Cecilia was buried in the catacombs along with other Christian martyrs. She is the patron of music and musicians.

Cecilia, teach me the inner songs that I can sing in my heart. May I have an ear for heavenly music and always hear the strains of happiness that come from living a decent life in accordance with God's will for me.

DEVOTIONAL PRACTICE

Take a favorite passage from scripture or a poem that inspires you. Select two or three lines and repeat them out loud, as a kind of singsong chant, until a melody emerges from the natural cadences of the words themselves. Play with the melody to tease out the music. In a short while, you will have a personal song. Sing it during the day whenever you need a quick dose of inspiration.

ST. CHARLES BORROMEO

"Play billiards till you die."

1538–1584

NOVEMBER 4

Charles Borromeo, the bishop of Milan, came from a wealthy, aristocratic Italian family. He was born in the family castle, and lived a rather lavish life, entertaining sumptuously as befit a Renaissance court. He personally enjoyed athletics, music, art, and the fine dining that went along with lifestyles of the rich and famous of the sixteenth century. His maternal uncle, from the powerful Medici family, was pope. As was typical of the times, his uncle-pope made him a cardinal-deacon at age twenty-three and bestowed on him numerous offices. He was appointed papal legate to Bologna, the Low Countries, and the cantons of Switzerland, and to the religious orders of St. Francis, the Carmelites, the Knights of Malta, and others.

When Count Frederick Borromeo passed away, many people thought Charles would give up the clerical life and marry now that he had become head of the Borromeo family. But he did not. He deferred to another uncle and became a priest. Shortly thereafter he was appointed bishop of Milan, a city that had not had a resident bishop for over eighty years.

Although raised to the grand life, Borromeo spent much of his time dealing with hardship and suffering. The famine of 1570 required him to bring in food to feed three thousand people a day for three months. Six years later a two-year plague swept through the region. Borromeo mobilized priests, religious, and lay volunteers to feed and care for the sixty thousand to seventy thousand people living in the Alpine villages of his district. He personally cared for many who were sick and dying. In the process Borromeo ran up huge debts, depleting his resources in order to feed, clothe, administer medical care, and build shelters for thousands of plague-stricken people.

As if the natural disasters facing Borromeo were not enough, a disgruntled priest from a religious order falling out of favor with Church authorities attempted to assassinate him. As Charles knelt in prayer before the altar, the would-be assassin pulled a gun and shot him. At first, Charles thought he was dying, but the bullet never passed through the thick vestments he was wearing. It only bruised him.

Borromeo combined the love of the good life with the self-sacrificing zeal one would expect of a Renaissance churchman. Once when he was playing billiards, someone asked what he would do if he knew he only had fifteen more minutes to live. "Keep playing billiards," he replied. He died at age forty-six, not at the billiard table but quietly in bed.

PRAYER

Charles, give me the sense of balance to enjoy both the good things of life and the hardships. Help me to not become deluded by riches, power, and fame. Show me ways to strike a healthy and holy balance between the pleasurable and the painful events that make up every life.

DEVOTIONAL PRACTICE

Death can be an ally. We enjoy the good things of life more acutely when we realize that death may deprive us of them at any moment. The next time you are playing your favorite game or sport, watching a movie or listening to music, imagine that you have only fifteen more minutes to live. Then in the spirit of Charles Borromeo, continue what you are doing, savoring it to the fullest. If you do not die at the end of the fifteen minutes, give thanks.

ST. CHARLES LWANGA

"Teacher of new traditions."

1865–1886

JUNE 3

In 1879 the first Catholic missionaries arrived in central Africa. Initially, a tolerant and open-minded chieftain in Uganda, named Mtesa, allowed the European priests to teach and share their views. Some Africans became Catholics. Mwanga, who succeeded Mtesa, however, felt very differently. He resented the European presence and intrusion into tribal ways, slaughtered a contingent of Protestants, and executed a recent convert, St. Joseph Mkasa, who criticized the sex ring that Mwanga operated within the ranks of his official pages. If Mwanga had hoped that the execution of Mkasa would silence his critics, he was mistaken. His Christian subjects became even more outspoken about his abuse of the royal pages.

Later, the chief brutally killed another young page, who had been teaching Christian traditions to some of the other boys, by personally stabbing him through the throat with his spear. Charles Lwanga succeeded the slain young man as director of the pages. But Lwanga, too, was a Christian, and he secretly baptized four of the younger boys who wanted to join the new religion.

When word of this reached Mwanga, he ordered all the pages to appear before him and to separate according to whether they practiced Christian or traditional ways. Then he asked all the Christians, young men from the age of thirteen to their early twenties, Lwanga among them, if they wanted to remain Christian. "To the death!" they are reported to have shouted. Outraged and ridiculed, Mwanga ordered their deaths.

On Ascension Day, Lwanga went to his death, along with some fifteen royal pages over whom he had charge. The young men were stripped, bound, wrapped in reeds, laid on a funeral pyre, and burned to death. One young man, however, died of a broken neck just before he was to be burned. The order came from his father, the chief executioner, who saved his son from the torment of the flames. In the days and weeks thereafter, the persecution continued, and many Christians, both Catholic and Protestant, young and old, lost their lives.

PRAYER

Charles, it takes great courage to abandon the old ways and adopt something new, especially when authority figures are opposed to change. Give me the courage and determination to make changes and to embrace the new when it is right for me to do so, even in the face of criticism. At the same time, let me not be seduced by change just because it offers something new. Always may I have the wisdom to discern what is the appropriate course of action and to take it.

DEVOTIONAL PRACTICE

When you need to learn something new or change a traditional way of doing something and you are having trouble adjusting to the changes or the newness, baptize yourself into the new ways. Simply take a bowl of water, perhaps from a special spring or creek, bless it, and offer it to heaven. Then say a prayer, such as the one above, for the strength and enthusiasm to learn something new and to adjust to it. When the prayer is over, take three palmfuls of water and drip each on your head. You could say a version of an old Celtic prayer to the Trinity as you do this: "A palmful for the God of Life; a palmful for the God of Peace; a palmful for the God of Joy."

ST. CHRISTINA THE ASTONISHING

"A holy and somewhat embarrassing fool for God."

1150–1224

JULY 24

Christina died when she was about twenty-one. Her open coffin was placed in the church for the funeral Mass, which went without a hitch until the Agnus Dei. At that point, Christina sat up in the coffin and flew to the roof beams, as everyone, except her older sister, scampered from the church in fright. The priest coaxed her down, and Christina proceeded to explain that she had indeed died, visited Hell, Heaven, and Purgatory, and saw friends in all three places. She was allowed to return, she said, to pray for the people in Purgatory.

What today we might call a near-death experience was just the beginning of a life that was truly "astonishing." Christina often climbed dangerously high (and easily) into tall trees and towers. She crawled into ovens without being burned. She could handle fire without endangering herself. She jumped into ice-cold rivers in the winter without harm. She was even swept under a mill wheel, only to emerge on the other side unscathed. At times, she curled herself up into a ball so that she no longer looked human.

Obviously there were various opinions about Christina. Some thought she was crazy or possessed by devils. Some found her dangerous; others considered her to be just an eccentric contortionist and somewhat fun to have around. She lived a homeless life, begging for alms, dressed in rags, and exhibiting the kind of erratic behavior typical of the mentally disturbed in every century.

But whatever the state of her mind and soul, Christina had friends and admirers. She lived into her seventies and ended her final years living with a community of nuns who found her obedient, respectful, and even wise. Count Louis of Looz invited her to his castle, asked her opinions, accepted her criticism, and before he died, made his confession to her. Others, too, saw in Christina not just a crazy lunatic, but one of "God's holy fools."

PRAYER

Christina, give me the insight to look upon the homeless, the poor, and the mentally disturbed as God's children, who may have much to teach me. Rather than just dismissing them as fools or less than human, may I realize that they, too, have souls precious to God and deserving of my respect.

DEVOTIONAL PRACTICE

It is hard to meet the homeless and treat them as our fellow human beings. Sometimes it is even hard to give them your loose change. The next time you have the opportunity, give a homeless person a handout of food or money, and also take the time to start a conversation. Ask the person's name, where he or she lives or hangs out, and whether the person would like you to bring food or clothing. In some way, acknowledge the person's humanity and individuality before you part.

ST. CIARAN

"The tree of life."

512–545

SEPTEMBER 9

Ciaran came from an interesting mix of family traditions. His maternal grandfather was a poet, bard, and keeper of the folk memory in the long line of druidic wisdom characteristic of Celtic spirituality. His father was a carpenter, craftsman, and chariotmaker. Ciaran himself combined both traditions. As the founder of the monastery at Clonmacnoise, he constructed the groundwork for the most important learning center in the early medieval world.

Ciaran loved learning and tapped into the wealth of knowledge and wisdom of the great scholar St. Finnian, abbot of the monastery at Clonard. As a young monk Ciaran began developing an important network of "soul friends," the Celtic custom of seeking spiritual advice from close friends whom one trusts with issues of the soul. By the time of his death, he numbered the great Irish monks among his spiritual friends: Columcille of Iona, Finnian of Clonard, Enda of the Aran Islands, Senan of Scattery Island, and Kevin of Glendalough.

On one occasion, he visited his friend and mentor Enda, on Inishmore. The two men had similar visions, which they shared with each other. The visions showed a great tree growing by a river in the center of Ireland. Its branches stretched across the entire land and protected the island. Birds from around the world flew to the tree to pluck its fruit and carry it back to their homelands. Enda interpreted the vision as follows: Ciaran is the great tree; his grace protects all of Ireland; the setting is a monastery by a river in the center of Ireland; its reputation will attract scholars and pilgrims from all over the world.

Ciaran returned to the mainland, found a site on the Shannon River near the center of Ireland, and began constructing the great monastic learning center of

Clonmacnoise. Ciaran really was just the seed bearer, however, because in less than a year, he died, at age thirty-three.

Three days later, his soul friend, Kevin of Glendalough, arrived to find the monks in grief over their leader's death. But when they opened the chapel where the body lay, Ciaran's soul returned to his body so the two men could converse and bless each other one more time, pledging their love and friendship that would survive even death.

PRAYER

Ciaran, help me to lay practical foundations beneath my dreams. Guide me in putting my ideals to work by finding the appropriate structure and plan to turn them into realities that benefit me and others.

DEVOTIONAL PRACTICE

Often, visualizing our dreams helps them come true because visualizations begin to construct our dreams internally, a necessary step for realizing their outward manifestations. Choose a dream or a hope that is important to you. In quiet meditation, see yourself planting the dream or hope as a small seedling. Then water it and watch it grow. In your meditative vision, see the tree grow and develop through all the seasons, withstanding all forms of weather, until it becomes a large, healthy, commanding tree. Continue the visualization for ten minutes, and repeat it regularly or whenever you feel your dreams and hopes need a spiritual boost.

ST. CLARE

"Tasting the hidden sweetness."

1194–1253

AUGUST 11

When Clare was seventeen, she heard Francis of Assisi preach a Lenten sermon. So moved was she by the man's humility and joy, she ran away from home on Palm Sunday and sought out her fellow Assisian and his companions where they were living outside the town. Clare immediately declared her desire to follow in his footsteps, so he began the ritual of receiving her as one of his companions. She removed her clothes and donned the sackcloth robe Francis gave her, and then tied it with a rope. Next he cut her hair. She renounced her aristocratic family's wealth and social position. Francis had no arrangements for women to live with his friars, so he found room for Clare in a nearby Benedictine convent.

Immediately, Clare's family threatened to bring her home, so Francis moved her to another convent. Her fifteen-year-old sister, Agnes, ran away and showed up at the convent, declaring her desire to live the austere commitment to Jesus' poverty. At this point, the family hired twelve armed men to remove the young women by force, especially Agnes, whom the family thought was too young to embark on such a severe life. But Clare prayed that they would be saved, and Agnes became so heavy that the men could not forcibly pick her up and carry her off.

Francis then placed Clare and Agnes in a house belonging to the church of San Damiano, just outside Assisi, where he made Clare superior. She remained there for the next forty years. Then, as if a fire of self-transformation had swept through the area, others came, ready to change their lives for Jesus. Clare's mother and another sister joined them, along with three members of one of the most influential families of Florence.

Clare's order, known as the Poor Clares, practiced the strictest poverty. They wore no shoes, stockings, or any other type of foot covering; they slept on the ground, ate no meat, practiced the rule of silence, and engaged in other physical austerities. Their rule of poverty was so severe that it became a source of dissension among other women who joined, and the controversy eventually reached the highest levels of the Church, the popes themselves. One pope relaxed the rule and encouraged the order to hold lands in common in order to provide rent to support themselves. Some Poor Clares opted for this arrangement, but Clare herself resisted, wanting the nuns to rely solely on daily contributions rather than a yearly income.

Clare petitioned Rome. The next pope also sought to relax the rule. Again Clare held her ground. Finally, two days before she died, Rome granted the Poor Clares at Damiano the right to live in perpetual poverty without any fixed income.

Clare was sixty years old when she died from long years of illness. She had worked and prayed for over forty years to be, as she wrote in a heartfelt prayer, "transformed into the image of God through contemplation . . . in order to taste the hidden sweetness God has kept from the beginning for those who love him."

PRAYER

Clare, give me the steadfastness to stand my ground no matter who opposes me. When I know I am following God's will, may I be firm even in the face of authorities who disagree.

DEVOTIONAL PRACTICE

One of the most dramatic features of the followers of Clare and Francis of Assisi was their refusal to go along with the stylish fashions popular among their social class. As a witness to the timelessness of God's truth, they snubbed the trendy and ephemeral clothing fashions of the day. Although it is probably not possible to do this to the same extent as they did, occasionally wear old clothes or out-of-style clothing as a test of your ability to look out of sync with the times. You might feel somewhat embarrassed or awkward presenting yourself in public in clothing that makes you look square, dull, or uninteresting, but that is exactly the point: the real value of a human being is timeless in God's eyes and is not dependent on what he or she wears.

ST. COLUMBA

"Every leaf filled with angels."

C. 521–597

JUNE 9

Columba (or Columcille) left Ireland in 563, censured by his fellow churchmen, for what today we would think of as a strange theft: Columba had copied a manuscript owned by Finnian, the abbot of the monastery at Moville. King Diarmaid ruled against Columba, arguing that it was thievery. He made the analogy that a copy of a book is like a calf, and that every calf should stay with its mother. The decision, coupled with further confrontations between Columba's clan and other feuding families, triggered a war that caused considerable death and destruction. Columba was condemned, left Ireland with other family members, and founded the monastery on Iona.

Columba is one of the great Celtic monks who blended the older Celtic spirituality with new Christian practices. On one occasion, he refused to allow oak trees to be cut to build a chapel because the oak was long considered a sacred tree. On thinking about Ireland, he wrote, "Every oak leaf there is filled with angels." He boasted that "Christ is my Druid," a statement that honors both the Christian and pre-Christian traditions. Indeed Columba continued to practice the old druidic magic in the context of being a Christian monk. For example, he used a white stone from a river to cure illness, similar to the mysterious druid's egg or stone. After he blessed the stone, it floated on water. He calmed storms and wild animals, and once when he was living and preaching among the Pictish tribes, he quelled the Loch Ness monster.

Columba had the gift of prophecy, and when he prayed angelic light could be seen around him. He predicted that a crane would be blown by a storm from Ireland to Iona, and he told his monks to care for it for three days, and then it would return. The crane was a sacred bird in Celtic lore, representing old age, longevity, the wise old woman, and the feminine aspects of divinity. The crane arrived just as Columba had predicted.

On one important occasion, Columba returned to Ireland and argued successfully against a movement to strip Irish poets of some of their privileges. Columba believed that the poet played an important role in Celtic society, carrying on many of the spiritual and healing traditions of the druids. A poet's talent was the power of the word to express visionary experiences of the other realities, a feature of Celtic life that was important in both pagan and Christian times, past and present.

In the course of his life, Columba founded several important monasteries at Derry, Durrow, Kells, and of course Iona, to which monks from all over Europe traveled to discover the mystical experiences and traditions that Columba and the island itself engender in those who go there. Even today Iona is considered one of the world's most sacred places.

PRAYER

Columba, help me to appreciate the visionary experiences of life, whether they be angels in oak leaves, cranes as symbols of wise old women, or the power in river stones to heal illness. There is more divine power around us than meets the eye. Show me how to see with inner vision the mysteries and magic of creation.

DEVOTIONAL PRACTICE

Look for an oak leaf or a small oak twig that seems to draw your attention. Treat it with the respect due a fellow creature made by the same Creator who made you. Bless the leaf or twig, and ask it to come with you as a sign of God's power in your life. Handle it with the care and devotion you would a sacred relic, for it is sacred and stands for the sacred in your life. Place it on your altar. When you need help, carry it with you and be aware of the divine energy that it brings to you. Thank it regularly as a friend, companion, or relation.

ST. COLUMBAN

"Understanding the Creator through creation."

C. 543–615

NOVEMBER 23

At his birth, Columban's mother dreamed that she was giving birth to the sun. Indeed, the Irish saint's later travels and teachings across Europe would radiate in a sunlike fashion.

Columban grew up in Leinster, was well educated, and as did many young men before and after him, felt strong inclinations to enjoy a life of sensuous pleasure. Being a spiritually sensitive youth, however, he sought advice from a holy woman who had lived as a hermit for many years. She suggested that he dedicate himself to God, abandon the secular life, and even impose exile upon himself and leave Ireland.

Columban entered the monastic life on Cluain Inis, an island in Lough Erne, where he prayed, studied, and lived the life of a monk until he was about forty-five years old. At that time, he gathered twelve followers and embarked for the continent. Together they established monasteries in what is now France, Germany, Switzerland, and Italy. Columban's rule for his monks embodied the severe austerities typical of Celtic monasticism: harsh fasts, self-inflicted beatings, and the recitation of the long Divine Office each day.

Columban's spiritual path soon ran afoul of local authorities. The members of various noble families took sides over his practices and teachings. In general, he could be faulted for introducing Irish and Celtic customs into societies that had their own traditions. Behind the plottings may have been the Frankish court bishops who followed the Roman Catholic Church's structure and dogmas, especially the tradition of organizing Church authority around bishops rather than abbots, as was the Celtic custom. Columban was banished from the continent in

610, and he headed back to Ireland. But bad weather grounded his ship, and he remained in Europe, only to begin establishing more monastic communities in Switzerland and northern Italy, where he enjoyed better political support.

Columban preached the love of God and neighbor, and he encouraged people to discover God and his divine power in nature itself. He said, "If you want to know the Creator, understand created things"—an idea rising right out of his Celtic heritage of seeing the unity of the Creator and creation.

PRAYER

Help me, Columban, to find the Creator in all creation and to love the Creator as he loves all that he has made. May I receive your spirit so that I too can find the meaning of my life in following the truths of creation wherever life takes me, even if it be far from home.

DEVOTIONAL PRACTICE

Set up a special vase in your home for flowers. Whenever you change the flowers, remind yourself that by understanding their beauty and fragrance you understand the Creator who made them. Spend a few minutes each time you put new flowers in the vase, contemplating their beauty.

ST. CONRAD OF PARZHAM

"On the threshold of sanctity."

1818–1894

APRIL 21

Conrad was born in Bavaria to a farming family, with whom he lived and worked the first thirty years of his life. In 1849, he entered the Capuchin order as a lay brother, and he took his vows four years later in 1852.

For the next forty-one years he had the same job in the monastery. He was a doorkeeper. Although it might seem that his life was narrow, boring, and uneventful, Conrad was actually at an ideal place for spiritual (and secular) growth. It was through the doorway that visitors came to the monastery. In a sense the whole world passed through Conrad's doors: pilgrims, retreatants, important people, average people, those needing healing or food, the worried, the anxious, the grateful, old and young, rich and poor.

Rather than suffering burnout or midlife crises, as so many people do today when they are stuck in the same job or way of life for a long time, Conrad lived into his seventies doing routine tasks day after day without complaint. We might wonder what the effect of being continually at a threshold might have had on his outlook.

Doorways are liminal places, connecting the exterior and the interior, the outside and inside, one reality with another. The image of the "gates of heaven" is another example of the mystical truth that life is not meant to be lived in one realm only but there awaits us another world, more beautiful, truthful, and joyful than the one we now inhabit. Perhaps Conrad thought of these things as he went about his daily routines, letting people in and out, inviting them to leave the outside world of secular distractions and escorting them into a holy interior world of song, prayer, and spirit.

Conrad, teach me how to find the spiritual truth behind the worldly tasks that make up my day. Even in ordinary places I want to find the mystical meaning that shapes these tasks and allows them to serve as entryways into the greater universe and heaven.

DEVOTIONAL PRACTICE

Find three physical places (besides the door) in your home or place of work that have metaphorical significance for your spiritual life. These might be a favorite window, a porch, a backyard, a courtyard, a lobby, or a rooftop. Write a short prayer or affirmation about each place and get in the habit of reciting it to yourself when you are in or near these places.

STS. COSMAS AND DAMIAN

"The holy moneyless ones."

D. 303

SEPTEMBER 26

Cosmas and Damian were twin brothers born in Arabia in the third century. They studied medicine in Syria, possibly with Arab doctors, who were among the best medical teachers and practitioners in the ancient world. When the brothers began their own practice, they refused to charge for their services, offering them free to all. They became known as the "holy moneyless ones."

Cosmas and Damian used their practice—and the intensive contact with people that it brought them—to share their beliefs and values as Christians. They made many converts to the Christian faith by being dedicated, selfless servants of others. But in addition to this, they were good at what they did, having a widespread reputation as healers. Among the more difficult conditions that they cured were blindness, paralysis, and possession. They were even known to bring the dead back to life. Like other early saints, they had a special rapport with animals and included veterinary services in their practice.

When persecution against Christians broke out, Cosmas and Damian were arrested and put in prison. They were tortured and put to death but not before their sanctity foiled several attempts to kill them. They were thrown in the sea to drown, but angels rescued them. They were cast into blazing fires that did not burn them. When stones and arrows were hurled at them, the projectiles were deflected and did them no harm. Finally, they were beheaded.

After their deaths, miracles occurred that were attributed to them, and they became the patron saints of physicians and barbers.

Cosmas and Damian, help me appreciate my skills and knowledge in ways that do not depend on monetary value. Remind me that we are meant to give of ourselves generously and to share our talents and services with others, even those who cannot afford to pay money for them.

DEVOTIONAL PRACTICE

If you have a skill or service that you do professionally, find ways to offer it to those who cannot afford it. You might provide your services as an outright gift, but you could also barter your work for something that your client can do. If you find yourself resisting this practice, pray over it, asking for the courage and trust you may need to let an opportunity to make money go by. Have faith that what you give to others will come back to you threefold.

ST. CUTHBERT

"Finding a place of resurrection."

C. 646–687

MARCH 20

When Cuthbert was about fifteen years old, he had a vision that convinced him he should dedicate his life to God. While praying on the pastures of Northumbria where he was tending sheep, he saw a flash of light that swept across the night sky. Through the light, he saw angels carrying a ball of fire upward to heaven. In Celtic tradition, the soul is often seen leaving a dying person in the form of a fiery globe. Cuthbert knew intuitively that it was the soul of the Irish monk Aidan. Later, he was told that Aidan had indeed died the night of the vision.

The vision profoundly moved Cuthbert, but he postponed his decision to join a monastic community for a number of years. When he finally went to Melrose Abbey, he was no longer a shepherd but a warrior, mounted on a horse and carrying a spear. It seemed he had fought in local wars for a few years before giving up the secular life.

Eventually Cuthbert became prior at Melrose, and later at the famous Celtic monastery on Lindisfarne. The council at Whitby in the 660s decided that the Celtic Church should conform to the Roman Catholic Church regarding the liturgical calendar, monastic tonsure, and other issues. The previous prior, Colman, and all the Irish monks who were there left the island and went to Ireland where there was less meddling by the Roman Catholic Church. Cuthbert then became director.

In 676 Cuthbert longed for a more remote life, away from even the daily commotion of the Lindisfarne community, so he retreated to a more isolated and desolate island, but his reputation as a healer (he was called the "wonder worker of Britain") lured so many visitors that he had to build a guest house for them.

In 685 when Cuthbert was chosen to become bishop of a more distant diocese, he regretted having to leave the islands where he had found his peace—his "place of resurrection," as it is called in the Celtic tradition. So he devised a plan. He accepted the bishopric but asked to stay in his hermitage for the six months before his consecration. During that time he convinced another bishop to swap dioceses with him so that he could remain at Lindisfarne.

Cuthbert lived not quite two years after his consecration. When he knew his end was near, he went to his favorite little island, and in three months he died of a fever.

PRAYER

Cuthbert, help me recognize places where my soul comes alive. I know there are places and times in which I need to be alone and turn my mind and heart to divine mysteries. In these times of prayer, I can grow in wisdom and grace. Show me how to make the necessary "swaps" in my life so that I always have some place of retreat where I can become more fully alive.

DEVOTIONAL PRACTICE

Find some place in nature—the woods, fields, shoreline, hillsides, parklands—where you find peace, and go there whenever you feel the need. Bring some token of that place—a stone, a twig, a clump of soil—back home and place it on your altar. Think of this place as a place where your soul can come alive, a place of resurrection.

ST. DAMASUS

"Crypts and catacombs."

C. 306–384

DECEMBER 11

Damasus was a Spaniard, born in Rome. His father was a priest, and Damasus himself followed in his father's footsteps, although he never married. He became pope when he was sixty, at a time when clashing forces in the Church used violence against one another to get their ways. His papacy was opposed by a faction of supporters who resorted to armed conflict, and the political powers that backed Damasus fought with equal cruelty. Damasus' side won out.

As pope, Damasus lived through momentous events. Theodosius I, the eastern emperor of the Roman Empire, and Gratian, the emperor in the west, both declared that the official religion of the state would be Christianity as interpreted by the bishops of Rome. Damasus and the Christian senators in Rome had the altar of Victory removed from the senate chamber as a symbolic statement of the new order. From these years on, the Church and the state would be intricately intertwined in European history.

Damasus also supported the work of St. Jerome in translating the scriptures; this translation would be known as the Vulgate version of the Bible, used for centuries thereafter. But perhaps Damasus is best remembered for his work on the catacombs.

The catacombs were the underground tunnels and passageways beneath Rome where the first generations of Christians met to pray and worship. During the violent persecutions by the Roman state, it was dangerous to be a Christian or to be caught participating in Christian rituals. To escape the authorities, Christians met in the caverns under the city.

When Christianity became the state religion, Damasus ordered that the catacombs be drained and cleaned up and that the relics of the martrys whose bodies were buried there be preserved and honored. He also had inscriptions written and placed at important places in the catacombs so that pilgrims visiting the sites would be inspired by the significance of these passageways.

When he was about eighty, Damasus put up his own epitaph in the papal crypt where he was to be buried. It read: "I, Damasus, wished to be buried here, but I feared to offend the ashes of these holy ones." So he was buried beside the bodies of his mother and sister at a church he had built earlier.

PRAYER

Damasus, let me find in your example the spirit of honoring the dead and showing respect for the ancestors who have passed on into the next life. Help me overcome fearful or negative attitudes about death so that I might think of the deceased as still my companions.

DEVOTIONAL PRACTICE

Visiting the graves of deceased friends and family members used to be a regular practice for many people. Today we tend to forget or ignore those who have passed on, possibly because we have fearful attitudes about death and a weak belief in the goodness of the next world. But visiting and tending a grave need not be a morbid activity. In fact, it can be a celebration and a time of renewal for yourself and the memory of the person buried there.

Take food, drink, and flowers. Bring a poem or passage to read that the deceased was fond of. Make the occasion a kind of picnic. Toast the deceased, leave some food and the flowers, be joyful. The dead are among the ancestors, the saints, and the angels. We hope to be reunited with them after our deaths, but we do not need to wait until then to begin to celebrate with them.

ST. DAVID

"Prayer in nonprayerful moments."

C. 520–589

MARCH 1

David was born to Non, an Irish nun who was raped by a local ruler named Sant. Non, one of the great saints of the early Celtic Church, raised David alone. After being ordained, he studied with St. Paulinus on some unidentified island, where he is credited with having restored his teacher's failing eyesight. How or where he lived after returning from his studies is not clear, but he established monastic communities in many places, and in time he founded the great monastery at Mynyw in the remote southwestern area of Wales.

David's rule for the monks at Mynyw was intense. They engaged in hard manual labor and were not allowed the use of oxen to till the soil. They could speak only on the rarest occasions or when absolutely necessary. Their diet consisted of bread, vegetables, salt, water, and a little milk. He forbade alcohol, and was consequently known as the "waterman."

David led a devout spiritual life, conversed with angels, and often held such deep communion with angelic beings that others could see or sense the presence of angels around him. His advice to his followers was to never cease praying, even while working or engaged in nonprayerful activities. David's belief was that one could always be praying mentally, simply by renewing the intention to do so. In the tradition of Celtic spirituality, David was a "soul friend" to many people in his life. Others would visit him to share their souls' hopes, dreams, sorrows, and joys.

At his death, David left his followers and companions with this advice: "Keep your faith, and do the little things you have seen and heard with me." The patron saint of Wales had lived a life in which the smallest of activities were occasions for prayer, angelic companionship, and divine consolation. As he died, he looked upward, his eyes brightened, and he said, "Take me with you."

PRAYER

David, show me the ways to make even small tasks and humdrum activities occasions for prayer. Kindle in me the love of God so that even when I am doing nonspiritual work I will be able to keep the spirit of prayer and have a strong awareness of the divine presence.

DEVOTIONAL PRACTICE

Wear a thin rawhide or leather cord around your neck or wrist as a reminder of the ascetic practices that were common in the early Celtic Church. A simple chain or bracelet bought especially for this practice can substitute for the cord. As you become aware of the cord during the day, state your intention to be always in the presence of God and then offer a short prayer of gratitude for life, health, friendship, or love.

ST. DOMINIC

"Reasonableness and moral persuasion, not threats."

1170–1221

AUGUST 8

In 1208 a papal legate was killed by a member of the Albigensians, a Christian movement that held among its many beliefs the notion that the earth and material reality were created by dark forces and should be shunned. Pope Innocent III launched a crusade against them, primarily in southern France, where the movement flourished most successfully. The Albigensians had organized churches, bishops, laity, and liturgical services similar to Catholics. They read the Gospel and the Epistles of St. Paul incessantly in their own French dialect at a time when the Catholic Church provided no vernacular scriptures for the laity to read. They were obviously a threat to the Roman Catholic Church.

Dominic, a Spanish priest and friar living under the Rule of St. Augustine, who had been appointed prior of his friary at age thirty-one, after seven years of the contemplative life, accompanied the army led by Count Simon IV of Montfort. He preached to the Albigensians to give up their contrary views of Christianity and accept Roman Catholicism, but his admonitions went largely unheeded. The seven-year war between the two factions killed many in the movement but converted few. Nevertheless, Dominic was convinced that the way to reach Christians who held alternative opinions to the Catholic Church was by preaching with reason and reasonableness, not with threats and dogmatic pronouncements. He wanted peaceful, not warlike, encounters with non-Catholics who opposed the Church.

In 1214 Dominic founded the Order of Preachers, later called the Dominicans, to convert non-Catholics and reconvert lapsed Catholics through learning, scholarship, and preaching. Moral persuasion and scholarly argument were to be the new order's approach. By 1221, the year that Dominic died of an illness at age fifty-two, the order had over sixty friaries spread across eight provinces. Dominicans were in Poland, Scandinavia, Palestine, England, Spain, France, and Italy.

PRAYER

Dominic, when I lose an argument or fail to convince others of my position on something, keep me from resorting to insults, name-calling, anger, and abuse. Put into me the gentle, peaceful spirit that guided you through bitter crusades and bloody battles. Guide me in the ways of peaceful persuasion.

SPIRITUAL PRACTICE

Often the image we carry of ourselves greatly determines the outcome of our endeavors. If we think of ourselves as failures, we fail. When we visualize ourselves as friendly and helpful, we act in a friendly and helpful manner. If you have an ongoing conflict with someone at home, at work, or among your social acquaintances, spend five minutes each morning and evening visualizing yourself speaking gently and reasonably with that person. Even practice saying what you want to say in terms that are not confrontational, rather than abusive or insulting. In addition, visualize your antagonists agreeing with you; see them smile at what you say and nod their heads. Visualize yourself dealing with them in a friendly manner, no matter how much you resist doing so. Then carry these images with you throughout the day.

ST. DOMINIC OF THE CAUSEWAY

"The garden, the friend, and the road."

D. 1109

MAY 12

It would be helpful if we had a photograph of Dominic of the Causeway. His early life met with a series of rejections because of his uncouth appearance. He tried several times to join monastic communities, but they turned him down because he looked so slovenly. He was also thought to be somewhat stupid. It appears that this humble man from the Basque country of Spain had little going for him.

So Dominic became a hermit, built his own cabin, and cultivated a flourishing garden in the wilderness around it. He lived there respectably for some time. When St. Gregory of Ostia visited the area to preach, Dominic latched onto him and became his companion. Gregory, like the former garden, provided a setting for Dominic that enhanced his life as he traveled with the preacher and saw something of the world. When Gregory died, however, Dominic was left to his own devices to make something of his life.

Once more Dominic returned to his life as a hermit, this time in a dense wilderness area called Bureba. The trees and vegetation were so thick that a regular road had never been cut through the forest, and yet there was a popular route through it that pilgrims used to visit the famous shrine of St. James at Santiago de Compostela. The route was dangerous, because bandits lurked in the brambles and frequently attacked and robbed pilgrims. Dominic decided to build his new cabin and oratory in this unlikely area.

After Dominic established himself, he began to clear trees and build a proper road. Word spread, and others settled near him and took part in the construction work. Eventually, they built a bridge over a river and a hospice for pilgrims. Dominic's improvements created safety and comfort for many travelers. Once again Dominic proved that an uncouth appearance and what others considered ignorance did not prevent him from carving out a decent life for himself.

When he died, the hermit became known as St. Dominic of the Causeway because of the road he had built. He was buried in a grave which he also constructed and which later became the site of pilgrimages and miracles.

PRAYER

Dominic, show me how to find goodness in simple people whom I think of as uncouth or stupid. Teach me that God's wisdom and grace can be found in individuals of all sorts, not just in those who appeal to me.

DEVOTIONAL PRACTICE

When he started out, no one thought that Dominic would amount to much. And yet at three different periods in his life, Dominic took advantage of the opportunities that God gave him and managed to make a respectable life for himself. He made a garden, a friend, and a road. We might imagine that his perspective grew from the natural world of his narrow garden where he lived alone, to the love and friendship that took him out into the broader world, to a desire to use his talents to provide comfort and safety for others.

Consider your own life at the present. Can you find a garden, a friend, and a road? In other words, is there some private place (either physically or spiritually) where you can be alone and nurture your interior life? Is there a friend (or friends) who introduces you to a broader and more various world beyond your own narrow interests? Are you providing assistance in some way so that others might lead a better life?

If you have these three in your life, give thanks, and promise to use them wisely. If not, ask yourself how you might create the missing ones to enhance your life.

ST. DOROTHY

"The miracle of roses and apples."

D. 303

FEBRUARY 6

Dorothy was born in Caesarea, where her Christian parents had fled to escape the persecutions taking place in Rome. The Roman emperor Diocletian stepped up his harassment of Christian communities around the time that Dorothy was a young woman of marriageable age. When marriage to the Roman prefect Fabricius was arranged for her, Dorothy refused, saying that she wanted to remain a virgin. To compound her insults to the Roman authorities, she also refused to take part in the ceremonies to the old gods. She was thrown into prison.

Legends of how she was tortured are various. She was boiled in oil, locked in a dark cell for nine days without anything to eat, hanged by her feet and whipped, and singed on her breasts with flaming torches. Through them all, she felt nothing painful, but was soothed instead. Her wounds always healed overnight.

Along the route to her place of execution, Dorothy met a young clerk in the legal network, named Theophilus, who made fun of her belief that when she was dead, she would be transported to a heavenly garden filled with flowers and fruit. "Send me flowers and fruit, then, when you are dead," he mocked. In one version, the young man watched Dorothy kneel down before she was executed, and while she was praying there, an angel appeared to him carrying three roses and three apples. In another version, after her death a strange boy appeared at Theophilus's door in the dead of winter, carrying a basket with three red roses and three red apples.

Theophilus was converted and later martyred by being beheaded, after which his body was thrown to wild animals.

Dorothy, help me to believe in the sanctity of creation. Let me recognize in the flowers and fruits of the garden divine messages about the goodness of the earth, the seasons, and the Creator who makes them all.

DEVOTIONAL PRACTICE

During the winter months, place on your altar or in a special area in your home three apples and three roses. See them as reminders of the eternal garden that exists within you even in the dead of winter. Thank God for allowing you to have faith in this vision.

ST. DROGO

"When one door closes, another opens."

1102–1186

APRIL 16

Drogo was born to noble parents, but his mother died in childbirth, a fact he learned when he was ten years old. As many children before and after him, Drogo believed he was responsible for his mother's death. Overcome with guilt, the boy never responded to life with joy or enthusiasm. At age eighteen he rejected his inheritance and left the Flemish countryside where he could have had a comfortable life. Instead, he took to the open roads as a pilgrim.

Drogo journeyed through many lands seeking the holy places and shrines that were the destinations of pilgrims like himself in the Middle Ages. The open air, the change of scene, the camaraderie with strangers, and the lives of the saints whose shrines he visited lifted his spirit. Returning a new man, Drogo settled at Sebourg near Valenciennes and found work as a shepherd and handyman on the estate of a wealthy woman. He gave his wages and any gifts that came his way to the poor, and he acquired a reputation for being a saint. Many people reported seeing him in several places at the same time. In fact, a local expression was "I cannot be in two places at the same time because I am not St. Drogo."

After working six years on the estate, the wanderlust claimed Drogo once again, and he embarked on more pilgrimages. But then catastrophe occurred. The joyful traveler developed a hernia, which grew to repulsive proportions and prevented him from walking to any great extent. His pilgrimage days were over. Drogo retired to a cell in Sebourg, where he continued to be revered by local people who considered him a living saint. His physical condition prevented him from appearing in public, but for the next forty years, his presence in the community inspired many people. He died at age eighty-four.

Drogo, I hope to enjoy my life no matter what accidents or mishaps occur. I pray that I will get over feelings of guilt for past events and walk through the rest of my life with pride and the confidence that I will be of service to God and others.

DEVOTIONAL PRACTICE

Sometimes life deprives us of the very things we enjoy the most, even our spiritual practices. For Drogo, a painful hernia ended his days of wandering the countryside to visit sacred places.

Consider the aches, pains, injuries, and illnesses that prevent you from living as fully as you might wish. If you have actually stopped doing certain things because you are no longer physically able, reflect on how you have replaced them, if at all. We should not curtail our lives when our favorite activities are no longer possible. If we have eliminated one thing from our lives, whether because of disability or age, we should replace it with something of equal value. Reflect on the totality of your life, and ask yourself how you can enhance and enrich it.

ST. EDMUND CAMPION

"Sedition, treason, and the truth."

C. 1540–1581

DECEMBER 1

When the Jesuit order sent the newly ordained Edmund Campion back to his native England in 1580, many English Catholics were outraged. It was too dangerous, they thought, to have a priest who was so well known and (formerly) well respected among the highest people in the English government, including Queen Elizabeth herself, preach publicly on English soil. In fact, they were right. One of the most intensive manhunts in English history was soon launched against him.

Twenty-five years earlier, the brilliant young Campion had become a fellow at St. John's College, Oxford, at the early age of fifteen, and then proceeded to become one of the best-known orators in England. Called "one of the diamonds of England," he took the Oath of Supremacy, acknowledging Elizabeth as the head of the Church of England, and became an Anglican deacon in 1564. But on a trip to Dublin, Campion began to have doubts about the Protestant movement and returned to Catholicism. He fled to France, joined the newly formed Jesuit order, and was ordained in 1578. Two years later the order established its first English province by sending Campion and another Jesuit to England.

Campion preached almost daily, even though Catholicism was outlawed and harboring priests was considered treason. He wrote a pamphlet on "ten reasons" why Protestantism should be challenged. When the pamphlet was distributed at the university church at Oxford, it greatly troubled the political and religious waters. Government officials condemned the "seditious Jesuit's" activities, spies were ordered to pursue him, and official efforts were stepped up to trap him. In time he was betrayed, captured, and sent to the Tower.

As a prisoner, Campion was offered bribes, tortured on the rack, and eventually hanged, drawn, and quartered. The technical charge was treason, but the real reason was that he was a Catholic priest. His dying message was, "In condemning us, you condemn all your own ancestors. . . . God lives. Posterity will live."

PRAYER

Edmund, there are times I feel as if I am an outsider among people who do not understand me or my values. I try to live by the spiritual lights that guide me, but so many things in our society attempt to put them out. When it is hard for me to live up to my commitments, give me the strength that carried you through times of persecution and betrayal.

DEVOTIONAL PRACTICE

Campion was keenly aware of his place in a long line of believers. His death message invoked his ancestors and posterity. Light three candles on your altar: a white one for your ancestors who are now with God, a red candle that represents your struggle to live a spiritual life today, and a blue candle that represents the younger generation (and generations to come), which can be inspired by your daily witnessing to spiritual values. Resolve to be a better witness to what you believe.

ST. EDWARD THE CONFESSOR
"Finding spiritual substitutes."

1003–1066

OCTOBER 13

The young prince Edward and his brother Alfred were sent to Normandy when Edward was ten years old to assure their safety. Edward's father, Ethelred, and his Norman mother, Emma, felt that the political turmoil and civil wars in England made it dangerous for the heirs to stay there. Indeed, when Alfred returned in 1036, he was killed by opponents. Edward did not return until he was forty years old and declared king.

Edward was a good king. He was tall, well-built, pleasant, and fun-loving, and his reign was marked by peace and wise rule. He eliminated some of the taxes that were hardest to bear, he administered the realm in harmony with his council, and he removed from Canterbury a Norman archbishop who was irksome to the anti-Norman factions within the kingdom. Edward was fond of hawking and hunting and spent a great deal of time engaged in those sports. But he was always a devout Christian and attended Mass regularly.

While he was in exile in Normandy, Edward made a vow to go on a pilgrimage to Rome to visit the tomb of St. Peter. When he became king and began preparations to fulfill that vow, it became evident that a king could not just abandon his realm to go traveling. But troubled by the vow, he sought guidance from the pope, who suggested that he use the money he would have spent on the pilgrimage to care for the poor and to endow a monastery in England in honor of St. Peter.

Edward gladly accepted this substitute. He rebuilt and financed an old abbey on what was the west side of London. Called West Minster (to distinguish it from another church in the city), the abbey was dedicated on Christmas Day in 1065.

Edward, however, was not present. He had taken ill, and would die a week later. The king was the first to be buried in the now famous Westminster Abbey.

PRAYER

Edward, let me not be troubled when I cannot keep all the promises I make, both spiritual and nonspiritual. Help me to see that circumstances often prevent us from fulfilling our best-laid plans. But also encourage me to find realistic substitutes for the things I cannot do. May I throw myself into the alternative plans with the same enthusiasm I had for the originals.

DEVOTIONAL PRACTICE

Once a month, take the money you would have used for some personal enjoyment and give it to the poor or a charitable organization. Or spend the money on someone dear to you, surprising them with a gift or a treat. If you have any reluctance or misgivings about doing this, offer them up as spiritual energy to help people less fortunate than you who never have extra money to spend on luxuries.

ST. ELIZABETH ANN SETON

"From setbacks, great steps forward."

1774–1821

JANUARY 4

Elizabeth Bayley was born on Staten Island on the eve of the American Revolution. Her mother was the daughter of a rector in the Episcopal Church, and her father, a doctor, lectured on anatomy at what was then called King's College in New York City (later to be renamed Columbia University). At age twenty Elizabeth married a prosperous merchant, William Seton, and had two sons and three daughters. But within ten years the family fortunes were reversed and William Seton was bankrupt. Probably because of the stress, he fell ill, and when nothing seemed to help his condition, the family moved to Italy to find a cure. William died there in 1803.

Although Elizabeth lost her husband, she found a religion. Impressed with the Catholic culture of Italy, Elizabeth converted to Roman Catholicism in 1805, the year following her return to America. Family and friends were horrified, her influential parents distanced themselves from her, and she was in financial distress. Not sure what to do, she accepted the invitation from a priest to open a school for girls in Baltimore. Previously Seton had founded the Society for the Relief of Poor Widows with Small Children in New York City, so she had some experience in this kind of work.

In 1809 Seton founded the Sisters of St. Joseph in Baltimore and the same year moved to Emmitsburg, Maryland, where the order eventually became known as the Daughters of Charity of St. Joseph. The nuns ran hospitals and orphanages, but their shining accomplishments were in their work in developing the parochial school system, part of the educational reforms of the nineteenth century that paralleled the rise of the public school system.

Mother Seton found time to compose music, write lyrics for hymns, and produce spiritual essays. When Seton, the first saint born in America, died at age forty-six, her religious order, the first to be established in the United States, numbered over twenty communities scattered across the country.

Elizabeth, help me accept the setbacks in life as part of God's plans. You found a new life after your husband died. Remind me that there are always new opportunities that lie ahead, and that God can use misfortune to call us to lives of great service and devotion.

DEVOTIONAL PRACTICE

One of our most common secular rituals is balancing our bank accounts each month. It is easy to think of money as strictly secular, having no connection to the sacred. But if our lives are meant to be whole, then financial matters should have some link with our spiritual concerns. One way to find this link is to create it intentionally by viewing money as part of the spiritual universe in which you live.

When you sit down to balance your checkbook each month, offer a special prayer of gratitude for the money that has come in during the month. If you are currently affluent, acknowledge this gratefully, and vow to use some of your money for gifts and charitable causes. If you are not currently affluent, offer a prayer of trust that God can organize the universe around you so that the money you need will come your way. In both instances, build into your prayer a commitment to live frugally and simply and not to squander money on purchases you really do not need.

ST. ELIZABETH BICHIER DES ANGES

"Mastering change and getting the upper hand."

1773–1838

AUGUST 26

Elizabeth Bichier des Anges's brother had fled France during the chaos of the French Revolution. Then her father died in 1792, and the National Assembly moved to confiscate the family estate under its edict that émigrés, or ex-patriots, like her brother, could not inherit or own property in France. The estate was considerable, since Elizabeth's father had been the lord of the manor of Anges. She was determined not to let the revolutionary government take the family home.

Elizabeth asked her uncle, the Abbé de Moussac, to teach her about French law so that she could defend the property in court. The civil case dragged on, but Elizabeth's knowledge of law and accounting kept the estate solvent, and she eventually won the suit.

In 1796 Elizabeth and her mother moved to another home in Poitou, where she noticed that the ravages of the Revolution and the current antireligious policies of the government had practically destroyed religious life for rural families. She gathered farm families together in the evenings for prayer, hymns, and spiritual reading in lieu of traditional parish activities. Soon she heard that a priest 25 miles away was holding similar services in a barn for the rural people of that region. She went to meet him, and they hit it off. The priest was Andrew Fournet, also destined to achieve sainthood.

Andrew's plan for Elizabeth was that she direct a small community of nuns to teach and care for the sick. Although she had never been a nun or lived in a convent, Elizabeth's prior leadership in managing and saving her family estate impressed Fournet. He arranged for Elizabeth to have a year's novitiate in a Carmelite convent, but thinking she might like the life too much and not want to leave, he moved her to a less strict convent, where she spent about six months. Then Fournet recalled her to be superior of the handful of nuns he had recently organized. Again Elizabeth Bichier's innate intelligence and quick ability to learn and master new situations paid off.

In 1807 the Daughters of the Cross, as they would be called, took temporary vows. By 1811 the order numbered twenty-five women. By 1819 they were running thirteen convents. In the next six years the order opened fifteen houses in twelve dioceses. By 1830 the Daughters of the Cross had over sixty convents, and Mother Bichier was on the road supervising a very successful enterprise. But the work and travel schedule proved detrimental to her health, and in 1836 she was beginning to show signs of slowing down. Two years later, in pain and bouts of delirium, Elizabeth Bichier des Anges, a powerful woman who kept pace with the powerful and disruptive changes of her era, died.

PRAYER

Elizabeth, you seem to have never let the most devastating changes in society stop you. So often I worry about the changes I see taking place, and long for "the good old days," or I grow despondent over my lack of control over change. Show me how to bounce back, adapt, and triumph over the changes going on around me, as you did so well in your own life.

DEVOTIONAL PRACTICE

When there are serious changes going on in your life, try this meditation plan: On a piece of paper write out your exact complaint and why the change disturbs you. Then brainstorm for as many alternative ways as you can think of to *respond* to the change (not necessarily prevent it). When you have several responses listed, take that many days to meditate on each one individually.

Spend ten to fifteen minutes each day meditating on what your life would be like if you adopted one of the responses. Get a sense of how your life would be different, and ask God to show you the pros and cons of each one. When you have finished the series of meditations, you should be able to handle the changes going on from a position of strength, understanding, and self-knowledge.

ST. EMILY DE RODAT

"Discernment of spirits."

1787–1852

SEPTEMBER 19

At Villefranche in the south of France, Emily de Rodat grew up with her maternal grandmother during the turbulent years of the French Revolution. When she was eighteen, she returned to Maison Saint-Cyr, the school that she herself had attended, to help the nuns who ran it. Emily was put in charge of recreation programs, preparation for First Communion, and geography courses.

About ten years later, while Rodat was visiting a dying woman, she overheard some of the mothers who were present talking about how all the schools in the area were too expensive for them and how their children could not get a good education. Rodat realized how fortunate she had been, having come from an aristocratic family and having been educated in the exclusive school where she now taught. Her heart went out to the women, and she decided to do something about their situation.

It took Rodat less than a month to make arrangements and begin teaching the children of poor families in her own room at Maison Saint-Cyr. Soon she had forty children and three assistants, providing free education for the poor. She knew almost immediately that her project would require larger facilities, with more teachers and assistants.

The following year, in 1816, Rodat rented outside space and launched her free school. The women who taught with her would soon become the Congregation of the Holy Family, an order of nuns recognized by the Church. As fate would have it, the community at Saint-Cyr disbanded, and within two years of leaving it, Emily returned and obtained legal rights to the building. Her project now had substantial facilities, a hundred students, and nine nuns, including herself. Over the next two years the school expanded even more.

Then strange events began to occur. A series of mysterious deaths befell the community. Doctors were mystified; no explanation made any sense. There was talk among some churchmen that the deaths were demonic and that Rodat's project was cursed or the work of the devil. Rodat herself began to have second thoughts, not that the devil was afoot in her classrooms but that God was giving her a sign that she was not to found a new order. She considered merging with another community of nuns.

Rodat's own community, however, convinced her otherwise. The sisters refused to have any superior other than her, and so they proceeded, took perpetual vows, and adopted a habit. The year was 1820. Over the next thirty-two years the congregation's work continued to expand until the order administered thirty-eight operations, including prison work, orphanages, halfway homes for women, a hospice for the aged, and several cloistered convents. Emily de Rodat died of cancer in 1852.

PRAYER

Emily, when things go wrong, we need great discernment of spirits to see if the signs are from God and what they mean. Too often we can jump to conclusions that are inappropriate. Help me to be aware, as you were, of signs and omens, especially the messages that seem commonplace and come from my own family and circle of friends, for God speaks through them as well as through mysterious occurrences.

DEVOTIONAL PRACTICE

In your journal, practice discerning the spirits that operate in your life each day. Look back over the day's events and find the ones that seem to be teaching you something important. Ask for help in discerning their true meaning, and resolve to follow the guidance that comes through them. You can use the spirits of the major virtues and vices, such as patience, envy, sloth, forgiveness, joy, and kindness. These were the spiritual energies that influenced you positively during the day, so think of them as spirits to be discerned.

ST. ENDA

"An island of protection."

D. C. 530

MARCH 21

Oengus, ruler of the Irish province of Munster and brother-in-law to Enda, at first questioned the saint's request to be given the Isle of Aran, the most distant and the largest of three rocky islands off the western Irish coast. For all intents and purposes, it was uninhabitable. Even today the lack of soil is only offset by rigorous conservation practices and the addition of seaweed as fertilizer. The king rebuked his brother-in-law and suggested he look for more fertile grounds on which to build his monastery.

But Enda insisted. The Isle of Aran was his "place of resurrection." Oengus conceded and gave him the island, and Enda built the great monastery of Killeany, along with ten smaller houses. He lived there until he died, serving God, establishing monastic practices for the many students who followed him, and being a "soul friend" or spiritual adviser to men and women who came for his inspiration. Among them was St. Ciaran, who had a vision while he visited Aran that he saw a magical tree in the center of Ireland. He told the vision to Enda who had had the exact same vision. They interpreted it to mean that Ciaran would found a great monastery and center of learning in the middle of Ireland. The vision came to pass, and the monastery was called Clonmacnoise.

One's "place of resurrection" was an important concept in Celtic Christianity. This longing to find a spot, remote from the hustle and bustle of society, lured many men and women, like Enda, to seek out a hermitage where they could pray, work, sing praises to God, and stay mindful of eternity and the heavenly mysteries that awaited them at the time of their personal resurrection. So typical of Celtic spirituality is the blurring of time that just by being in a sacred spot where one finds the divine, one is already in heaven, even while on earth. The place of resurrection is where one comes alive.

In such a place miracles can happen. On Aran, Enda would ask his monks to test their holiness at the end of each day by going out alone in a small wicker boat without its watertight leather covering to see if it would float. If the boat sank, it indicated the person had failed in some important spiritual practice or virtue. The reports are that no one ever sank except a cook, who admitted that he had stolen a little food for himself from another brother. Enda asked him to leave the island.

PRAYER

Enda, show me how important it is to be always mindful of eternity and not to get lost in the fads and fashions of the modern world. The fashionable quickly passes, and only the spirit endures. May I remember this, and keep, at least in my imagination, a little island of protection around me where the eternal values never get lost.

DEVOTIONAL PRACTICE

Find a photograph of a small island that appeals to you for its beauty or sense of mystery. Place it on your altar or in a special place where you will see it and look at it each day until you can recall its details from memory. Then, whenever you feel that the pressures to conform to mindless fads or wasteful activities are too great, recall the island and think of your soul enjoying its peace and calm. Say to yourself that this is your place of resurrection, and it will revive you.

STS. ETHNE AND FEDELM

"Tell us about God."

FIFTH CENTURY

JANUARY 11

We know very little about Ethne and Fedelm, the two young and beautiful daughters of King Loegaire of Connacht, except the following story about their encounter with St. Patrick.

One day, Patrick met the two women at a well. They asked him the following questions about the nature of God, typical of young people being trained in druidic knowledge. "Who are you, and where do you come from?" they asked. "Who is your God, and where does he live? Tell us about him, how he is seen, how he is loved, how he is found. Tell us if he is youthful or very old; if he lives forever; if he is beautiful; if many people have fostered his sons; if his daughters are recognized by the men of the world as dear and beautiful."

Patrick's reply also echoes the ancient Celtic understanding of the Creator as being inseparable from the universe. "Our God is the God of all things, the God of heaven and earth, of sea and river, of sun and moon and stars, of high mountains and low valleys, the God above heaven, the God in heaven, the God under heaven. He has a dwelling around heaven and earth and sea and all that dwell in them. He inspires all things, he gives life to all things, he dominates all things, he sustains all things. He lights the light of the sun and the light of the light. He put springs in the dry land and islands in the sea, he set the stars to minister to the greater lights." Then Patrick went on to explain the Trinity: that the Father and Son are not younger or older than each other, and that the Spirit breathes in them, and that the Three cannot be separated.

On hearing these wonderful things, Ethne and Fedelm became Christians and, according to legends, passed into the next world in death immediately. They were buried by the well, a traditional Celtic entryway into the otherworld.

PRAYER

Ethne and Fedelm, give me the curiosity that inspired your questions about God. I pray that I will always have the searching attitude that wonders where I might find God, know him, and love him and his sons and daughters.

DEVOTIONAL PRACTICE

The description of God that moved and inspired the two saints is typical of Celtic thinking: it sees the Creator intimately flowing through and living in all created things. Compose a description similar to Patrick's, but include specific places from the area where you live: rivers, hills, mountains, creeks, towns, local animals and birds, and so on. Examples: "My God is the God of the Black Creek, of Mohonk Mountain, of the Hudson River; he lives in the Catskill Mountains and their valleys. He is the God of the deer and the badger, of the fox and the crow," and so forth.

Memorize the list, add to it now and then, and become aware of the Creator's presence whenever you pass, see, or think about the natural places and elements that surround you.

ST. EUSTACE

"A friend of animal teachers and companions."

D. 118

SEPTEMBER 20

The Roman general Placidus was hunting one day in Italy when he saw a stag. He chased the deer, came upon it, and discovered in the stag's antlers an image of Jesus on the cross. The stag told him that the charitable works that he did were pleasing to Jesus. His wife, Theoptista, also had a vision that told her the family should become Christian. Greatly moved by these apparitions, Placidus, Theoptista, and their two sons were baptized. Placidus took the name Eustace.

Shortly thereafter, the stag appeared to Eustace again and made predictions of misfortune and crises that would befall him. The predictions came true. Eustace's servants died, a thief robbed him, and his horse even passed away. He and his wife became separated in an attempt to flee into Egypt, and their two sons were carried off by a lion and a wolf. Through a series of happy circumstances, the two boys were saved by farmers and shepherds, Eustace and Theoptista were reunited, and the family enjoyed new prestige when the emperor promoted Eustace in the army.

But after a successful victory, Eustace refused to honor the Roman gods, and the emperor ordered him to be thrown into an arena with wild lions. The lions became tame, however, and left Eustace alone. The order was then changed to put Eustace and his family inside a brass bull in which a fire was set. The family died, even though their bodies remained unburned. Eustace is the patron saint of hunters.

PRAYER

Eustace, you enjoyed the help of animals on important occasions. Help me to understand how animals can teach us many things, sometimes in supernatural visions, sometimes just by being themselves. In whatever ways animals appear to me, help me to see them as fellow creatures with whom I share the planet and whom God put here to help us through life.

DEVOTIONAL PRACTICE

If you have a special animal that seems to be part of your dreaming, visionary, or spiritual life, pay particular attention to the ways it appears to you. Close your eyes and meditate on your animal spirit, using a drum or small rattle to call it to you. Animal spirits respond to the sounds of a steady drumbeat or rattle. Sit and be with your spirit animal, drumming or rattling, and ask it questions, listen for answers. The Divine Spirit speaks to us through animals who are sent into our lives.

ST. FIACRE

"Gardens and taxis."

D. C. 670

SEPTEMBER 1

Monasteries in ancient Ireland were more like tribal villages than the great imposing complexes that we think of today. At the time of Fiacre, they were often just a cluster of a few huts and a small central building in which to pray. Religious life was organized around little more than working the fields, growing crops and herbs, and daily devotional practices. Yet this is what appealed to Fiacre the most.

Fiacre studied herbal literature and agricultural practices at a monastic school, and then he built a hermitage for himself on the Nore River where he developed a garden that became famous far and wide. In Fiacre's day, medicine was based on a knowledge of herbs, and the saint's reputation as a healer grew. Soon he was inundated with visitors to the point where he had to move his hermitage to a more remote location where he would be less distracted from his work and prayer. Still people sought him out for his knowledge of herbs and his talent at healing.

At one point, his father, a warrior-chieftain, asked him to return home to take over leadership of the tribe, but Fiacre refused and went to France where he settled about thirty miles from Paris. The local bishop gave him land for a new hermitage, and again Fiacre's reputation soon spread so that great numbers of visitors were coming for healing remedies from his garden. Eventually he needed more land.

Fiacre asked the bishop for additional acreage and was told he could have all the land that he could plow in one day. As he marked off the area to dig, the land miraculously turned over, rocks cleared themselves away, trees were uprooted, and the soil was mysteriously cultivated. A witness saw Fiacre kneeling in the field praying. When the bishop heard of the miracle and came to see what had happened, he discovered an immense area cleared and cultivated.

Fiacre's written records about herbs and gardening became standard sources of information for many years. Today he is the patron saint of gardeners and, surprisingly, Paris cab drivers. This latter patronage began in the seventeenth century when large numbers of pilgrims hired carriages at the Hotel St.-Fiacre to take them to the saint's grave outside Paris. The carriages were called *fiacres*, and the word is still used today in France for taxicab.

PRAYER

Remind me, Fiacre, that even if I don't cultivate a garden, I am always planting seeds: seeds of inspiration for others by what I say and do. Show me how to do this well, and to be willing to share my knowledge and expertise in whatever field with others who have need of it. In this way, I will continue the great tradition of helping to be a healer for others.

DEVOTIONAL PRACTICE

In your garden, mark off one area that you designate as your "healing garden." No matter what you plant here, care for it mindfully and ask that the energy you expend in watering, weeding, and cultivating the plants there be dedicated to healing the sufferings of others, perhaps someone you know personally. Offer prayers for that person (or persons) each time you water or work in that area of your garden.

ST. FINDBARR OF CORK

"The friend behind the friend."

C. 560–C. 630

SEPTEMBER 25

Findbarr of Cork was the illegitimate son of a smith and a slave, and was raised by three monastics to whom his parents assigned him. One day a rich man named Fidach came to the place where young Findbarr was being brought up. Fidach was looking for a soul friend. Findbarr's tutor told Fidach to kneel before the young boy, for already miracles were occurring around the child's activities. The rich man objected to bowing before a child, until Findbarr's tutor said that he would also kneel before the lad. From an early age Findbarr was involved in the soul-friend network of the early Irish church.

Years later Findbarr himself was going through a period in his life when he had no friend with whom he could share the deepest thoughts and feelings of his soul. His former soul friend had died. So Findbarr went to Eolang, the head of a monastic community, and told him how troubled he was that he had no soul friend. Eolang said that he would get him a soul friend worthy of him. Then the two men had a vision of God being in their presence and of Eolang putting Findbarr's hand into the hand of God, his new soul friend. At that moment, God began to lead Findbarr to heaven, but Eolang protested, "Lord, do not take Findbarr from me now, but wait until he dies and his soul leaves his body." God released Findbarr's hand, which he kept covered with a glove for the rest of his life because it was so radiant that people could not look on it.

When Findbarr died, his companions saw angels taking him to heaven, where he sat down with those who would be his soul friends throughout eternity: saints, angels, and the Holy Trinity.

Findbarr, help me to appreciate the friends that God has sent into my life. Remind me of the goodness they bring, and show me ways to return the goodness and blessings to them.

DEVOTIONAL PRACTICE

One of the great teachings of the life of Findbarr is that behind every true soul friend is the one and ever-present soul friend, the Divine Spirit. It is good to get in the habit of seeing the friendship of God working through our closest friends. Collect photographs of one or two of your best friends, and with a yellow marking pen, trace an outline around their bodies or just their heads, similar to a halo. Put the photographs where you will see them, and let the yellow aura around them remind you that it is the friendship of God that comes to you through these friends. Be aware of this as much as you can when you are physically with them.

ST. FLANNAN

"The blemished king."

SEVENTH CENTURY

DECEMBER 18

Flannan's father, Turlough, was king of a district in Ireland at Killaloe where Flannan became the first bishop after his pilgrimage to Rome. When Flannan began talking about going to Rome, his family and friends opposed it. Travel in those days was hard and dangerous, but Flannan persisted in his dream, knowing he would find a way. Like other Irish adventurers before him, he hoped to go by sea, but not having a boat, he prayed for some other means. Legend tells that a large floating stone drifted up to where he prayed on the shore. He climbed upon it, and it carried him to the Eternal City.

On his return Flannan preached, prayed, and engaged in the ascetical practices common to Celtic monastics, such as reading his prayers while standing in the cold waves. The altered state of consciousness required for such feats was conducive to visionary experiences, which were highly prized in early Christianity.

Flannan's preaching convinced his father to abdicate his kingship and become a monk in his old age. Turlough asked Colman, a local bishop, for a special blessing for his family, since three of his sons had been killed in wars. Colman said that his seven other sons would become kings in their own right.

Flannan worried about this blessing, not because he begrudged his brothers the privileges of kingship, but because he was afraid that he would be in line at some point to assume the role. But Flannan thought of a way out. In the old Celtic tradition a king who was physically deformed or blemished was required to abdicate—and a man with any deformities could not become king. This was in keeping with the belief that the king received his authority from the goddess of the land, represented by the queen. Only through the goddess's own sovereignty could the king have power. So Flannan prayed that he would be blemished, and, according to a biographer, "scars and rashes and boils began to appear on his face so that it became dreadful and repulsive." Thus Flannan escaped the fate of being king, and he lived out his days as a man of the Church.

PRAYER

Flannan, help me to be resourceful in finding ways to stick to my goals. I pray that I will find the courage to do what I know I must do, even if others have different plans for me.

DEVOTIONAL PRACTICE

In the spirit of St. Flannan, make your next blemish (or ache, pain, or headache) a cause of grace. Rather than complain about it, accept the embarrassment and discomfort as a teaching that the beauty of the soul is not dependent on what we look like physically or on our state of health. Certainly take steps to recover, but be patient and allow the blemish or pain to bring you closer to understanding what is required for the inner health of your soul.

ST. FRANCES XAVIER CABRINI

"A heart to embrace the universe."

1850–1917

NOVEMBER 13

When Frances Xavier Cabrini was a little girl growing up in Italy, she knew that she wanted to be a missionary. She dressed her dolls up as nuns, placed them in little boats she constructed out of paper, filled the boats with flowers, and sent them down the river, imagining the dolls would become missionaries in far-off lands. The major problem with her dream, however, was that there were no women missionaries in the Church at that time.

When Cabrini approached the local bishop at age twenty-seven, with her desire to be a missionary even though there was no institute for women missionaries, he replied, "Found one." So Cabrini did: the Missionary Sisters of the Sacred Heart. Nine years later, it was recognized by Rome.

In 1889 Cabrini and six of her sisters sailed to New York City where they hoped to establish orphanages in Little Italy, much as they had done at home. The New York archbishop was against the idea, mainly because there was no money for the project. Cabrini raised $5,000 from the wife of the curator of the Metropolitan Museum, and in a short time her nuns were caring for four hundred children off the streets of New York.

About that time, Cabrini had a dream that her children were playing, working, and learning in a beautiful woodland setting along a calm majestic river, rather than in the orphanages she had opened in Manhattan, Staten Island, Brooklyn, and Hoboken, New Jersey. The archbishop took her up on her dream and arranged a carriage ride that took them eighty miles north of the city to a 150-acre Jesuit monastery on a high bluff above the Hudson River. The Jesuits' well had run dry, and they wanted to sell.

In 1890 the sisters acquired the property rights, just as the summer drought was setting in. Confident that God would show her where there was water, Cabrini walked the grounds, observing every feature, plant, and slope of land. Finally, she tapped her walking stick on the ground and said, "Dig here." The water that bubbled up flows to this day.

By the time of her death (brought on by an earlier bout with malaria), Cabrini had crossed the ocean thirty-nine times and founded over sixty missions in places as diverse as New Orleans, Denver, Seattle, Chicago, Los Angeles, Burbank, South America, France, Spain, England, her homeland of Italy, and the famous New York prison, Sing Sing. It seems that her final prayer, "Dear God, give me a heart that can embrace the universe," had already been answered.

PRAYER

Frances, enlarge my own heart so that it can embrace the universe. Let me not turn my back on people and places that need my service. Show me how to throw open my arms to those in need and respond generously and joyously.

DEVOTIONAL PRACTICE

Cabrini's childhood game (like many children's games) touches something deep in human nature: the need to symbolically and ritually express our hopes and desires. Following her example, construct a small paper boat, take it to a nearby river, and place in it a slip of paper on which you have written a wish, dream, or goal. As you launch the boat and watch it float downstream, restate your confidence in God's universe, and believe that you send your wish or dream out into the world, where it will come true.

ST. FRANCIS CARACCIOLO

"Signs and synchronicities."

1563–1608

JUNE 4

In 1588 Ascanio Caracciolo received a letter from John Augustine Adorno suggesting the need for an order of priests who would combine both the active and the contemplative life. The idea appealed to Caracciolo, a priest who was already engaged in this type of active life—namely, helping prisoners prepare to die peacefully. The curious thing, however, is that the letter was not meant for him but for a relative with the same name. But Caracciolo felt it was a sign from heaven and immediately took steps to meet Adorno.

Caracciolo, Adorno, and ten others founded the Minor Clerks Regular, and Ascanio took the name Francis. Their headquarters was in a house in a suburb of Naples, but they set off for Spain to set up houses there, only to be rejected. When they returned to Italy, their numbers increased, and the priests dedicated their work to missions, hospitals, and prisons. The order also maintained hermitages for members who sought lives of deeper contemplation.

Caracciolo's life, however, did not go as he planned. He fell seriously ill again, reminiscent of the period earlier in his life at age twenty-two, when it was thought he would die of leprosy. At that time, he vowed that if he survived, he would dedicate his life to God, and almost instantly he recovered. But now as he got well, his good friend and companion, Adorno, died at age forty, leaving Francis bereft. On top of this, he was asked to become superior of the order against his better judgment and contrary to his desire to lead a simple, humble life within the order.

But under Francis's administration, the order flourished. Three houses were established in Spain, and more young men flocked to the order. After seven years, he resigned as superior general to become novice master to the new recruits.

Francis died in the Abruzzi where he had gone to help set up a new novitiate. On his deathbed, suffering from a high fever, he shouted, "Let us go! Let us go!" A companion asked, "Where?" Francis replied, "To Heaven! To Heaven!" He then expired at age forty-four.

PRAYER

Francis, your life took a dramatic turn through a serious illness, a letter that was never intended for you, and the death of your best friend. I know that heaven sends signs like these all the time, but usually we just ignore them or consider them to be strange coincidences. Help me to recognize these synchronicities and omens, to read them accurately, and to find in them the divine messages that can deepen my spiritual life.

DEVOTIONAL PRACTICE

Keep a journal of synchronicities and meditate on them to discover God's will for you. At the end of each day, think back over any unusual coincidence or occurrence and write it down in a notebook. After a few weeks, study these entries for patterns and repeated similarities. Meditate and reflect on them as you would dreams, especially the startling ones, looking for messages or insights that indicate how your life is going. They may suggest changes to make, or confirm your present course of action.

ST. FRANCIS DE SALES

"Go simply; fear nothing."

1567–1622

JANUARY 24

"Go courageously to do whatever you are called to do," advised Francis de Sales, a man whose life epitomized this practice. Born in the family castle, Château de Sales, in Savoy, near Geneva, Francis had a private tutor throughout his childhood and youth, attended the Jesuit College at Clermont where he studied philosophy and theology, and earned a law degree from the University of Padua when he was twenty-four. As an aristocratic heir to an important family, he was offered a high position in the local government, but he turned it down. Francis wanted to devote his life to God. His father was not pleased. Eventually, however, with his father's blessing, Francis became provost of the Geneva chapter, and six months later he was ordained a priest.

At once Francis embarked on a courageous mission. The region on the south shore of Lake Geneva was strongly Calvinist, and the Duke of Savoy was attempting to reconvert the area by military force. The people were in rebellion. Francis volunteered to be assigned to that violent and war-torn area. Attacked by wolves, threatened by assassins, several times roughed up by angry mobs, and with a price on his head, Francis pursued his missionary activities. He wrote and published leaflets explaining the Roman Catholic Church's positions in contrast to Calvinism. He emphasized, for example, the belief in free will, as opposed to Calvin's theory of predestination. Within four years, he had made considerable progress, and many former Catholics had returned to the Church.

Francis was appointed bishop of Geneva where he continued to preach and write, found schools, instruct children (with whom he had an easy and comfortable rapport), and eventually organized a new order, the Order of the Visitation. He never seemed to let his position and power go to his head.

Francis's published works, *Introduction to the Devout Life* and *On the Love of God,* the latter written for the Visitation nuns, continue to be classic texts on living the spiritual life. Repeatedly he encouraged people to find holiness in everyday matters, emphasizing the freedom each individual has to choose to do good and reject what is bad and harmful. In whatever state of life men and women find themselves, they can discover the way to God, joyfully and without fear.

In 1622 Francis met with Louis XIII at Avignon to obtain certain favors for his diocese and became ill on the way home. He suffered a stroke and died over the Christmas holidays at age fifty-six. He is the patron of journalists and writers.

PRAYER

Francis, help me live by your wise instruction: "Go simply. If you have any fears, say to your soul that the Lord will provide for you. Trust in him, depend on his providence. Fear nothing."

DEVOTIONAL PRACTICE

Create a small altar, and place there some symbol or talisman that represents your work or career. For the next three days, and whenever you feel the need thereafter, look at this symbol and remember that the hours you spend engaged in this work are not spiritually useless, but that God can be found even there. Whenever you have specific fears or worries about your work, carry the talisman with you as a reminder that God will help you to go simply and fearlessly through your day.

ST. FRANCIS OF ASSISI

"Spiritual joy and sincerity."

1181–1226

OCTOBER 4

The turning point in the life of young Francis of Assisi is the fateful day he stripped in public, handed his clothes back to his father, and walked out of town naked. Considered mad by his family, who were prosperous silk merchants, Francis went to live in a ruined chapel which he set about repairing. The carefree days when he was a popular figure among the boisterous, fun-loving youths of the town were over. The former soldier, so profoundly moved by two visions of Christ, now dedicated his life to poverty and hardship.

Remarkably, others followed Francis's example, including some of the leading citizens of the town. In a short time, he had disciples who joined him in living the life that took the Gospel message literally and applied it radically. Francis and his companions based their lives on poverty, love for all people and nature, and the need to identify with the sufferings of Jesus. Essentially homeless and jobless, but joyful and childlike, they took seriously Jesus' admonition not to worry about tomorrow. They sang songs to their brother, the sun, and their sister, the moon.

Francis's new way of life gained official status in the Church in 1210 when the pope approved the order, and two years later St. Clare joined him to create a community that would become the Poor Clares. By 1223 Francis had attempted two unsuccessful pilgrimages to the Holy Land (he was shipwrecked once and became ill on the other) and one unsuccessful attempt in Egypt to convert the Muslims. He returned to Italy to combat a movement in the order to relax the rule. Rather than fight against the reformers, Francis retired from organizational duties and devoted himself to the simple practices of the spirit that had originally inspired him. He created the first crèche for Christmas celebrations; he prayed in solitude; he received the stigmata; and he went blind.

But remaining true to his love for all the elements of nature, Francis prayed to the Fire that was used to painfully cauterize his eyes. "Brother Fire, God made you beautiful and strong and useful; I pray you be courteous with me." He continued to commune with all the creatures of nature with an inner gladness and an abiding sense that all things in creation are children of a loving God. He died at Assisi on October 3.

PRAYER

Francis, give me the serenity to live simply and distinguish my needs from my wants. Help me recognize in all living creatures the same life force that flows through me. Give me the willingness to acknowledge other forms of life as my brothers and sisters, for we are all children of the same Creator.

DEVOTIONAL PRACTICE

Whenever you first see the sun, moon, rain, or any other element of creation, honor it with simple greetings, such as the following:

"Blessings on you, the Great Sun of Heaven, for returning today to warm us and light up our lives."

"Sweet Light of Moon, shine gently on my evening activities and bless my sleep."

"Thank you, Sister Rain, for coming to wash the earth and refresh all growing things."

ST. FRANCIS OF PAOLA

"Prayers for the neighborhood."

1416–1507

APRIL 2

Young, eccentric, and charismatic, the fifteen-year-old hermit, Francis of Paola, living in a cave by the sea, won the hearts and admiration of his neighbors. Two other men joined him before he was twenty, and a new spiritual community was in the making. Neighbors helped them build three cells to live in and a chapel where they sang the psalms and heard Mass said by a priest who lived in the area.

It seemed destined for Francis to live this kind of life. His childless parents had prayed to the great saint of Assisi for a child, and naturally named him Francis when he was born a boy. When he was thirteen, he studied with the Franciscans, but he soon returned home to begin life as a hermit, modeled on his namesake.

In 1452 Francis and his companions founded a community, which they named the Hermits of St. Francis of Assisi. Again, friends and acquaintances in the neighborhood responded and helped them build a monastery. Francis encouraged his monks to practice the virtues of penance, charity, and humility. They were also to abstain from meat, dairy products, and eggs. Francis himself slept on the ground or a plank, using a stone or a log for a pillow. In 1492 Francis renamed the order the Minims, to refer to their goal of being the *minimi*, or least important, among God's people.

In 1481 Louis XI of France became terminally ill and fell into a deep depression over his impending death. By this time, Francis had gained a reputation for insight, compassion, wisdom, and healing, so the king invited him to the court. But Francis felt that to pray for the king's recovery would be against the will of God. Even kings, he told the monarch, have limited life spans and should trust in God to take them at the right time. Instead of healing the monarch, he helped him to die. Many conversations took place between the monk and the king which, according to observers, were inspired, as if the Holy Spirit spoke through Francis. Louis died peacefully in the humble hermit's arms.

Charles VIII, Louis's son, admired Francis's work, and on becoming king, he threw his influence behind the Minims. Francis lived for the next twenty-five years in France and died on Good Friday, after receiving Communion while standing barefoot with a rope around his neck, a practice developed by his order. He was ninety-one.

PRAYER

Francis, I know it is important to live as a useful member of my neighborhood. Help me find the right balance between pursuing my own spiritual and personal needs and being an active force for good for those who live nearby. Give me the grace to be a good neighbor.

DEVOTIONAL PRACTICE

Build into your spiritual practice regular prayers and rituals for the good of the neighborhood where you live. Occasionally light a candle or a stick of incense, and let it burn down as a symbol of your prayerful intentions for the health and well-being of all who live near you.

ST. FRANCIS XAVIER

"Songs and costumes for conversions."

1506–1552

DECEMBER 3

Francis Xavier, a thirty-five-year-old Jesuit priest and one of the original "Company of Jesus" founded by Ignatius Loyola, was on a ship bound for India. It was a rough trip and took twice as long as scheduled. When he arrived in Goa in 1542, he found a roisterous Portuguese community, mired in the corruption typical of colonial ports of call. He immediately began working with the Christian community there, trying to bring them back to the religious truths from which they had wandered.

Xavier worked in hospitals, prisons, and the leper community, as well as roaming the streets ringing his bell to call Catholics to Mass and services. In general, he was well received. Among the lower classes and less educated, he taught religion by writing song lyrics that incorporated religious truths and principles, then set the new lyrics to popular tunes of the day. These "spiritual" versions of the songs became great hits, and people sang them at home and work, in the city streets as well as in the fields.

Xavier was quite flexible when it came to reaching people and spreading the Gospel message. On an island near Ceylon (now Sri Lanka), he "went native" by wearing local clothing, eating traditional foods, learning the language, and living as poorly as the indigenous people. He found many receptive to Christianity. Among the upper Brahmin caste, however, he was less successful. He converted only one person in twelve months.

In Japan a few years later, Xavier took the opposite route, although the principle was the same. He discovered that the affluent Japanese were not interested in a poor, simply dressed priest. So he dressed regally, as if he were a representative of the king of Portugual, and asked his fellow missionaries to play the subservient role as if they were his attendants, rather than colleagues. It worked. The local officials even gave him an empty Buddhist temple to preach in.

Xavier had an unquenchable thirst to spread the Gospel message and the teachings of his mentor, St. Ignatius. Realizing that China was a key to the Asian-Pacific world, he hired a Chinese boat captain to smuggle him onto shore. China was officially closed to foreigners at that time. He arrived on an island six miles off the China coast and about one hundred miles south of Hong Kong, where he fell sick and died at age forty-five.

PRAYER

Francis, help me find ways to adapt to society so that I might be a force for good and be able to serve others. If my religious style is offensive to others, show me ways to temper it without giving up the essential truths. By being flexible and trying to meet people halfway, even wearing their clothes as you did, I will be able to inspire others to lead a more spiritual life.

DEVOTIONAL PRACTICE

Try writing your own lyrics to your favorite songs. Write them so that they reflect your spiritual concerns or the religious truths that are most important to you. If you feel embarrassed singing them, whistle or hum them. You will know inside that the tune carries more important meanings than the original lyrics. This practice works especially well when you can't get an obnoxious jingle from a television commercial out of your head. Just rewrite the lyrics!

ST. GALL

"The servant bear."

C. 550–635

OCTOBER 16

Gall was one of the twelve missionaries who accompanied St. Columban on his trek from Ireland to establish monastic learning centers in what is now France, Switzerland, and Italy. During the so-called Dark Ages, after the collapse of Rome, it was primarily Irish monastics and scholars who kept the light of learning alive. The monks founded the great monastery at Luxeuil, in Burgundy, then eventually moved on to the Alps where they founded settlements near Zurich. Gall was in poor health when the others left for Italy, so he stayed behind near Lake Constance. He desired the more isolated life of a hermit anyway.

In time, many followers joined Gall, and the site of his hermitage grew into the Monastery of St. Gall, one of the preeminent cultural centers for literature, music, and art in the Middle Ages. Several times Gall was offered prestigious positions as bishop and abbot, but he turned them down to remain a simple hermit.

Like many forest-dwelling saints, Gall enjoyed personal relationships with wild animals. On one occasion, when Gall was lying prostrate on the ground with outstretched arms, a favorite position for prayer among Irish ascetics, a bear came into the camp and began rummaging through the food supply. Gall simply commanded the bear to fetch a log for the fire, and the bear did so. In exchange, Gall gave the bear a fresh loaf of bread from the meager larder and told it not to come back to harm anyone near the monastic settlement again. This may have been the same bear that Gall befriended by removing a thorn from its paw. In any event, Gall and his companions had no further trouble from the bear.

Gall, help me develop compassion for all living things and to see them as fellow creatures of the same Creator. This is especially hard with animals that can do harm or do not exhibit the warm, friendly demeanor that makes loving them easy. But help me realize that all things fit into God's plan.

DEVOTIONAL PRACTICE

It is important to see the face of God even in creatures that are not physically attractive or those whose behavior repulses us, such as insects, reptiles, and animals that are often portrayed in movies and artwork as monsters. The Creator made everything for a purpose and put some good in all beings.

As a spiritual practice, say the following blessing whenever you see an animal, insect, or any creature that you find disgusting either in its appearance or behavior:

"Blessings of life be yours,
Blessings of joy be yours,
Blessings of the God of Life be yours."

ST. GENEVIEVE

"Prayer and more prayer."

C. 422–500

JANUARY 3

Genevieve, the patron saint of Paris, was born at Nanterre and dedicated her life to God when, at age seven, she met St. Germanus, who made a remarkable impression on the little girl. After her parents died about eight years later, she moved to Paris and joined a community of nuns.

Throughout her life, Genevieve combined her interest in civic welfare with her unusual abilities at prayer and prophecy. Typical of urban life in any century, her political activism made both friends and enemies. Genevieve's prophecies about locally powerful people antagonized them if the predictions were not favorable, of course. Her call to create a moral society outraged citizens who were content to ignore the welfare of others. At least one attempt was made on her life to put an end to her political and spiritual challenges.

When Childric, chieftain of the invading Frankish tribes, occupied Paris, Genevieve pleaded successfully with him to convince him to release captives, using the moral weight of her reputation. Later she negotiated with another Frankish chieftain, Clovis, on the same issue. He, too, released captives and political prisoners.

During the Franks' occupation of Paris, Genevieve organized a rescue squad to bring in boatloads of food during a famine. Later she predicted accurately that Attila the Hun would bypass Paris if the citizens would pray to God to save them. She organized a prayer crusade for the purpose, calling on the citizens of the city to join in seeking divine intervention. The prayer campaign paid off, and the marauding Huns left Paris alone. On another occasion, the prayers of Genevieve were accredited to bringing rain and ending a drought.

Even after her death, Genevieve's protection continued to safeguard Paris. Throughout history, Parisians have turned to her in time of trouble, praying that she intercede with God for the good of the city. In 1129, for example, an epidemic plagued Paris, taking the lives of countless citizens. When no hope seemed in sight, Parisians turned to the method that Genevieve had taught them six hundred years earlier: prayer. The city prayed, and the epidemic came to a remarkably sudden end. Genevieve died in Paris on the day that is now her feast day, January 3.

PRAYER

Genevieve, sometimes when things look bleak, even prayer doesn't seem to help. It is easy, then, to stop praying, and to give in to despair. Teach me to conquer the fatalistic attitude that can see no hope by continuing to pray. Help me to pray always, even when things look hopeless.

DEVOTIONAL PRACTICE

Get in the practice of praying every day. It helps to establish a regular prayer time, perhaps five or ten minutes at lunch, before breakfast, or just before going to bed at night. Use the time to pray for family, friends, and any troubling situations you know of. Include one prayer or short petition for something that seems hopeless to you.

ST. GILBERT OF SEMPRINGHAM
"Food for the Lord."

C. 1083–1189

FEBRUARY 16

In the monastery that Gilbert of Sempringham founded in England, a special custom was practiced at meals. Gilbert called it "the plate of the Lord." The best portions of dinner were put on an extra plate, and it was given to the poor. Gilbert's concern for the less fortunate people, however, went back into his earlier life.

Gilbert, the son of a wealthy Norman knight, studied in France and was ordained a priest. Through his father's connections, he received, in 1123, the benefices of Sempringham and Tirington, which provided a sizable income for him. As lord of the estates, he saw to it that the revenues went to the poor in the parishes, and he kept for himself only the minimum amount that he needed to live.

A group of seven women living near one of his parishes requested that Gilbert draw up regulations for them to live as nuns. When the congregation grew, he added lay sisters and lay brothers to assist the nuns, primarily working their land. He petitioned for the new order to become members of the Cisterians but was turned down. Not to be defeated, he decided to found his own order and called it the Gilbertines. Later he added canons regular to be chaplains for the nuns. The Gilbertines were the only English order founded in the Middle Ages. Its popularity spread, and by the sixteenth century, the Gilbertines held twenty-six monasteries. Henry VIII's suppression of Catholic monasteries, however, put an end to the order.

Gilbert himself lived an admirable and humble life, considering that he had been born to great wealth and held the title of lord. He wore a hair shirt, ate very little, and rose many nights from sleep to pray. He was imprisoned in 1165, charged with aiding the exiled Thomas of Canterbury, but the charges were later dropped.

Gilbert eventually became blind and resigned as superior. He died well over the age of one hundred.

PRAYER

Gilbert, no matter how much money I have or how comfortably I live, let me not forget the less fortunate that live around me. If I can help them physically, let me do so. If not, may I remember them in my prayers.

DEVOTIONAL PRACTICE

The small sufferings we willingly take on can be endured for the sake of those who have much greater sufferings. When we deny ourselves, we symbolically identify our plight with others who are also denied the good things of life, and our discomfort serves as a reminder to pray for them.

As often as you are able, deny yourself the best portion of a meal or a dessert and let someone else have it. Instead of reaching for the best part or the largest slice, take a less attractive piece and silently offer a prayer for those who never get the best part or may not be eating at all that day. Obviously, tell no one that you do this, so that you do not receive any praise or honor for it.

ST. GREGORY THE GREAT
"The chants that enchant the soul."

C. 540–604

SEPTEMBER 3

Gregory seemed destined to be pope, coming from a family that had produced two popes already, one being his great-great-grandfather. His own father was one of the wealthiest men in Rome, with extensive estates in Sicily. And after years of turmoil, there were not many patrician families left in the Eternal City. Rome had been sacked four times in one hundred and fifty years and conquered four times in twenty years. It had also suffered earthquakes. As prefect of the decaying city, Gregory, who was then around thirty years old, was one of the few remaining public servants. But he resigned in the hopes of living quietly in the monastery he established in his own home.

While still abbot of his monastery, Gregory met three blond young men whose beauty captivated him. When he asked them where they were from, they replied that they were Angles, which Gregory heard as "angels." The youths inspired him with a desire to leave immediately as a missionary for England, but the Roman populace pressured the pope to bring Gregory back. Later, in 590, when the pope died, the same Roman people unanimously acclaimed Gregory pope. Then, as head of the Church in Rome, he sent the great St. Augustine to bring the Gospel to England. He also bought some English slave boys in their late teens to educate as Christians, so fascinated was he by this land of fair-haired people.

Gregory was a man of many interests and humane sensibilities in an age when peace and compassion were in short supply. He ordered that Jews be left alone and not be coerced into Christian practices, or forced to give up their synagogues. Once when a converted Jew turned a synagogue into a church, Gregory ordered him to give back the synagogue to the Jewish community. Gregory also had a list of poor citizens to whom he gave regular grants for food and clothing. But threatened by Lombard tribes in the north of Italy and from encroachments by the Byzantine emperor, who claimed authority in Italy, he gradually built up the Church's position as a temporal, military power.

Throughout his fourteen-year reign, Gregory wrote sermons, letters, biographies of the saints, and songs and hymns, and he put his weight behind reforming the liturgy. In time, his name would be synonymous with the magnificent stylistic chant—Gregorian chant—one of the greatest forms of sacred music in the Catholic Church.

When Gregory died in Rome, the Roman people, true to form and loyal to the man they loved, acclaimed him a saint immediately.

PRAYER

Gregory, you called yourself the "servant of the servants of God," a title that every pope since you has used. Help me find value in serving others, even those who are servants. I pray for the humility to place myself under others and serve for motives higher than prestige or recognition for the work I do.

DEVOTIONAL PRACTICE

Gregorian chant has made a comeback in recent years. Although it may sound like old-fashioned music, the timeless, ethereal quality of the singing still touches the heart and moves the soul. As a spiritual practice, buy and listen to Gregorian chants along with your favorite music, and witness to the importance of the spirit by having sacred music in your music collection.

ST. GUY OF ANDERLECHT

"A bitter lesson in not being true to your values."

C. 1012

SEPTEMBER 12

Guy grew up in a poor family, and when he reached adulthood, he wandered around a bit, looking for some kind of job or calling. He had been raised by devout parents who instilled in him solid Christian virtues, among them the desire to live simply and not go running after the world's riches. Guy eventually settled down near Brussels, where he worked for the local church as a sacristan. He enjoyed the work and managed to save some money, but he always prayed that he would not get too attached to wealth and comfort. He worried that he would develop a fear of losing it and then not be content to live more modestly.

Guy was by no means rich, but he fell into a worldly scheme that went wrong. A local merchant sought investors for a shipping venture, and Guy invested his savings in the project and left his job, thinking he would make money. His motives were quite noble: he hoped to make a lot of money so he could give it to the poor. But the ships sank before they got out of the harbor, and all the contributors, including Guy, lost their investments. Guy also discovered that his job as sacristan had been filled by someone else. He was now homeless and unemployed.

Guy realized that investing money did not fit his character or temperament, nor was it really in line with the spiritual values that had sustained him since boyhood. He set out to visit Rome, Jerusalem, and other sacred shrines, and spent seven years wandering as a pilgrim across Europe. By the time he returned to Brussels, he had worn himself out. Sick and exhausted, Guy entered a hospital, and he died shortly thereafter.

Guy, may I never become so attached to a certain level of income or standard of living that I could not be happy with less. Everything is relative, especially the relationship of money to happiness. It is an old cliché that money cannot buy happiness, but it is often hard to truly believe that. Help me find happiness in ways that do not require a great deal of money and be ready to accept whatever setbacks God chooses to send me.

DEVOTIONAL PRACTICE

Get a bowl (about the size of a cereal or soup bowl) and fill it with pennies. Put the bowl on your altar or in a special place. Let the pennies represent your current wealth or standard of living. Each day take one penny out and make an affirmation or say a prayer similar to the one above. Do this until the bowl is empty.

As you watch the bowl becoming emptier and emptier, find ways each day that give you joy or happiness that do not require money (or that require considerably less money than you currently spend). Imagine that these will be the only sources of happiness and comfort once the pennies are gone. Reflect on these ways to be happy, and try to make them as important as your current activities that require money, or even more important.

ST. HALWARD

"Quick decisions."

D. C. 1043

MAY 14

Halward, the patron saint of Oslo, Norway, was the son of Thornez, the sister of King Olaf the Fat. As a nobleman he invested his wealth and influence in a shipping enterprise, trading among the islands of the Baltic Sea. Little of his life has come down to us, but his death was dramatically recorded.

One day as Halward and his men were preparing their ship to return to Norway, a desperate woman ran down to the wharf and begged that they take her with them. Enemies, she said, were chasing her and wanted to put her to death. The woman was in the last months of a pregnancy and pleaded that Halward help her escape. As they spoke, three angry men ran up demanding that Halward turn the woman over to them because she was a thief. She denied their accusations.

Halward then made a quick decision out of compassion for the pregnant woman. He obviously knew none of the facts involved in the dispute, nor did he know any of the individuals personally. He told the woman's pursuers that he would not release her, but assuming that she had stolen from them, he offered to make retribution by giving the men the value of whatever it was she had taken. The men refused the offer, which might imply that there was something else going on in the dispute in addition to (or perhaps even instead of) simple thievery.

Intent on capturing the woman, one of the men grabbed his bow and arrow and shot Halward. He died of the wound immediately. But to vent their anger even further, the three thugs took his body, tied a stone around his neck, and threw him into the sea. Remarkably, however, the body floated and washed ashore along the Gothland coast. Halward's remains were taken back to Oslo and interred in a stone church that his family built for him. The church became popular in the Middle Ages as an important shrine to Halward and as the burial place of Norwegian kings.

PRAYER

Halward, help me make decisions based on compassion, even if to do so means I must put some of my own resources into the process, as you did when you offered to pay for whatever the woman had stolen. I pray that I, too, might realize the blessedness of going out on a limb to save the weak and less fortunate.

DEVOTIONAL PRACTICE

In the spirit of Halward, whenever you have to make a quick decision, ask yourself which option is the more compassionate position, and then evaluate the alternatives in light of compassion. This is not to say that you must always take the more compassionate option, although that would be the ideal. There may be other circumstances (perhaps life-threatening) that warrant a different decision that is not the most compassionate. But if you allow compassion to inform your decision making, you know that you are operating under the highest values.

ST. HELEN

"Finder of the true cross."

C. 250–330

AUGUST 18

Social life in the Roman Empire was always fraught with risk, danger, and betrayal. Nothing was certain, as St. Helen discovered. Born to an innkeeper in Bithynia, Helen never dreamed that she would one day be the Roman empress. But around 270 she met the Roman general Constantius Chlorus, who overlooked her humble background and asked her to marry him. She did. In 283 he was appointed Caesar under the Emperor Maximian, whereupon he succumbed to political pressure to divorce Helen and marry the emperor's stepdaughter, Theodora. Jilted for a younger woman, Helen bided her time.

In 306 Chlorus died, and Helen's son by him, Constantine (born sometime between 274 and 288), was appointed Caesar by the popular acclaim of his troops, at that time stationed in England. The young Caesar, enjoying the enthusiastic support of his armies, was acclaimed emperor eighteen months later. In 313, Constantine announced the official toleration of Christianity in the Roman Empire by the Edict of Milan. Religious prisoners were released and churches were rebuilt.

Helen, who was sixty-three at the time, became a Christian and threw herself enthusiastically into spreading the Gospel and bringing the once-persecuted Christian communities to fuller status within the Roman Empire. She found treasure and wealth within the Empire to give to the poor and homeless. When Constantine became head of the eastern Empire in 324 and moved the capital to Constantinople, Helen used the opportunity to visit the Holy Land. Once there, she supervised the building of a church in Jerusalem, and had basilicas constructed in Bethlehem and on the Mount of Olives. Helen became fascinated by the possibility of discovering the cross on which Jesus died. With her support, searchers explored and eventually found three crosses in a rock cistern east of Calvary. The finding of these crosses is still celebrated on May 3.

Helen, you searched for the true cross on which Jesus died. Help me to search also for the spiritual truths on which life should be lived. Inspire me to find the personal goals that will keep me on the road to happiness as I seek to follow God's will. May I find in your own life the courage not to allow temporary setbacks to deter me from leading a holy life.

DEVOTIONAL PRACTICE

Buy or make a small wooden cross, and wear or carry it as a symbol of your steadfastness in the face of life's disappointments. When you feel betrayed or let down by friends or family members, meditate on this cross and let it be a sign of your determination to be patient and to make the most of any crisis.

ST. HENRY MORSE

"A spiritual alias."

1595–1645

FEBRUARY 1

Henry Morse was arrested four times for being a priest. He had been born in Suffolk to Protestant parents, was a student at Cambridge, and then pursued law studies in London. In 1614 he became a Catholic while in France and embarked on training for the priesthood. He was ordained in Rome in 1623.

The following year Morse was back in England where he was almost immediately arrested in the suspicious and treacherous times when English officials viewed Catholic priests as enemies of the realm. He was imprisoned in York where he met John Robinson, a fellow prisoner and a Jesuit priest. Morse studied under Robinson over the next three years, which constituted his novitiate. While still a prisoner, he took his vows as a Jesuit. Eventually he was released and banished, and he then went to Flanders where he ministered to English soldiers fighting for the king of Spain.

In 1633 Morse returned to England under the name Cuthbert Claxton and began serving both Catholics and Protestants during the great plague epidemic of 1631–1637. Morse himself caught the plague three times in the course of his work but recovered each time. Soon he was arrested on the charge of being a priest and perverting the king's subjects. Through the queen's intervention, he was released on bail. In 1641 he left England in obedience to the royal proclamation that banished all Catholic priests from the realm. He would have defied the order had he not wanted to jeopardize his bail-bond holders.

Henry Morse was, however, undaunted and determined to continue his work as a priest in his native country. He returned two years later to work with the sick. He was arrested, escaped, and was apprehended again. This fourth time was to be his last. He was taken to London and sentenced to death by virtue of his conviction nine years earlier. Although Catholic priests were continually suspected of fomenting plots against the king, or being involved in them, Morse stated before his execution that he was working solely for the good of his countrymen and had never plotted against the government. He died praying aloud for himself, his persecutors, and for the people and land of England.

PRAYER

Henry, bring me to find the strength never to give up in the face of opposition. Help me gather the courage I need to practice my faith and lead a spiritual life according to my soul's deepest purpose even when people around me mistrust me or think unkindly of me. Let me remember how willing you and others have been to suffer imprisonment, torture, even death to witness to the love of God.

DEVOTIONAL PRACTICE

Henry Morse worked as a priest under the alias Cuthbert Claxton. Although you do not live in such treacherous times, it can help your spiritual practice to create a "spiritual alias" who is strong, courageous, and unshakable—and known only to you and God. Select a name, possibly from the saints who inspire you, and imagine this person as your higher, more spiritual self, who has all the devotional qualities to which you aspire. Recall your alias during the day when you feel discouraged, and let his or her energy strengthen you.

ST. HILARION

"Remembering the lives that inspired us when we were young."

C. 371

OCTOBER 21

One would think that if a monk did not change his tunic until it was worn out or wash the sackcloth after he put it on, no one would want to visit him. But conventional wisdom defied the life of Hilarion, a holy hermit who spent much of his life trying to escape the great numbers of visitors who came to see him in spite of his less than hygienic grooming habits.

Hilarion studied at Alexandria and converted to Christianity when he was fifteen. Shortly thereafter, he decided to visit the great St. Antony of Egypt, the original "desert father" and inspiration for generations of men and women who sought to escape the world and retire into the desert and wastelands to pursue an intensely spiritual life. Hilarion spent only two months with Antony before the influx of visitors coming to be healed, inspired, or cured of diseases by the famous hermit became too much for him. He left Antony and retreated deeper into the wastelands of Egypt to a place bordered on one side by a swamp and on the other by the sea.

For years Hilarion provided the meager necessities of life by weaving and selling baskets. He managed to get by on only fifteen figs a day and lived in a rough shelter made from woven reeds and grasses. Later he built a cell, but it was far from commodious. It measured four feet wide and five feet high, and extended only a little beyond the length of his body when he was lying in it. Indeed, it was more of a tomb than a regular monk's cell.

When Hilarion was sixty-five, he had a vision that Antony, his old mentor, had died; and being plagued by visitors who came to hear him talk or be healed, he decided to move on. People gathered to prevent him, so he threatened to go without food or water until they let him pass. After he had fasted for seven days, the crowd left, and he departed with some monk companions. They wandered until they arrived at the mountain where Antony had lived. Intrigued, the monks climbed to the top and found Antony's two cells.

Hilarion asked to see Antony's grave so that he could pay tribute to him, but learned that the old hermit had left strict orders not to let anyone know the location of his body for fear that someone would construct a church for it.

Again, Hilarion moved on, this time searching for a place where he did not know the language in the hope that visitors would not come to see him. But he soon learned that, even without words, his mere presence and the miracles that occurred around him drew crowds.

Eventually Hilarion went to Cyprus where the distractions continued. He moved inland twelve miles and finally found a place of quiet and solitude. He died at age eighty.

PRAYER

Hilarion, help me appreciate the people who have influenced my life. Without the help, encouragement, and support of others when I was young and unsure of what direction to take, I could have embarked on the wrong path and never found the life that I now enjoy. I pray for them, too, and ask you to intercede in their own lives if at all possible to help them in whatever difficulties they may now find themselves.

DEVOTIONAL PRACTICE

After some fifty years of living as a hermit, Hilarion went to visit the grave of his original mentor, St. Antony of Egypt. Do you have some mentor from years ago: a teacher, priest, nun, relative, or older companion who inspired you to pursue the life or career that you now have? If you do, call that person or write a letter just to say hello and express your gratitude. If possible, arrange a visit. People who have played important roles in our earlier lives are among the greatest of God's gifts to us.

ST. HILD

"A stretch for the soul."

614–680

NOVEMBER 17

Hild was a holy woman of Anglo-Saxon bloodlines but influenced by the Celtic Christianity of northern England, where she grew up. St. Aidan encouraged her to found monasteries in Northumbria, since she had a charismatic personality and inspired others to follow in her footsteps. One of the communities she established was the monastery at Whitby, a double monastery catering to both women and men. She was abbess of Whitby during the famous council held there in 664 to force the independent Celtic communities to bow to the rules of the Roman Catholic Church regarding the liturgical calendar, the monks' tonsure, and other practices that the Celtic monks found unsuitable. Hild sided with the Celts.

Hild was famous as a soul friend to many people in northern England, encouraging them in their spiritual practices and advising them on the movements of their souls. She was known for challenging others with what we might call "soul stretches." Usually she exhorted them to spend time each day reading and studying the scriptures and doing good works. Hild was counselor to Caedmon, the first known poet in the English language.

Caedmon was an older man who joined the monastic community late in life. He believed that he had no talent for stories, songs, or poetry, and he would frequently leave the feasting hall when the musicians came forth.

One night he left and went out to tend the cattle, fell asleep in the barn, and saw a dream figure approach him, saying, "Caedmon, sing me something." When Caedmon asked what he should sing, the figure replied, "Sing about the beginning of Creation." Caedmon did, and from then on, his career as a singer of songs, teller of tales, and poet of the English language was confirmed. He frequently learned his words from visions he had while asleep, continuing the old druidic practice of using altered states of consciousness for training poets. Also like those of other Celtic bards, Caedmon's poems were about the beginning of time, other universes, the history of humankind, and the stories and adventures found in the scriptures.

Hild died after a long illness. Her final message to the members of her monastery was to live in peace.

PRAYER

Hild, give me strength to stretch beyond the normal routines of my life. Show me how to deepen my spirituality by doing the things that I find hard or disagreeable. I pray that I might never sell myself short by staying within the safe confines of the same old routines.

DEVOTIONAL PRACTICE

It is good now and then to stretch ourselves by doing something that seems to be a little beyond our normal activities or capabilities. By stretching, we grow. Hild often took this approach in working as a counselor with those who came to her for spiritual direction.

Choose a spiritual practice (such as the ones in this book) that does *not* appeal to you for some reason or other. Perhaps it is fasting, meditating, scripture study, spiritual reading, visits to sacred places, or donating money to the poor. Consider your reasons against it. Then commit yourself to doing it. Stretch yourself to perform the activity, and see what effect it has on you.

ST. HILDEGARD OF BINGEN

"The World of all Beauty and Music."

1098–1179

SEPTEMBER 17

"Music," wrote Hildegard, the abbess of a monastery in what is now Germany, "is a half-forgotten memory of a primitive state . . . [it is] a bridge of holiness between this world and the World of all Beauty and Music." This insight was just one of many that flowed from this remarkable medieval woman who began her spiritual career at age eight, when she went to live with a hermit, Jutta, who taught her how to write and sing in Latin. At fifteen, Hildegard herself became a nun and eventually succeeded Jutta as director of the hermitage that had grown into a community of religious women. Around 1147, Hildegard moved her nuns to a monastery near Bingen.

Hildegard's visions and writings worried her at the start. She feared that people would think she was crazy. Indeed, throughout her life there were those who thought she was either crazy, a fraud, or a sorceress engaged in evildoing. But early on, the Church officially examined her revelations and deemed them authentic and good for the Church. A pope even ordered her to publish them, and a monk was assigned to be her secretary. Over ten years she recorded twenty-six visions about God, creation, redemption, the Church, and other spiritual topics.

But visionary writing was not Hildegard's only work. She also composed music and lyrics, including hymns, canticles, and anthems. Her mystical paintings are on par with the sacred artwork of other cultures and centuries. She composed fifty allegorical homilies, wrote a morality play, and maintained an ongoing correspondence with many people that involved hundreds of letters. Her entire life was a renaissance outpouring of mystical and spiritual work that continues to inspire people of all countries.

Hildegard's view of music as a sacred realm leading to God was written in response to the vicar general who had placed her abbey under an interdict, a punishment for allowing a young man who had once been excommunicated to be buried on the abbey grounds. Hildegard took her stand and refused to have the body removed. The interdict itself was eventually removed, and Hildegard's argument still inspires. She wrote the authorities who had closed her abbey that anyone who imposes "silence on churches in which singing in God's honor is wont to be heard, will not deserve to hear the glorious choir of angels that praise the Lord in Heaven."

Near the end of her life, Hildegard was exhausted from her grueling schedule. Crippled, unable to stand upright, needing others to carry her, she passed on to that World of all Beauty and Music that she had seen in visions throughout her life.

PRAYER

Hildegard, help me to find God's power and goodness in works of beauty, whether music, art, sculpture, film, dance, or any other creative expression. May I value my ability to create, treasuring it as a great gift from the divine Creator, in whose image and likeness we are created.

DEVOTIONAL PRACTICE

Find some piece of instrumental music that moves you or puts you in a sacred mood. It should be the kind of music that has a luring quality that easily carries you off into a dreamlike state of reverie. Save this music for special occasions when you want to experience what Hildegard calls the "World of all Beauty and Music." Play it when you feel depressed or you are in need of spiritual uplift. Do not formally meditate or pray when you listen to it. Instead, let this devotion be wordless, just a sacred time to feel the goodness and beauty of God.

ST. HUGH OF LINCOLN

"Hands-on sanctity."

1140–1200

NOVEMBER 17

The diocese of Lincoln had not had a bishop in eighteen years when Henry II bestowed it on the Carthusian abbot Hugh in 1186. It was to the king's advantage to keep bishoprics vacant, because the revenues from the land and estates went to the crown. But as part of his penance for the murder of Thomas Becket, Henry appointed Hugh the bishop of Lincoln. From the start, Hugh was a hands-on bishop. He ordered the cathedral to be repaired, and he personally carried stone, cut it, and socialized with the masons and builders, whose company he genuinely enjoyed.

Hugh defied other social customs by working directly with the leper community, a group of people shunned by the vast majority of healthy people in the Middle Ages. When he was criticized for allowing a leper to kiss him, he replied, "St. Martin healed the body with his touch; it is my soul the leper heals by his kiss." Hugh displayed his personal involvement in funerals as well. He attended every funeral in his neighborhood, including those of the poor, to which he also contributed money. He was known to break dinner engagements with the king to attend a funeral.

When the Jewish communities in the diocese were attacked by anti-Semitic mobs, Hugh placed himself physically between the rioters and the Jews to prevent bloodshed. He personally tore down a shrine to a teenage boy who was thought to have been killed by Jews. Actually the boy was a thief, murdered by his partner, but local feeling, running high against the Jews, had turned him into a martyr. Under Hugh's reign, the Jewish community in Lincoln suffered no massacre, as did the Jews of York.

Hugh confronted his benefactor, the king, on many occasions. He criticized the Forest Laws which gave royal foresters great latitude in punishing the poor who hunted in or collected firewood from the king's forests. The foresters, it was said, hunted the poor as ruthlessly and callously as they hunted deer or boar. Hugh also withheld money and manpower from Richard I's levy to support a war in France, the first time in history that military support was refused the crown.

Throughout his tenure, Hugh used his power of excommunication rather than monetary fines, so that the punishment would fall equally on the rich and the poor. Once when a convicted criminal was being taken to the gallows, Hugh intervened and took the man into his own lodging, on the grounds that the protection of sanctuary should not be limited to the actual church precinct but should extend to wherever the bishop happened to reside.

At a council meeting in London in 1200, Hugh died, but not before he got his last swipe at those who would try to thwart his will that left all his possessions to the poor. Anyone on his staff, he warned, who attempted to keep anything for himself would be excommunicated.

PRAYER

Hugh, I pray for the same faith that allowed you to see how a leper's kiss can heal the soul. Help me to take the same bold steps to become intimately involved in charitable works, especially those that most people choose to ignore. Let me see in these occasions the healing of my soul.

DEVOTIONAL PRACTICE

Consider the many issues you pray for or about, and in the hands-on spirit of Hugh of Lincoln, become personally involved in whatever ways you can. Select some cause or concern that you feel is important, and attend a meeting, volunteer time, contribute financial support, or join an organization that works for the cause.

ST. HYACINTHA MARISCOTTI

"The pouting nun."

1585–1640

JANUARY 30

When Clarice Mariscotti entered the convent, she threatened her family and the nuns who received her with words to this effect: "Okay, I'll be a nun, but you won't like it! You'll be sorry." Being a nun was the last thing on her list of priorities.

Clarice was born into a noble family in central Italy and had absolutely no inclination to the religious life, even though she had been educated in a Franciscan convent. When her youngest sister was married to a wealthy marquis, Clarice felt that she had been snubbed; *she* should have been the bride. She began to pout, grew morose, complained, and made a pest of herself, until finally her parents couldn't take it anymore. They sent her to a nunnery.

On arriving at the Franciscan convent, Clarice (who took the name Hyacintha at her profession) let it be known that she would live by the letter of the rules but not the spirit. She was a noblewoman first and foremost, a nun second, and she planned to take full advantage of her upbringing and aristocratic connections. In accordance with the customs of the times, she was able to acquire considerable comforts and personal luxuries to enhance the austere Franciscan lifestyle. Even in following the rules, she kept to the bare minimum. For ten years, Hyacintha lived in the convent, scandalizing other nuns and proving that the religious life could not prevent her from making life miserable for everyone.

Then while suffering some illness, Hyacintha received a priest into her room to hear her confession, and he immediately noticed the luxuries. He asked her how she could live such a hypocritical life, and something shifted within her. She resolved to tighten up her devotions and conform to the spirit of the life she professed to embrace. But her conversion was short-lived. Soon she was reveling in her lax ways once again. Then, as often happens, God sent a more serious illness, which alarmed her again, and this time when she reformed her life, it took.

Hyacintha became such a model religious that eventually she became novice mistress and a much-sought-after spiritual counselor. Her standard for spiritual growth was the exact opposite of what had characterized her life before. Concerning ways to deepen one's spiritual life, she said, "The sort of people who most appeal to me are those who are despised, who are free of self-love, and who have little tangible consolation. To suffer and to persevere bravely in spite of the lack of all sweetness and rewards in prayer—this is the sign of the spirit of God."

Hyacintha devoted much of her time to collecting money and supplies for the poor, sick, aged, and homeless, mostly by begging. She died at age fifty-five.

PRAYER

Hyacintha, help me to live consistently with what I profess. Show me where my life is not conforming to the values and practices that I claim are important, and pray that I can reform my life to be free of all hypocrisy.

DEVOTIONAL PRACTICE

Hyacintha thought that as a nun she needed the same luxuries she would have had as a noblewoman. How many luxuries and comforts do you have that are not really necessary and which in fact may be contradicting your deepest spiritual values? What are your true needs as opposed to your wants?

Make two columns on a sheet of paper and title them "Wants" and "Needs." List the possessions, activities, people, hobbies, pastimes, and so forth that make up your life, putting each in its proper column. Over the next few days, meditate on this list, observe your life, being mindful of these categories, and see if it is possible to transfer some of the "needs" into the "wants" column. Then try to reduce the number of items in the "wants" column by changing the way you live. Even if you eliminate only one, you have made some progress in simplifying your life so that you can concentrate on what is really important and needful.

ST. IA OF CORNWALL

"The miraculous leaf boat."

SIXTH CENTURY

FEBRUARY 3

The quaint little town of St. Ives in Cornwall has a very unusual patron saint. She is Ia, an Irishwoman about whom little is known. But like many saints, the one or two pieces of information about her continue to haunt us.

Ia may have been related to the chieftains of Irish tribes. At some point she was inspired to lead a holy life as a missionary to foreign lands. The era she lived in witnessed the dispersal of many Irish missionaries, both men and women, to other parts of Europe and Britain to teach the Gospel. Ia had planned to sail for Cornwall with three companions, but she arrived at the shore too late. The others had already set sail. Disappointed, she began to pray, when a small leaf floated up in the waves.

Possibly looking for some sign in nature to reflect her own misfortune, Ia poked the leaf with a rod she carried to see if it would sink. Perhaps the sinking leaf would carry her own sinking hopes beneath the waves, and she would begin to feel better. But on the contrary, the leaf did not sink. Instead, it grew larger, and finally the leaf was as big as a boat. Like other Irish voyagers before and after her who trusted their boats and fates to the winds of God, Ia climbed upon the leaf and pushed off. Not only did she reach Cornwall safely, but legend says she arrived before her three friends.

PRAYER

Ia, help me to find the will of God in disappointment when plans do not go as I had hoped. Help me realize that in some sense, there is no totally bad luck.

Everything is part of God's grand scheme if we but know how to interpret it. Give me the confidence to pray and to expect a sign to show me where to go next after a plan or project fails.

The next time you suffer disappointment over plans that go wrong, take a few minutes to go outside and to be quiet in nature. The natural world is always unfolding as God planned, following the processes and workings that were begun at the beginning of creation. Ask God to give you some small sign—a leaf, a bug, a twig, a movement of air, a scent, a sound—that will show you how to interpret your disappointment, how to get over it, or which direction to move in next. Give thanks for this teaching and resolve to follow it.

ST. IDA OF HERZFELD

"Death: a teacher of the good life."

D. C. 813

SEPTEMBER 4

Ida was the great-granddaughter of Charles Martell, who defeated the Muslims and united the Franks, and grew up in the imperial court of Charlemagne where her father was a well-respected retainer and adviser. Ida's family was greatly devoted to Christianity. Her mother became a nun and later the abbess of a monastery. Her two uncles were monks and later were honored as saints.

Charlemagne arranged a marriage between Ida and Egbert, a count in his court, and as part of the wedding gifts he gave the couple extensive estates from which they derived considerable income. The extravagant generosity was in part a gift in exchange for the service that Ida's father had rendered to Charlemagne. Ida and Egbert were a happy couple, enjoyed their life together, and mutually supported each other in their desire to do good works for the people under their care. Egbert died, however, while Ida was still young.

Ida never remarried but remained a single widow committed to using the revenues from her estates to help the poor. She also increased her own spiritual practices of prayer and asceticism, built a chapel for herself inside a church she founded in Westphalia, and led an exemplary life of the spirit that outshone many people in cloistered life. In general, however, she hid her spiritual practices from the public, desiring that they be known only to God. Her example encouraged her son Warin to become a monk and later an abbot.

One of Ida's practices involved a stone coffin that she had made for herself. Each day she filled the coffin with food to be distributed to the poor in the neighborhood. When the coffin was emptied, it reminded her that this was to be her final destination. In this way Ida stayed mindful of her obligation to the poor and of her own death. Her final years found her suffering from a painful illness which she bore with great dignity.

Ida, teach me to think about my death in positive ways. Death can be an ally and a teacher to remind me of what is really important in life. And if I stay mindful of death, I will be inspired to do the important things in life joyfully and well.

DEVOTIONAL PRACTICE

On a blank piece of paper make a list of all the things that are most important to you today (people, places, activities, objects). On another piece of paper list all the things that were important to you at some happy period in your life in the past, such as during adolescence, college days, early adulthood, the years you were raising children, working at a good job, or living in a favorite place. You might end up with some of the same items on each page.

Reflect on these two lists, and circle the three most important items on each sheet.

Then visualize St. Ida, a guardian angel, or some other saint or deceased relative telling you that you have only a couple of hours to live. Meditate on the six items you have circled, asking yourself which of these, if any, you would want to spend your last hours involved with. If none, then how would you want to spend your last few hours? What does this tell you about your priorities and values? Are there changes you should make in the way you are now living?

ST. IGNATIUS LOYOLA

"Journey into the sacred past."

1491–1556

JULY 31

In 1521, the same year that Martin Luther took his stand against the Roman Catholic Church at the Diet of Worms, a young noble soldier named Ignatius Loyola was wounded in the leg at the battle of Pamplona in Spain. The wound would leave him with a limp for the rest of his life. But more important, it confined him for a long period of time to a convalescent bed, where he hoped to relieve his boredom by reading romances. When he was told there were none, only books that dealt with the lives of the saints, he read them instead. Gradually, the lives and legends of the holy men and women of the past began to work a strange effect on the soldier. He found their commitments, trials, sufferings, and joys admirable, and he resolved to imitate them.

When he recovered, Ignatius Loyola made a pilgrimage to the shrine of the Our Lady of Montserrat and stayed in a friary near a cave, where he prayed, did penance, and began to write what would become his famous instructions called *The Spiritual Exercises*. When he went back into the world in 1524, he resolved to study Latin, philosophy, theology, and other disciplines to make himself a valuable "soldier for Christ." At age thirty-three, he returned to school, and eventually he received a masters degree from the University of Paris where he began to meet other men attracted to his lifestyle.

In 1534, the year that Henry VIII took control of the Church in England, Loyola and six companions took vows and were soon calling themselves the "Company of Jesus," later to be known as the Society of Jesus, and then simply the Jesuits. In 1540 the order was approved by the pope. It consisted of ten men.

Loyola continued to train men for the Society of Jesus, using the innovative meditation techniques he pioneered in his *Spiritual Exercises*. For the next fifteen years, he was the superior of the order, which went from ten to a thousand members. By the time Loyola died unexpectedly in 1536 at age sixty-four, the Jesuits were working in nine countries and provinces in Europe, India, and South America. A new order had been born to reform and strengthen the Church in a world of conflicting Christian traditions.

PRAYER

Ignatius, help me to find the resolve that motivated you to go anywhere, do anything for the greater glory of God. Especially strengthen me when I am so easily tempted to take the easy way or comfortable way, thinking only of myself.

DEVOTIONAL PRACTICE

One of Ignatius Loyola's meditation techniques is to imagine yourself in the place where Jesus or a saint you admire lived and taught, or in some scene from the Old or New Testament. This scene then becomes the basis of your meditation. It might be the Nativity, the Crucifixion, the Sermon on the Mount, or Moses on Mount Sinai. Use all your senses: see the scene, hear the sounds, smell the scents, touch the objects, animals, or people. Try to get as much sensory input as you can so that you feel you are truly there. Take part in the scene in some way. Then reflect on what you have seen and heard, and draw some inspiration from it that you can apply to your life.

ST. ILLTUD OF WALES

"The loss of friends."

SIXTH CENTURY

NOVEMBER 6

One day Illtud, a cousin of King Arthur, was out hunting with a group of friends when some mishap occurred and several of them were killed (the details of the accident remain unknown). So shaken was he by the precariousness of life that he decided to leave the world of courts, military campaigns, and aristocratic hunts and lead a more contemplative life. His days of knighthood were over. He resigned his military position with a chieftain of Glamorgan and made plans to retire from society.

Trynid, Illtud's wife, joined him in his new resolution, and they built a house of reeds on the banks of the river Nadafan where they lived simply and quietly. Eventually Illtud seems to have developed a need for an even more austere life. He had a vision of an angel who encouraged him to leave Trynid and his home and take the tonsure at a monastery. Early one morning he headed out. It appears Trynid was not totally in agreement on this, for she tried to visit him sometime later, but he refused to see her. What their relationship was like is not clear.

After spending some time as a monk, Illtud quit the community and embarked on a solitary life once again. He built a hermitage by a stream, and soon others joined him. The community prospered, its reputation spread, and Illtud's center became the first important monastic school in Wales.

Miraculous events surrounded Illtud's life. On one occasion a local chieftain attacked the monastery, and Illtud fled to a cave where an angel brought food to sustain him. When floodwater threatened the monastic grounds, the monks repaired the damaged seawall, but it did not hold. Only through prayers by Illtud did the water miraculously not submerge the fields. Illtud also organized relief for others suffering from natural catastrophes. He sent a boatload of grain to Brittany during a local famine there. Because of this, many churches and places in Brittany are named after him. It is not clear whether he died in Wales or Brittany where some legends claim he was born.

Illtud, your calling to the spiritual life grew out of your loss of friends, and your pursuit of the spiritual life enticed you to leave your wife. I pray for guidance in knowing how to balance my own needs for solitude and contemplation with my obligations to family and friends. Help me make wise decisions that allow my love for God and my love for others to nurture each other.

DEVOTIONAL PRACTICE

The death of friends can change our own lives. People we thought we would know longer and grow old with are suddenly gone. While it's true that new friends move into our lives, they can never replace the friends who played important roles in our past.

Occasionally do something to celebrate the lives of friends who have died, perhaps on the anniversaries of their deaths. Go out to dinner in a restaurant that you used to frequent together, rent a video of a movie that the friend enjoyed, read the friends' favorite poets or sing their favorite songs, visit a place you used to go to together. Make these joyous occasions, remembering the fun and good times you had. Thank them for having been part of your life, and express your desire to be reunited with them in the next life.

ST. ISIDORE OF SEVILLE

"A sifter of the world's knowledge."

C. 560–636

APRIL 4

Every age produces its men and women with voluminous appetites for knowledge. In Spain in the late-sixth and early-seventh centuries, such a person was Isidore, bishop of Seville. He had been tutored by his older brother, Leander, and was his personal secretary when Leander became bishop. Isidore succeeded him on his death and used his position as bishop to continue his own studies, but he also became an activist in the educational system of his day.

Isidore founded cathedral schools, which were somewhat like modern seminaries, for each diocese in Spain. The schools offered not just the usual classical studies but also such innovations as astronomy, medicine, law, geography, languages, and—remarkably for Isidore's time—the works of Aristotle, which were often thought to have disappeared in western Europe until reintroduced by the Arabs centuries later.

Isidore's personal interests resulted in prolific writings on many of these topics, but he also wrote brilliantly on theology and philosophy, devised a set of rules for monks, created the Mozarabic missal, and authored biographies of Old and New Testament figures, as well as of other illustrious individuals in history. If this were not enough, he also wrote a compendium or history of all the important events since the creation of the world! Isidore pulled his writings and far-flung knowledge together in his greatest work, *Etymologies,* or *Origins,* which was an encyclopedia of all the world's knowledge.

When Isidore grew weak in his old age and knew his death was imminent, he died in the classical manner one might expect of an early medieval scholar and churchman. He donned sackcloth and had ashes poured over his head. He raised his arms to heaven, publicly confessed his sins, forgave his debtors, gave his possessions to the poor, and retired to his private quarters, where shortly afterward he died.

Isidore was one of the best minds of his time, the last of the ancient Christian philosophers, and much to his credit, an open-minded and forward-thinking public servant. He was interested in creating educational opportunities to preserve and disseminate the world's knowledge for the sake of human advancement.

PRAYER

Isidore, we live in an age when information can smother us. Help me to juggle the information that comes from all the many media sources we have today and not to become discouraged about trying to know everything there is to know. Most of all, show me ways to manage my time, as you must have done, so that I can do and learn the really important things.

DEVOTIONAL PRACTICE

Try this exercise to test your need for news and gossip: Think of it as a kind of fasting, except instead of going without food, you will go without the day's news. Simply choose a day, or several days, in the coming week to be your media fast. Do not read the daily paper, watch television programs that cover news events, or listen to the news on the radio. When you find yourself longing for your "news fix," say a brief prayer, asking for the ability to discern the really important news events from the trivial ones.

ST. ITA

"The sacred three."

D. C. 570

JANUARY 15

Ita was part of the ancient Celtic tradition of finding sacred meanings in the number three. A mystical number in many cultures, three holds special power for the Celtic imagination. Probably one reason the Irish accepted Christianity so effortlessly was the belief that the Divine Spirit had three important aspects—that is, the Godhead was a trinity. Even the pre-Christian Celts found threeness interwoven in the concept of divine power.

Ita was a woman of an important Irish clan, and from a young age had visions and intimations that she was called to lead a saintly life. One night she dreamed that an angel gave her three precious stones. The next day she wondered what they meant, and the angel appeared and told her that the stones represented the three aspects of the Blessed Trinity that would come into her life in a remarkable way. The angel also said that her dreams and night vigils would be occasions for angels and God to appear to her.

Ita's father initially resisted her wish to live the monastic life, but eventually he gave in. Ita moved to the base of a mountain, and in a short time, other women joined her there. They established a school for young boys, and many future saints and leaders in the Irish church passed under her tutelage, including the famous St. Brendan the Voyager.

Ita founded a monastery at Killeedy in County Limerick, and supervised it wisely and generously for many years. Once Brendan asked her what three things pleased God the most. Her answer was direct and to the point: "Three things that please God the most are true faith in God with a pure heart, a simple life with a grateful spirit, and generosity inspired by charity." Then Brendan asked what three things displeased God the most. Her answer: "A mouth that hates people, a heart harboring resentments, and confidence in wealth."

Ita lived to a great old age, and was the soul friend of many men and women, counseling them on their spiritual needs. When she died, it was said that the presence of the Holy Trinity was felt to be closely and lovingly around her.

PRAYER

Ita, teach me how to acquire the three things that please God. Help me overcome the three things that displease God. Most of all, help me to value the things that please God wherever I find them, and to shun all that displeases him.

DEVOTIONAL PRACTICE

Find three small stones that hold some fascination for you. Preferably look for them in some natural place that you enjoy. In the ancient Irish tradition of blessing with fire and water, pass each stone over a candle flame three times, dedicating each to one of the three things that pleases God. Then bless each with three drops of water, again assigning each to one of the things that pleases God. Lay them out on an altar or shrine, and carry a different one with you on the day that you wish to deepen your commitment to what it represents.

You could also find three stones to represent the things that displease God and use them in a similar way to overcome the things that displease him.

ST. JAMES THE GREATER THE APOSTLE

"A man with a spiritual nickname."

D. 42

JULY 25

James, a fisherman, was mending nets with his father, Zebedee, and his brother, John, when Jesus appeared and said, "Follow me." Without any questions, the two brothers rose, left their father and the nets, and became disciples. James, called "the Greater" to distinguish him from the younger disciple also named James, acquired a divine nickname from Jesus: Son of Thunder.

On the occasion when Jesus and his disciples were poorly treated in a Samaritan town, James and John suggested that they ask God to strike the town with fire from heaven. But Jesus, who was not interested in revenge, rebuked the two men and called them "Sons of Thunder," possibly referring to the impetuousness with which they responded to such incidents. The name stuck, especially with James. John would acquire his own identity as the "disciple whom Jesus loved."

James was in the inner circle of Jesus' followers. He was one of the three privileged to be with Jesus on the mountain of Transfiguration, where they saw his divine nature. James was also with Jesus in Gethsemane the night he was arrested, and it was James who was curious about whether he would be able to sit beside Jesus in the kingdom of heaven.

James became the head of the Christian community in Jerusalem and was the first apostle to be martyred. He was beheaded by Herod Agrippa I in a political execution to appease certain Jewish factions in the city. A tradition grew up that James had journeyed to what is now Spain and preached the Gospel there, and that after his death, his relics were moved to Santiago de Compostela, a Spanish town that became a favorite pilgrimage site during the Middle Ages. James is still the patron of Spain.

It is good to have energy and enthusiasm and to respond to life's adventures with gusto, but sometimes I may hurt the feelings of others when I do. James, help me to be sensitive to others and not to fly off the handle when I feel slighted or attacked. Especially pray for me that I will not seek revenge for the little slights and insults that occur daily.

DEVOTIONAL PRACTICE

James was given the name "Son of Thunder" by Jesus to acknowledge his impetuous personality. What would your spiritual nickname be if Jesus were to give you one? One way to get some insight into this is to do a prayerful meditation to find out. Ask Jesus to let you hear your nickname while you meditate.

Light a candle, burn incense, relax, and clear your mind. Put yourself in the divine presence and watch your slow, steady breathing for about ten or fifteen minutes. During this time, observe the images and thoughts that cross your mind, noticing the ones that seem to be the most persistent or the most appropriate to your spiritual life. Ask if that is your nickname. If you sense the answer is yes, then for the next few weeks, think of yourself as having that name. How does it fit? What can you learn about yourself from it? How comfortable do you feel with it? Consider it a teaching.

ST. JANE FRANCES DE CHANTAL

"Displaying what you truly are."

1572–1641

DECEMBER 12

"There is something in me that has never felt satisfied, but I cannot tell you what it is," Jane Frances de Chantal told her spiritual adviser, Francis de Sales. When she was still in her early thirties, Jane's life changed when her husband died in a hunting accident. What would she do with the rest of her life? she wondered.

Born in Dijon, the daughter of the president of the Burgundian parliament, Jane lived as other wealthy aristocratic women of her day. She married Christopher de Rabutin, Baron de Chantal, when she was twenty and had seven children, three of whom died soon after birth. Eight years later in 1601, the baron was shot in the thigh while hunting and died the following week. Jane and her children moved in with her father-in-law, a feisty, ill-tempered, tryannical old man. Living conditions were strained.

Then in 1604, during a Lenten service, Jane heard a sermon by Francis de Sales, the visiting bishop from Geneva. She recognized him as the spiritual director she had longed for and had seen in an earlier vision. She asked if he would become her spiritual father and eventually he agreed. De Sales asked her if she intended to remarry, to which she replied that she did not. Commenting on all the jewelry that she wore, de Sales suggested, "Well, then, why don't you lower the flag?" Jane complied by trimming back her lavish lifestyle, visiting the sick and dying, and devoting herself to caring better for her children. She continued to live alternately with her father and her father-in-law.

When Jane asked de Sales if he thought she should join a nearby Carmelite order, he advised against it, saying he had a new project in mind for her. In 1610 they formed an order for women specifically unable to bear the severity of established convents either because of age, infirmity, or other circumstances. They called the new order the Visitation of the Virgin Mary. Jane Frances, Mary Favre, Charlotte de Brechard, and Anne Coste became the first members, and were soon joined by ten others.

De Sales died in 1622, leaving Jane bereft of her closest friend and adviser. A few years later her son was killed in war, other friends died, and plague ravaged the region. Her sadness was compounded by spiritual doubts and depression. But as the years went by, additional convents were founded until there were over sixty-five. Jane's last years were spent administering them and the many ministries in which the order was involved. In 1641 at age sixty-nine, she was honored in Paris by the queen, became ill on the way home, and died at Moulins. She was buried near her best friend, Francis de Sales.

PRAYER

Help me to pray with utmost sincerity your prayer to know the will of God. "What is your will for me, O God? I await your plan. I want to live only for you and be guided by you always."

DEVOTIONAL PRACTICE

Consider your lifestyle and ask how you might "lower the flag." In what ways are you broadcasting values, principles, or desires that are not in line with your true spiritual goals? Find something in your life—clothes, jewelry, home furnishings, or playthings—that you can do without. Then bless these things and give them to the poor.

ST. JEROME

"Putting words into practice."

C. 342–420

SEPTEMBER 30

Jerome was a whiz kid with languages. His native language was Illyrian, spoken in the area that would become the border between northern Italy and the former Yugoslavia, but as a young student he learned Latin and Greek and read all the classical writers. In his thirties, he retreated to the Syrian desert to live a more hermitic life and there learned Hebrew. The result of his linguistic studies was a translation of the Old and New Testaments, called the Vulgate, that would be the official text of the sacred scriptures for the Catholic Church well into the 1970s.

Jerome was ordained a priest but never really aspired to having a priestly ministry. He agreed to ordination on the grounds that he not have to serve any church in a pastoral capacity. He also never celebrated the Eucharist during his life. Jerome's primary interests were scholarly and ascetic. While living in Rome in the 380s, he inspired others with the value of living a celibate life. He even organized a community of wealthy Roman women to practice celibacy, and he wrote denunciations against Church thinkers who questioned the need for celibacy or virginity in the religious life. Jerome also fought against those who believed that Mary was not a virgin and that she had had other children besides Jesus.

Jerome's temperament was prickly, and he made enemies, among them Rufinus, a scholar who had been his friend for twenty-five years, and the formidable St. Augustine, who quarreled with him over an interpretation of St. Paul's epistles. Once a band of armed monks attacked the monastery of men and women under Jerome's direction to protest his attacks on Pelagius, the theologian who inspired their own thinking.

In 410 the tribal chieftain Alaric sacked Rome, and many Christians fled to Palestine where Jerome lived, translating scriptures and directing religious communities. He and his followers provided shelter for the refugees. In doing so, Jerome realized the true importance of scriptures: namely, putting them into practice. He said, "I have put aside all my study to help them. Now we must translate the words of Scripture into deeds, and instead of speaking holy words, we must do them." He died peacefully about ten years later at Bethlehem.

PRAYER

Jerome, help me not to alienate others with my own spiritual views. Let me learn from your experience how important it is to be tolerant of others who are sincere in their spiritual quest even though it might be different from my own. Most of all, give me the resolve to put what I believe into practice for others.

DEVOTIONAL PRACTICE

Select from the Gospel ten or twelve inspirational admonitions that encourage us to live a more decent life, such as "forgive each other, live meekly, do not judge others, do not worry about tomorrow." Jesus' Sermon on the Mount has many that you could use. Write each one on a strip of paper and put the strips into a jar or basket. Each morning before you begin your day, place yourself in the presence of God, and draw a slip from the jar to be your focus for the day. Ask for help in putting the admonition into practice as often as you can during the day. In the evening reflect on how well you succeeded. The next day you can continue with the same admonition, or select a new one. When you feel you have practiced the ten or twelve sufficiently, replace them with others.

ST. JOAN DE LESTONNAC

"Let time heal all wounds."

1556–1640

FEBRUARY 2

Joan de Lestonnac was what we would call today a "late bloomer." She was forty-seven when she began the spiritual career for which she would become famous.

Joan was born into an aristocratic family in Bordeaux, and her early years with her parents reflected the strife ripping apart French society. Her father was a good Catholic, but her mother, Joan Eyquem de Montaigne, the sister to the celebrated French essayist, Michel de Montaigne, converted to Calvinism. She tried to undermine young Joan's faith, and when that failed, mistreated her badly. It was these early years, while she suffered her mother's abuse, that stirred Joan's desire to turn to a religious life of prayer and asceticism.

When she was seventeen, Joan married Gaston de Montferrant, who was related to royal families of France, Navarre, and Avignon. Clearly the call to the religious life would have to wait. They were happily married and had four children. In 1597 Gaston died, and Joan spent the next six years caring for her children until they were off on their own (two daughters became nuns). Then at age forty-seven, she decided to enter the Cistercian monastery at Toulouse, but she had been there only six months when her health failed under the rigorous schedule. After she left, her health returned.

Joan went back to Bordeaux and spent two years at her country estate preparing for the spiritual work and service that she longed to do. Young women gathered around her to volunteer to nurse the sick and help victims of the plague. Eventually, under the guidance of two Jesuit priests, Joan founded the order of Notre Dame of Bordeaux, a community of religious women dedicated to the education of young girls and modeled on the rule and constitution of Ignatius Loyola. In 1610 Joan was elected superior, and the mission flourished.

Later, another member of the order, Blanche Hervé, circulated rumors that Joan was not a fit director of the order. Blanche seems to have desired Joan's downfall, and she persisted in spreading malicious gossip, until the cardinal, believing Blanche, had Joan removed from office. When Blanche was elected superior, she mistreated and physically abused Joan. After considerable time, the two women were reconciled, primarily because of Joan's unswerving patience and goodwill throughout the period. Getting on in years, Joan did not want administrative duties again. She lived quietly within the order and died peacefully.

PRAYER

Joan, when others misunderstand me and say untrue things about me, help me withstand the abuse with grace, goodwill, and dignity. Let me find comfort in God, knowing his love for me can pull me through the darkest hours.

DEVOTIONAL PRACTICE

Time heals all wounds, according to the folk belief found in many parts of the world. When you are troubled by something, light a stick of incense and sit before it, noticing the slow burning and the sweet fragrance that comes from it. Let your thoughts focus on the way time passes, and remind yourself that with courage and goodwill, a sweet fragrance will come even from the difficulties that you currently find yourself in. Continue watching the incense until it completely burns out.

ST. JOAN OF ARC

"Clothes make the saint."

1412–1431

MAY 30

An often-overlooked fact about the fate of Joan of Arc is that she was burned at the stake for wearing men's clothing. The bizarre outcome of her brilliant career as the woman warrior who almost single-handedly saved France is indeed strange.

Joan was a thirteen-year-old peasant girl when she heard the first Voice and saw the blazing light that accompanied it. The Voice returned, accompanied by others, which, in time, Joan understood to be Sts. Michael, Catherine, Margaret, and others. Their message to her was to rally the French forces around the Dauphin, the uncrowned prince, and to lead military campaigns against the English troops and their Burgundian allies in the civil war raging across France. At first, French military commanders thought she was crazy, but when her prediction that the French would suffer a serious defeat came true, Joan was listened to more carefully.

Joan went to meet with the Dauphin, and requested men's clothing for the trip. When she won his confidence, a special suit of white armor was made for her, along with her own standard. Her successful campaigns at Orleans and in the Loire valley turned the tide for the French. The Dauphin was crowned king at Rheims, with Joan standing beside him.

Joan's subsequent battles met with defeat, possibly because they were not part of the visionary plan that her Voices had originally proposed. She was captured by the Burgundians, sold to the English, and put on trial as a sorceress and heretic. During that time Charles and the French armies made no attempt to rescue her. The tribunal questioned her about the Voices, her faith, her desire to wear men's clothing, and her willingness to obey the Church. The judges decided she was in league with diabolical forces.

Joan initially refused to deny her beliefs and actions, but eventually a retraction was made. The details of it are the source of controversy. Possibly she retracted to receive a prison sentence instead of death. Part of her retraction was not to wear male clothing. For some reason not evident from the historical record, back in prison she resumed wearing men's clothing, which outraged prison officials. She continued to state her belief in her visions and the divine will behind her mission. The authorities declared her a lapsed heretic. She was burned at the stake, and her ashes were thrown into the Seine. Twenty-three years later, her mother and brothers had the case reopened, and Joan was officially vindicated by a papal commission.

PRAYER

Joan, help me be open to divine voices. Kindle my belief that heavenly messages can come to me if I am open-minded and open-hearted and live a devout spiritual life. And most of all, share with me your courage to carry out the will of God in my life as I see it and hear it, no matter what others may think.

DEVOTIONAL PRACTICE

Joan's mission and sense of identity required her to wear men's clothing, which became a source of controversy and led to her death. Clothing can be a powerful reminder of who we are, what our intentions are, and how others see us. Religious clothing, liturgical vestments, and spiritual garb are important in many traditions.

As an experiment, buy some article of clothing or style of clothing or jewelry that is not part of your customary way of dressing. Bless it for some special intention, such as to be more forgiving, to be aware of God's presence in daily life, or to be a reminder to offer prayers or aspirations during the day. Then wear it, and see what effect it has on you in terms of understanding yourself and your intention. Also be ready for others to question you about it. Will you have the courage and self-assurance to share with them your spiritual practice and beliefs?

ST. JOHN BAPTIST DE LA SALLE

"Friend of youth."

1651–1719

APRIL 7

The turning point in the life and career of John Baptist de la Salle, a French priest, was his 1679 encounter with Adrian Nyel, a dynamic layman with impressive ideas about education. When Nyel came to Rheims, where la Salle was a canon, to open schools for poor boys, la Salle encouraged him, even to the point of helping him launch two schools, hiring teachers, renting a house for them, and letting them eat in his own dining room. Eventually he invited the seven teachers to live in his own home. The young canon was clearly being lured into the world of childhood education.

The living arrangements and initial schools did not work out, mostly because of la Salle's strictness and the severity of the rules that he expected the men to live by. They left. But la Salle continued thinking and planning, meditating on the current theories and practices of education. In time, others joined him, and the Brothers of the Christian Schools—or Christian Brothers, as they came to be known—were born.

Four schools were opened, and soon la Salle began a novitiate to train applicants between the ages of fifteen and twenty to be brothers. Young men hoping to become lay schoolmasters also applied, and so la Salle began a program of teacher training. By 1705 the order was running a reformatory school for boys, and by 1717, they had begun an educational program for adult prisoners. What were la Salle's revolutionary ideas about education?

Although they are common features of modern schools, for the late seventeenth and early eighteenth centuries, they were avant-garde. La Salle proposed that children would learn better in classes where they would study the same sub-

jects together, instead of what had been the traditional method of individual instruction. He began the practice of teaching in vernacular languages—French,
Italian, English—rather than Latin, which had dominated education since classical times and was still the hallmark of an educated person. La Salle also insisted
on silence and obedience in the classroom. And so elementary education as we
know it in our own time came into being.

In 1717 la Salle resigned as head of the Christian Brothers and became a
simple brother like the rest of his men. Although a priest, he had resigned his
canonry years before and had written a stipulation into the order's rule that no
brother could become a priest and no priest could join the order. His final years
attested to his desire to keep the order free from a caste system. He died at age
sixty-eight.

PRAYER

John Baptist, help the children that I know come to understand the importance of
education. Give them and their teachers the motivation to use the school years
profitably, growing in wisdom and grace along with the practical knowledge and
skills they need to live successful lives.

DEVOTIONAL PRACTICE

Some of us have very few good memories of our school days. Yet we survived
them, and much of what we are today we owe to the teachers, subjects, activities,
and other classmates we had years ago. The purpose of this devotional practice is
to recall and recapture the strengths you had when you were in school.

Prepare to meditate in your usual way. After a few moments of silence and
relaxation, let your mind "wander the paths of memory," and ask to be shown a
scene from your school days that demonstrated one of your greatest strengths as
a child. When you see or sense yourself as a young student, ask this young image
of yourself if you still have that strength and, if not, how to regain it. Also ask for
help in being strong in that way in your present life.

ST. JOHN BOSCO

"Following a dream."

1815–1888

JANUARY 31

When John Bosco was nine years old, he had a mysterious dream that changed his life and gave him a goal that motivated him for over sixty years. In the dream, he was in the middle of a bunch of shouting, fighting, screaming children. At first he tried to calm them by talking with them, but that didn't work. Next he tried to restrain them physically, even threatening to beat them. That also failed to quiet them. Then a woman appeared who said, "Softly, softly . . . if you wish to win them, take your shepherd's staff and lead them into a pasture." The children turned into wild animals, then into gentle lambs. And with that, Bosco knew his calling was to help the struggling children of the poor find their way into a better life.

Bosco began almost immediately to influence the other boys in the poor neighborhood where he lived with his widowed mother. His father had died when he was two. Young John became a street entertainer, and on Sunday mornings gathered young boys around him with his juggling, acrobatic feats, and magic tricks. Then he would encourage them to go to Mass with him. At sixteen he entered the seminary with borrowed and donated clothes, as well as charitable donations for tuition. While studying theology in Turin, he continued his Sunday activities of finding street kids to entertain and influence in whatever ways he could.

Eventually this became Bosco's major mission. He even quit his chaplaincy at a hospice for girls when there were complaints that the boys he preferred to work with were noisy and threatening the peace of the hospice. With his mother as a housekeeper, Bosco opened his own refuge, a kind of shelter for homeless boys. Many of the boys found apprentice work during the day, but at nights, Bosco taught them shoemaking, tailoring, and Latin. He also set up a printing press so they could learn that trade and be able to support themselves later in life.

By the mid-1850s Bosco had ten priests assisting him. In 1859 he founded the Salesian Order (named after Francis de Sales, the bishop of Geneva), which was a congregation of priests to care for homeless boys. In 1872 a similar congregation, called Daughters of Our Lady, Help of Christians, was organized to do similar work with girls. By the time of his death, John Bosco had watched the Salesians grow to 768 members, with thirty-eight houses in Europe and twenty-six houses in the western hemisphere. Today there are thousands of Salesians around the world, and Bosco's childhood dream is a major enterprise in the Roman Catholic Church.

PRAYER

John, your work provided turning points in the lives of unfortunate boys and girls who might never have survived into adulthood without your influence. Help me be aware of the potential turning points in my own life, as well as how my influence can be a turning point in the lives of others, especially young people.

DEVOTIONAL PRACTICE

Think back to some incident in your childhood that was an early turning point (either for the better or the worse), and write it down on a piece of paper. Then think ahead year by year, and write down each major event that changed your life or started you in a new or important direction. Do this up until the present. Be mindful of these peak moments, and meditate on them, looking for what each had to teach you and whether you learned and grew from the occasion. Offer thanks for the opportunities they presented to you. Next resolve to forgive yourself for the opportunities you missed, and then forgive the people who hurt you along the way.

ST. JOHN CHRYSOSTOM

"Harsh words for the rich and famous."

347–407

SEPTEMBER 13

When John Chrysostom preached in his parish in Antioch, the congregation frequently applauded. He was one of the most popular orators of his day; his name, Chrysostom, means "golden mouth." As a youth John studied under one of the great teachers of oratory, and he could have had a shining career as an orator and philosopher. But at age twenty-three he became a Christian and went to live with monks in the mountains outside the city. He even spent a couple years as a hermit in a damp cave that harmed his health. He eventually returned to Antioch.

In 397 Chrysostom became bishop of Constantinople, and his sermons began to touch the nerves of people in high places. He frequently criticized the wealthy for not giving enough to the poor. He even included statistical breakdowns of the wealth in the city to show that the upper classes could well afford to contribute more to the care of the lower classes. To the rich, he preached, "When you are weary of praying and do not receive, consider how often you have heard a poor man calling and have not listened to him. . . . Stretch out your hands, not to heaven, but to the poor."

Chrysostom spoke against the conspicuous consumption of the aristocratic families, criticizing their dress and morals. Nudity in the baths and the entertainments was a prime target, not because Chrysostom disapproved of the human body but because of the social implications of certain practices that involved nudity. For example, the wealthy appeared nude before their male and female slaves in the baths because they assumed that slaves were not human beings with the same sensitivities that free people had. Naked dancers were exploited and abused as a matter of course, also on the assumption that they were not fully human.

231

Chrysostom preached against these practices and the ideas behind them. "Do not say that she who is stripped is a whore. Her nature is the same as yours. They are bodies alike, both that of the harlot and that of the free woman." Many people felt Chrysostom's outrage was aimed specifically at the empress, Eudoxia, who was known for her vanity, lack of charity, and sensuous entertainments.

Chrysostom had enemies within the Church as well as without, many of whom were sincere and morally upright individuals. But in time he was tried for a number of charges, which included "using words offensive to the empress." After years of religious and political wrangling, Chrysostom was finally banished by the emperor to a town on the far end of the Black Sea. He was marched there in the summer heat, a captive of guards who treated him brutally. After several months of travel he was exhausted and near death. He was taken to a nearby chapel where he died, his last words being, "Glory be to God for all things."

PRAYER

John, help me find the courage to say what I know is true, no matter how important the people are whom my words might offend. I do not want to be a coward and remain silent when my voice should be heard for the sake of truth and decency.

DEVOTIONAL PRACTICE

The words that came from John Chrysostom's mouth earned him the appellation "golden mouth." What words are golden for you? What phrases or short sentences do you find exceptionally moving or inspiring? Make a list of these, and try to work them naturally into your conversation in a way that is not self-aggrandizing. Drop them as little seeds of inspiration that may take root in the souls that hear them. One way to do this is to focus on using one phrase or statement each day.

ST. JOHN DAMASCENE

"Lover of pictures and poetry."

C. 690–749

DECEMBER 4

When he was a boy, John Damascene's father bought him an expensive tutor named Cosmas. Arab traders had brought Cosmas to Damascus from Sicily, and the elder John paid a handsome price for the valuable slave who taught his son grammar, logic, arithmetic, geometry, literature, and all the sciences. John's father was the chief of revenue for the Moslem caliph in Damascus, a hereditary position that John himself stepped into when he became an adult. The family were Christians and did not seem to have any problem living under and working for Muslim rulers.

After serving as revenue chief for a number of years, Damascene resigned and, with his adopted brother, who was also named Cosmas, joined St. Sabas's monastery outside Jerusalem. There the two brothers enjoyed the monastic life as well as their fondness for poetry and song. In fact, the other monks were somewhat scandalized by their activities. The two spent their free time writing books, composing songs and hymns, and actually singing them!

But more seriously, these were the times when Christians raged against each other over whether physical representations of Jesus, Mary, and the saints constituted idolatry. The iconoclasts were against images and ruthlessly destroyed them wherever they appeared. John and Cosmas argued for their usefulness as tools that would strengthen piety and religious sentiment among Christians. Damascene was frequently denounced by Byzantine emperors for upholding the practice of making and exhibiting images.

Cosmas became a bishop, and John was ordained a priest and served in Jerusalem for a while. But eventually he returned to the monastery, where he contin-

233

ued to write, compose poetry, and develop some of the leading texts in early Christian thinking. Damascene is now considered a doctor of the church. His works include texts on philosophy, theology, heresy, orthodoxy, the teachings of the Greek religious scholars, Scripture, morality, and asceticism. Some of his poetry and hymns are still used in the Greek liturgy.

John Damascene died at St. Sabas's monastery at an advanced age.

PRAYER

John, give me a love for poetry and pictures. Even though I live in an age glutted with the printed word and visual images, I pray that I always will be able to find and value those images and words that speak to my heart and soul.

DEVOTIONAL PRACTICE

We should be able to express our spirituality through art and poetry, even if we are not artists and poets ourselves. Find a painting or photograph of some person, landscape, or scenario that you think has spiritual meaning. Then look through a book of poetry for a poem that captures the same kind of sentiment. Put the picture and the poem in a place where you will see them and be reminded not only of the spiritual sentiment but also of your search for them.

ST. JOHN DE BRITTO

"Other lands, other customs."

1647–1693

FEBRUARY 4

Although John de Britto was a Portuguese Jesuit priest from Lisbon, he died a guru in southern India. The strange course of events that brought him to India began when he was a small child suffering from a serious illness and his mother called upon St. Francis Xavier for help and promised to dedicate her son to him if he survived. The boy survived, and his mother instilled in him a love and respect for that early Jesuit missionary to India. De Britto was destined to follow in Xavier's footsteps.

De Britto joined the Society of Jesus when he was fifteen, and he sailed for Goa with sixteen other Jesuits in 1673. His mission at Madura was near the equator, but he learned to adjust to the harsh climate. He also learned to adjust to the Indian way of life, which was so alien to him. Early on, De Britto knew that to be accepted by the Indians he would have to live like them. To be respected as a teacher, he would have to adopt the lifestyle typical of other Indian teachers.

To the best of his ability, De Britto adopted Indian mores, abstained from meat, wore Indian clothing, and respected all the laws of the area that he did not find morally objectionable. One area in which he refused to comply was the caste system, built on centuries of prejudice and ill treatment of the poor. His willingness to meet the Indians on their own terms paid off, and he made converts to the Christian faith.

In 1686, De Britto and his students were captured and tortured for several days for not participating in the local rituals to the god Siva. The priest-guru was near death, but he recovered and was called back to Portugal. Once back home, he longed to be at his mission in India. He returned for three years, but again was arrested by a local raja who saw his activities as subversive of local spiritual traditions. While awaiting his beheading, De Britto wrote in a letter, "I await death and I await it with impatience." He called death "the object of my prayers" and the "reward for my labors and my sufferings."

PRAYER

John, so often I see people intolerant of others and unwilling to meet each other even halfway. Teach me how to appreciate and honor the values and lifestyles of others. When people are different from me, this does not make them wrong or unworthy. Pray for me that my discernment sharpens so that I understand the variety of differences that make up the world, and not criticize or reject others unjustly.

DEVOTIONAL PRACTICE

Find a store that sells cultural articles from around the world and buy some small object or article of clothing that seems not to "fit" you because it comes from a culture that you know little about, or from one that does not particularly appeal to you. Take it home, bless it, and begin to use or wear it, asking that the spirit of the land from which it comes enlighten you to the richness and worthiness of this way of life.

ST. JOHN EUDES

"Fallen women, inept priests, and the Hearts of Jesus and Mary."

1601–1680

AUGUST 19

Throughout the history of the West, until rather recent times, sexual behavior was strictly circumscribed, especially for women. Rules laid down by male hierarchies, whether in politics or religion, severely controlled the sexual lives of women and provided rigid penalties for transgressions. "Unchaste" or "loose" women might never find a respected place in society. Many would never marry, and former sexual experiences would forever haunt them. In the 1630s Father John Eudes met Madeleine Lamy, a woman who was caring for women and young girls who were thought of as "fallen women."

Eudes became interested in this work while he was a volunteer helping plague victims in his native Normandy, where his father had been a prosperous yeoman farmer (and had hoped John would marry to inherit the estate). During the plague years of 1625 and 1631, the young priest was moved by the condition and fate of women who were trying to turn their lives around and find a respected place in society. He met Lamy and was inspired by her work. Both of them realized, however, that to make serious improvements, a more permanent arrangement was needed rather than the temporary homes that many women were able to find with people such as Lamy.

In 1641, Eudes and Lamy set up a rented house to rehabilitate women, and they invited Visitandine nuns to staff it. About ten years later, the nuns separated from the Visitandines and formed their own order, Sisters of Our Lady of Charity of the Refuge. In 1666 the order was formally recognized as an institution within the Church to care for and rehabilitate women. The work that Eudes and Lamy had begun thirty years earlier had finally paid off.

Eudes himself was involved in another important reform movement in the Church—namely, the improvement of clergy education. He founded the Congregation of Jesus and Mary, an order of priests to set up seminaries and teach in them. Over the course of his life, Eudes founded numerous seminaries, preached missions, and also promoted another devotion of his: adoration of the Sacred Hearts of Jesus and Mary, on which he wrote popular books. He composed the Mass of the Sacred Heart in 1668.

In the winter of 1675 Eudes ran a nine-week mission, preaching outdoors every day. He took ill and never recovered enough to continue his strenuous pace. He died five years later.

PRAYER

John, let me be mindful of the people in our society who need help in turning their lives around. When I see men and women who are "down and out," help me to be compassionate toward them, realizing that but for the grace of God, I too could be in their circumstances.

DEVOTIONAL PRACTICE

Prayer can be a powerful force in making changes, even in the lives of people who do not know they are being prayed for. Studies of praying for the recovery of hospital patients have demonstrated this again and again. On almost any day, your newspaper will have a story about someone or some family down on their luck. Cut out the article (and photo if there is one) and give it a place of honor on your altar or shrine. Pray for these people daily for nine days, or whatever length of time seems appropriate to you. Although you may never know what becomes of them, have faith that God hears your prayers, and that your prayerful concern will be an important part of the changes taking place in their lives.

ST. JOHN FISHER

"The voice of conscience."

1469–1535

JUNE 22

In 1502 John Fisher, the thirty-three-year-old priest and vice chancellor of Cambridge, resigned his post to become the personal chaplain to Lady Margaret Beaufort, the mother of the king, Henry VIII. Through her good offices and generous donations, colleges and chairs of instruction were founded at both Oxford and Cambridge. Two years later Fisher became a bishop and the chancellor of Cambridge, an office he held until he was executed for treason.

During his tenure, Fisher engaged in the intellectual and theological disputes raging across Europe concerning Roman Catholicism and the new ideas coming from the Protestant reformers. He wrote against Martin Luther concerning the efficacy of prayer and the sacraments. Fisher's writings and sermons won him an international reputation. In 1529 he became the personal counselor of the then-queen, Catherine of Aragon. As the issue of royal divorce emerged over the years, Fisher championed Catherine's side, arguing against the divorce.

When the crises in the royal marriage were eventually resolved in favor of divorce, Fisher withheld his consent. Then when Henry sought to assume leadership of the Church in England, Fisher sided with the pope, and argued against the monarch heading the English Church. Refusing to accept the Bill of Succession because it required swearing the oath of supremacy that acknowledged Henry as head of the Church in England, Fisher was imprisoned in the Tower of London as a traitor.

While in prison, Fisher was made a cardinal of the Church, a move that strained even further his position in the realm. A friend of Thomas More and Erasmus, Fisher had spent years discussing, teaching, and writing about religious principles in an age of tremendous change. The prisoner stated his own personal principles quite clearly. In 1534 Fisher said, "Not that I condemn anyone else's conscience. Their conscience may save them, and mine must save me." The following year he was beheaded.

PRAYER

John, pray that God may make me strong in my religious principles. Help me to value the voice of conscience that speaks to me about spiritual matters, and may I always stand up for what my conscience tells me is right and just. But also, may I never condemn other people if their consciences tell them differently.

DEVOTIONAL PRACTICE

We are given a conscience so that an internal voice will guide us through life. Occasionally, light a candle, burn some incense, and quiet your mind. Put yourself in the presence of God. Enter the stillness of your soul and listen quietly to what the voice of conscience says to you. If you are troubled by some particular issue, make the intention as you light the candle and incense that you are seeking guidance concerning it. Then for the next eight or ten minutes, consider the thoughts and promptings that come to you as spiritual instruction on that issue.

ST. JOHN GUALBERT

"Forgiveness versus revenge."

D. 1073

JULY 1

One day John Gualbert was walking a narrow passage in the winding streets and alleys of Florence, when he recognized the man who had murdered his older brother, Hugh. The man had supposedly been his brother's friend, but as in so many relationships in medieval Italy, deception, jealousy, and bitterness often transformed love into hate. Gualbert knew that he should avenge his brother's death. That too was the code of the day, especially for a noble family like theirs. He drew his sword and rushed the murderer, who fell on his knees and pleaded for mercy.

At that moment, Gualbert experienced a revelation. He recalled Jesus' own words of forgiveness for the men who crucified him. Gualbert sheathed his sword, helped the other man to his feet, embraced him, and asked his forgiveness. He pardoned the murderer, and they parted peaceably. Gualbert then dropped into a church of a nearby monastery and prayed before a crucifix. Suddenly he saw the figure on the crucifix bow its head. Gualbert knew instinctively that his act of forgiveness was being acknowledged and that forgoing his revenge was pleasing to God.

Gualbert then asked the abbot of the monastery to admit him as a monk, but the abbot refused, knowing that Gualbert's father would not approve. Undaunted, Gualbert cut off his own hair and borrowed a habit, and the abbot then admitted him to religious life.

In time, Gualbert founded his own monastic community at Vallis Umbrosa, which became the order of Vallombrosan Benedictines. He only allowed modest-sized buildings constructed of timber and mud, in contrast to the magnificent stone edifices being built at the time. He also required stricter behavior of his monks, compared with some of the lax rules of other monasteries. Gualbert's order was also the first to create the position of lay brothers, a custom adopted by other orders and today a mainstay of many religious communities.

A humble man, Gualbert refused minor orders for himself, content to be a simple monk. He gave generously to the poor, even on occasion dispensing the monastery's entire store. He was over eighty when he died in 1073.

PRAYER

John, let me vow never to seek revenge. May you give me the inspiration to swallow my pride and forgive those who hurt me. Help me to remember Jesus' great act of forgiveness on the cross and that his great commandments were to love one another and to forgive one another.

DEVOTIONAL PRACTICE

Vowing never to seek revenge is not the same as vowing never to *want* to get even again. People will hurt you and you will want to get even with them. This is just part of human life. But here is a ritual to help dissipate the desire for revenge. When you feel like getting back at someone who has hurt you, write out on a piece of paper your plan for getting even. Make one up if you don't actually have one. Then with prayers to become a more forgiving person, burn the paper in a small pot, in the fireplace, or over a candle. As the paper goes up in smoke, ask that your own desire for revenge go up with it. Then renew your vow never to seek revenge.

ST. JOHN MASSIAS

"Meals on donkey."

1585–1645

SEPTEMBER 18

Young John Massias was an intense, spiritually minded little boy, who preferred to pray and go to church rather than play games with other children. His parents were from an old Spanish family of noble blood, but they had fallen on hard times and were quite impoverished. They both died when John was still very young, and he went to live with an uncle who gave him the job of tending sheep. John often prayed the rosary three times a day: for sinners, for deceased souls that had not yet reached the rewards of heaven, and for his own salvation. He continued this practice throughout his life.

Massias also had visions of the saints, seeing them and speaking with them. He felt their presence strongly around him, especially when he prayed. The Virgin Mary and John the Evangelist were the most frequent spirits with whom he communicated. In fact, St. John encouraged him to leave Spain and go to the New World as many Spaniards were doing during this century of exploration. So he left his uncle, found passage on a ship, and sailed for Peru.

In his new country Massias worked for two years on a cattle ranch. He saved his money until he had enough to travel to Lima, the capital. There he joined the Dominican order, where he worked for the rest of his life as a lay brother and porter. Many people came for his advice and to share in the grace and sanctity that radiated from him.

Massias was particularly concerned about the poor in the city, often going out to find them when they were too embarrassed to come to the monastery for handouts. He even trained his donkey to make the rounds through the city streets so that charitable citizens could put food in its saddle bags for the poor. The donkey was well known as Brother John's messenger of charity. People who were hungry and too poor to buy a meal knew they could help themselves to whatever the donkey carried.

The humble lay brother was well respected throughout the city for his holiness and miracles. When Massias died at age sixty, the archbishop and viceroy both attended his funeral.

PRAYER

John, I pray that the devotion you had for the saints might rub off on me. Awaken my interior senses to see and hear the visitations and instructions from the holy ones who have lived before us and who now watch over our spiritual progress.

DEVOTIONAL PRACTICE

The saints, angels, and guardian spirits most often join us when we are in deep prayer or meditation. John Massias's practice of saying the rosary three times indicates that he spent a great deal of time in a meditative state of consciousness. The repetitious, mesmerizing prayers of the rosary quite naturally produce a deepened state of awareness. In fact, repeating any prayer, poem, or charm three times or nine times (three times three) is a traditional method to deepen your interior senses and prepare them for visionary experiences.

Memorize a prayer or inspirational poem (or compose one for your own intentions). Then ask your patron saint or guardian angel to advise you on an issue or problem you are dealing with. Next, repeat the prayer three or nine times with your eyes closed. You may hear or sense the answer as you pray, but if not, listen intently in the silence within you when you say the prayer for the last time. In the moments immediately following your prayers, you should hear a reply.

ST. JOHN NEPOMUCENE NEUMANN

"The loneliness of the spiritual immigrant."

1811–1860

JANUARY 5

John Nepomucene Neumann knew from his young days that he wanted to be a priest, so he studied well, entered a diocesan seminary, and continued theological training at a university in Prague. When he was ready to be ordained, however, he ran up against a brick wall. No diocese in his native Bohemia would ordain him. There were enough priests. So Neumann applied to dioceses in the United States, a growing, expanding nation of new immigrants and new states. He got no answer.

Finally, on a hunch and with a lot of prayer, Neumann said good-bye to his family and, with $40, sailed for the New World. He arrived in New York City in May 1836 and was ordained in June. He then went to Buffalo where he spent four years doing pastoral work with German immigrants. He described it as work fit for "only a poor priest" who can lead "a wandering life" and who needs "no pleasure, except the care of souls." It satisfied Neumann, but by 1840 he realized that the loneliness and hardship of the work required more spiritual support than he was getting. So he joined the Redemptorist order. During the next decade he continued his "wandering life," in Maryland, Ohio, Pennsylvania, and Virginia. Again Neumann worked with the many immigrants pouring into the new settlements forming along the frontier.

In 1852 Neumann was appointed bishop of Philadelphia. Here he plunged into the construction of churches, schools, and a cathedral. Neumann had always been interested in providing solid education for the children of immigrant families, both to deepen their religious commitments and to prepare them to get ahead in society. Two catechisms that he wrote were approved by the American hierarchy in 1852 and went on to become standard texts for most of the nineteenth century.

Neumann's life personally touched thousands of Americans through his articles in newspapers, his catechism, and the schools and churches he founded. He died of a stroke on a street in Philadelphia in the winter of 1860.

It is often hard to lead a dedicated spiritual life alone. John, help me to understand when and where I need community, as you did when you joined the Redemptorist priests and as you realized among the settlers coming from Europe to live on the frontier. May I overcome any reluctance to seek spiritual advice from others or to join—or form—support groups to deepen my spiritual life.

DEVOTIONAL PRACTICE

Reading inspirational books is one way to feel connected to others living a spiritual life. Commit yourself to reading spiritual literature, other than Scripture, at least three or four times a week, if not every day. Even ten or fifteen minutes can help overcome feeling isolated. If possible, suggest to family members or friends that you form a reading club to meet and discuss your thoughts and feelings about common books that you choose to read.

ST. JOHN OF THE CROSS

"The dark nights of our souls."

1542–1591

DECEMBER 14

In 1577 John of the Cross was imprisoned in Toledo in a cell that measured 10 x 16 feet, with only one small window so high up that he could not read his prayers without standing on a stool to get up near it. His captors beat him cruelly until he bled—he had the scars on his body until he died. Who were his captors? What was his offense?

His offense was his refusal to leave the monastery at Avila, where he had been invited by St. Teresa to help in her reforms of that community. His captors and persecutors: his own religious superiors and the representatives of the Inquisition. After nine months John escaped and found refuge in a reformed monastery.

The controversy John stumbled into was partly his own doing. He and his good friend, Teresa of Avila, founded a stricter order of Carmelites, called the Discalced Carmelites. The word "discalced" refers to their practice of wearing sandals or going barefoot instead of wearing shoes. This was just one of the more severe ascetical practices that they advocated. The new reformed order threatened the older Carmelites, and the tension came to a head in 1577 when John was arrested. Within two years, however, a separate province was established for the Discalced Carmelites, although disagreements continued even among the Discalced themselves.

It was while in prison that John wrote his famous work *The Dark Night of the Soul,* which is still a classic in mystical literature. It recounts the depression, dryness, lack of enthusiasm, and severe discouragement that most people experience now and then when pursuing a deep spiritual life. Perhaps the dark night is best summed up in John's comment "A bird can be held by a chain or a thread, still it cannot fly."

The accusations, slander, gossip, and ill will continued throughout John's life. Disappointment hounded him. He was reduced from the directorships he once held to the status of a simple friar. Teresa died in 1582. His enemies within the order claimed to have evidence of his wrongdoing that warranted his expulsion from the monastic life that he loved so dearly. Still he persisted. In his last year, he contracted a fever and underwent several medical operations, but he never regained his health. He died leaving behind his great spiritual masterpiece along with two others, *Spiritual Canticle* and *Living Flame of Love,* both about the joy of experiencing the love of God.

PRAYER

John, give me strength to persevere when things look their darkest. Help me to remember that the dark nights do eventually leave, that day returns and brings with it the bright light that helps me see clearly the great love that God has for us. Even when I feel that prayers such as this one are of no use, may I continue to pray and not give up hope.

DEVOTIONAL PRACTICE

When you are experiencing depression or confusion about anything in your life, whether in your spiritual practice or in your everyday activities, light a special, long-burning candle to dispel the darkness that clouds your soul. Whenever you see it, think of it as the beginning of a new light, a "living flame of love" that burns in your own heart and grows stronger as the candle declines. When the candle is spent, clean the holder and use it as a vase for flowers.

ST. JOHN OGILVIE

"Gossip and hearsay."

1579–1615

MARCH 10

Among the most exciting intellectual controversies in the late sixteenth and early seventeenth centuries was that of religion. Some of the best minds of the era vied with one another over religious principles, Church structure, matters of faith, and spiritual practices. The curious and scholarly John Ogilvie was swept up in these disputes at Louvain, where at age thirteen he was sent to pursue his studies. He arrived a Scottish Presbyterian, as were his noble parents (his father was a baron, his mother related to the Stewarts and Douglases), but in four years he was swayed from Calvinism and joined the Catholic Church. He then joined the Society of Jesus and was ordained a Jesuit priest in 1610.

Although there were strict laws about the entry of Catholic priests into Britain, Ogilvie volunteered for the Scottish mission, where he hoped to be part of a plan to win over King James I to Catholicism through the influence of Catholic nobles. He arrived in Scotland under the alias John Watson, supposedly a horse trader and returning soldier from the wars in Europe. He worked secretly among Catholic families, meeting in their homes, then took the bold step to serve Catholics in prison. Visitors to prisons were searched closely, as they still are today. Ogilvie ran the risk of being exposed as a Catholic priest.

In time, Ogilvie was betrayed by Adam Boyd, who posed as someone who was interested in becoming a convert to Catholicism. The two met at an appointed time in the Glasgow market, but the meeting was a trap by Boyd and a Protestant henchman. A fight broke out, and Ogilvie was apprehended and taken to prison.

Ogilvie was tortured to break his will and to make him reveal his knowledge of the Catholic underground. He was given no food for twenty-six hours and deprived of sleep for eight days. Whenever he fell asleep, he was prodded, kicked, shouted at, dragged from the couch, and thrown on the floor. His torturers even resorted to tearing out his hair. He was charged with high treason, not the more lenient charge of saying Mass. King James himself sent Ogilvie five questions regarding the relationship of Church to state, which, if he answered favorably, would assure his freedom. Ogilvie could not answer honestly and please the king.

Throughout his imprisonment, torture, and execution, officials tried to bribe Ogilvie into disclosing the identities of secret Catholics among the Scottish nobility—that is, the nobles who swore to the Oath of Supremacy in public but privately were still practicing Catholics. He refused. Even on the scaffold, he was offered his freedom and a comfortable position if he would renounce Catholicism. Although he was told that he was being executed because of his answers to the king regarding politics, Ogilvie knew that his true offense was being a Catholic priest.

PRAYER

It is often easy to go along with talkers and gossips, and to say things about others that we have no right to say. John, inspire me to keep my mouth shut as you did under the cruelest of torture. May I not indulge in vicious or vindictive conversation just to please my listeners. Give me the courage to remain silent, or if I speak, to speak well of others, as I would want them to speak well of me.

DEVOTIONAL PRACTICE

Carry a special coin or medal in your pocket blessed for the purpose of strengthening your resolve not to engage in vicious gossip. When you are with people who are maligning someone, reach in your pocket and grasp the coin firmly with the intention that your clenched fist is akin to your clenched tongue. Say to yourself that for as long as you hold the coin in your hand, you will also hold your tongue.

ST. JOHN THE APOSTLE

"The apostle of love."

FIRST CENTURY

DECEMBER 27

The relationship between Jesus and John has been a source of wonder and mystery for two thousand years. Known as "the beloved disciple" and "the disciple Jesus loved," John's place among the original followers of Jesus singles him out as someone special. He seems to have held a unique place in Jesus' heart.

John and his brother James left the fishing nets they were mending when Jesus said, "Follow me." He was the youngest of the apostles, one of the "Sons of Thunder" (along with James). John was with Peter and James at the Transfiguration, when Jesus revealed his divine nature. He accompanied Jesus into the Garden of Gethsemane the night he was arrested. Along with Peter, John was the first to rush to the tomb on Easter morning after they had been told by Mary Magdelen that the body was gone.

The fact that Jesus and John had some extraordinary regard for each other is clearly seen at the Last Supper where John shared Jesus' couch, lying with him (as was the Eastern custom for dining) and resting his head on Jesus' chest. He also was the only apostle to be at the Crucifixion and the one whom Jesus wanted to take his place in his own family. As he died, Jesus entrusted Mary, his mother, and John to each other's care.

Later, John accompanied Peter on his mission, was imprisoned with him, and played an important role in organizing the new Christian communities. He preached at Ephesus in Asia Minor, and tradition says that he was with Mary when she died. John wrote the fourth version of the Gospel, the most mystical and poetic of the Gospels. His visionary view of the Divine Spirit's role in human life and history was dramatically captured in his Revelation, also known as the Apocalypse.

John's version of the Gospel and his three Epistles celebrate the power of love and the ways that love is the essence of Jesus' message and the nature of God. "God is love," he wrote, "and those who abide in love, abide in God, and God in them." Jesus' final discourse at the Last Supper is a call to love one another and to use our ability to love as a means to know God and serve him. As John recorded it, Jesus' core teaching is to become united with one another, and the Creator, through a life of love.

Fittingly, Jesus seemed to exert a loving protection over the "beloved disciple" to the end of his life, for John was the only apostle not to be martyred but to die a peaceful death.

PRAYER

John, increase my capacity to love. Help me love myself, the important people in my life, and even the acquaintances with whom I share my daily work. Open my eyes so that I might recognize in all forms of love the Divine Creator who created us out of his own love.

DEVOTIONAL PRACTICE

We often talk about our love for God without feeling it. Love is many things, including an emotion. It would do us well to have ways to intentionally recapture the loving feeling that we experience now and then in our devotions but which can be illusive and transitory.

Although this may sound corny, find some instrumental music that you consider to be romantic and that puts you in a relaxed, reflective, and peaceful mood. A tape or CD that runs for fifteen or twenty minutes or longer is ideal. As a meditational practice, listen to the music when you are alone. Darken the room, light a candle, and use the time to stir up feelings that you associate with love, but keep your attention in the presence of God. You don't need any special words or prayers for this. The goal is simply to "feel," and to be mindful that, as John put it so simply, God is love.

ST. JOHN THE BAPTIST

"The courage to decrease."

FIRST CENTURY

JUNE 24

John lived as a hermit in the Judaean desert until he was in his late twenties, at which time he returned to civilization and began preaching on the shores of the Jordan River, baptizing people and encouraging them to abandon their selfish and wicked lives and turn to God. His message was simple: "I am a voice from the wilderness, calling you to have a change of heart, repent, and make clear the paths of God, for the Kingdom of Heaven is close at hand." Many heard, understood his teaching, and were baptized with the waters of the Jordan as a sign of their changed lives.

When Jesus, his cousin, appeared one day during his preaching at the Jordan, John recognized in him the teacher and healer that was sent by God to baptize with the fire of the Holy Spirit. At first John hesitated to baptize him, but Jesus told him it was right to do so, and so he baptized Jesus, thus inaugurating Jesus' public career. "From now on," John said, "Jesus must increase, and I must decrease."

But John continued to preach, gather crowds, and provoke many influential people with embarrassing public comments about their scandalous and self-serving lives. Among his targets was Herod Antipas, the ruler of Galilee. John criticized him for his incestuous and adulterous marriage to Herodias, the wife of his half brother. Under Herod's orders, John was imprisoned. Salome, goaded by her mother, Herodias, asked for John's head. Herod complied and John was executed.

John, give me the strength to overcome my fear of "disappearing"—of not being recognized, admired, fawned over, the center of attention. We are so addicted to the attention we crave from others that to be quiet, humble, and unassuming can hold great terror. Help me to truly believe that others must increase and I must decrease, that God's will must be done even if it means putting my own will on hold.

DEVOTIONAL PRACTICE

John's feast day occurs shortly after the summer solstice, when the days are the longest. The daylight hours begin to decrease as the days grow shorter. Celebrate the feast of John by building a bonfire (as is the custom in many countries) and honor the gift of light in your life, both physical and spiritual. As the fire dies to coals and ashes, commit yourself to increasing the spiritual light in your life, by following divine inspiration and putting the needs of others before your own.

ST. JOHN VIANNEY

"A patient ear for everyone."

1786–1859

AUGUST 4

The young John Vianney made his First Communion in secret. Roman Catholicism was inimical to the leaders of the French Revolution, which had begun when he was three years old. But the temper of the times did not abolish John's longing to be a priest. In his late teens he asked his father about studying for the priesthood rather than working the rest of his life tending cattle and sheep on the family farm. When he was twenty, he left home to study with the Abbé Balley.

Through a clerical error that kept his name off the role of divinity students, Vianney was drafted into Napoleon's army, but he fell ill and missed being sent to Spain with his contingent. Shortly after his health returned, he met a strange man on the road who invited Vianney to travel with him. The stranger led him to an encampment of army deserters living in the forests. Now technically a deserter, he hid out on a cousin's farm, several times narrowly escaping soldiers looking for deserters. When Napoleon granted general amnesty in 1810, Vianney could breathe easier and resume his studies.

Never a good student, Vianney only became a priest through the Abbé Balley's patience and private tutoring. After ordination in 1815, Vianney was assigned as curate to his friend and mentor. When Balley died, two years later, Vianney became the parish priest at the small, isolated village of Ars. But in a matter of years, the remote outpost would become one of the major sites of pilgrimages in France, not because of the place itself, but because of John Vianney.

Although Vianney had a narrow, judgmental streak (he was intolerant about such things as dancing, modern fashions, swearing, working on Sunday, and general "loose living"), the sanctity of his personality attracted many people. The parishioners themselves reformed their lives, and during the period from 1830 to 1845 an average of three hundred visitors a day came to go to Confession to Vianney. He often sat in the confessional twelve to sixteen hours a day, listening to people, advising them, encouraging them to live decent lives. In the last year of his life, over a hundred thousand people came to visit the famous Curé of Ars, many through the special ticket office in Lyons that sold eight-day-return train tickets especially for the pilgrimage.

Vianney always longed for the more quiet life of a contemplative monk, but he ended up staying in his parish, his celebrity status increasing yearly. In 1855 he was awarded the Imperial Order of the Legion of Honor, which he refused to accept. He died peacefully but was overworked and under too much strain for a man of seventy-three.

PRAYER

John, you knew how important it was to be available for people who needed you. Give me the dedication to listen to others' problems even when I would rather be doing something else, or when other people's lives frankly just bore me. We all need an ear to listen to us. When I can be of service in this way, help me to do it patiently and generously.

DEVOTIONAL PRACTICE

We often become impatient when we are forced to do things we don't want to do, but it is easy to imagine that more time is passing than really is. Time yourself for a minute, while you take slow, deliberate, deep, complete breaths. Count them. You may be surprised how many breaths you can take in a minute, even while breathing more slowly and deliberately. Now, the next time you are impatient, take that number of breaths, let a minute pass, and be mindful that the breath is a manifestation of your spirit. Breathe deliberately to strengthen your spirit and calm your mind. Breathe in the patience to continue your task with a more generous spirit.

ST. JOSAPHAT

"Robber of souls?"

C. 1580–1623

NOVEMBER 12

John Kunsevich and his good friend Joseph Rutsky became monks in 1604 at Vilna in what is now Poland. John took the name Josaphat, and the two young men began to plot ways to reform the Ruthenian church. (Ruthenia covered the area of present-day Belorussia and Ukraine.) In time the two men worked their way up in the Church, Rutsky becoming the metropolitan of Kiev and Josaphat the abbot at Vilna. Both were intent on reforming the abuses they saw in the Church, such as laymen controlling Church lands, secular clergy marrying several or many times, and the general decadence and laxity among the orders of monks. On one occasion, the monks at the famous Caves monastery near Kiev threatened to drown Josaphat in the Dnieper River for his attempts to reform their community.

Josaphat and Rutsky's goal was union with Rome, a hot and controversial topic. Many Church leaders and laypeople worried about arbitrary interference in their lives by the pope and the cardinals, who were Westerners and unfamiliar with eastern European customs. The argument against union was in some ways rather simple: Roman Catholicism was not the traditional Christianity of the various indigenous peoples living in that area between Europe and Asia. They had their own religious customs, spiritual traditions, and folk beliefs based on centuries of ancient native cultures. Some people accused Josaphat of "turning Latin" and being a "robber of souls."

The Catholic chancellor of Lithuania, Leo Sapieha, feared that the discord and dissension that reformers like Josaphat created made the area politically unstable (neighboring Cossacks might invade). He accused Josaphat, who had become bishop of Vitebsk, of using violence and closing down non-Catholic churches. The bishop of Polotsk, Meletius Smotritsky, who was elected by a group of dissident bishops, was determined to drive Josaphat, his rival, from the area. Smotritsky's followers hatched a plot against the reformer.

A priest named Elias went to Josaphat's residence and insulted his servants. He even rebuked Josaphat himself to his face. He was there to cause trouble, and he succeeded. After warnings, Elias was arrested and locked up in Josaphat's residence, and his supporters stormed the grounds. Josaphat released him with another warning, but the angry mob broke in and seized the archbishop, shouting, "Kill the papist!" Josaphat was hit on the head with a halberd, shot with a bullet, dragged from his home, and thrown into the Dvina River.

PRAYER

Josaphat, sometimes I am close-minded about the value of other people's spiritual beliefs and practices. Like you, I have my own ideas about what is right and wrong. Help me to be understanding about the people whom I think are wrong, just as I would want them to be understanding about my beliefs, which to them appear equally wrongheaded. The Golden Rule must be paramount, and I ask for the ability to live by it.

DEVOTIONAL PRACTICE

Undoubtedly there were many devout and sincere Christians in Ruthenia who would have felt that giving up their traditional spiritual customs to adopt Western, Roman practices that were alien to them would rob them of something important in their souls. Not all religious practices are right for everyone.

In order to become more sensitive to the "soul needs" of other people, as well as your own, choose one or more religions to read about, such as Judaism, Islam, Buddhism, Hinduism, or the various religious customs of indigenous people around the world. As you learn about other spiritual practices that seem alien to you, try to find a similar or analogous practice in your religious life that would probably be equally alienating and "soul-robbing" to someone from the other religion. Also try to imagine what you would lose, or how you would feel, if you had to give up that practice and adopt another that did not satisfy the deep longings of your soul.

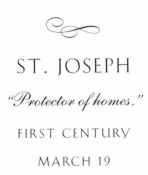

ST. JOSEPH

"Protector of homes."

FIRST CENTURY

MARCH 19

Except for a few stories in the infancy narratives in the Gospel, very little is known about Joseph, the husband of Mary and the foster father of Jesus. Joseph was from the royal house of David and grew up in Bethlehem. At some point, he moved to Galilee where he worked as a builder. It is likely that he and his family were prosperous but not wealthy, judging from the gift of two turtle doves which they gave to the temple on the occasion of Mary's purification after Jesus' birth. Doves were the offering made by the lower, working class.

Joseph was attuned to heavenly influence and divine messages, particularly as they came in dreams. He was told by an angel not to reject Mary when he discovered that she was pregnant. Later, when Herod threatened Jesus' life, Joseph was told in a dream to take his family to Egypt where they would be safe. Joseph had considerable influence in molding Jesus' character, since in the custom of the times, sons worked alongside their fathers, and Joseph was known to be a just man.

There was considerable devotion to Joseph in the fourth to seventh centuries in the East, but interest in him as a saint did not develop in the West until the fifteenth century, when, in 1479, the Church put Joseph on the liturgical calendar. St. Teresa of Avila and St. Francis de Sales promoted devotion to Joseph, and today he is the patron saint of fathers, workers, and, curiously, real estate.

Joseph's influence in the sale of real estate is difficult to document. There is a tradition that in the Middle Ages, a group of nuns buried a medal to the saint and prayed to him for help in finding a building that could serve as a convent. They were successful. Today, statues of St. Joseph are one of the hottest-selling items in religious stores. The current practice is to bury a statue of Joseph in the yard to facilitate selling your house. Almost everyone agrees that the statue should be buried upside down, but there is controversy over whether it should be buried in the front or back yard. Many people choose to bury it upside down in the front yard, facing the "for sale" sign.

Joseph, give me the perseverance to work diligently at my trade or career, and to provide for myself and my loved ones. Even when times are hard and it is easy to become discouraged, help me to work hard. Also, teach me how to be happy with a modest living and not hunger for great wealth that could so easily prevent me from enjoying the simple things of life.

DEVOTIONAL PRACTICE

As a carpenter and head of a household, Joseph is rightly the patron of a safe and prosperous home. Bless your home with a statue of Joseph which you might bury in the yard rightside up since you are not planning to sell. When the time comes to sell you can invert it.

Locate the statue in a place that you can use (or at least think of) as a sacred site. Occasionally leave seed or bread there for the birds. If it is a place where you can sit to read or meditate, do so. Also get in the habit of asking Joseph's protection over your home when you are away or when no one is there to watch the property.

ST. JOSEPH MARY TOMMASI

"A spiritual daydreamer."

1649–1713

JANUARY 3

Joseph Mary Tommasi came from a wealthy and politically powerful family that was as much dedicated to the spiritual life as it was to its place in the world. Tommasi was born in Sicily, the heir to his father's offices as Duke of Palermo and Prince of Lampedusa. But by the time Tommasi decided to enter the Theatine order at age fifteen, he had four olders sisters who were Benedictine nuns and a mother who had entered a convent, and even his own father had expressed the desire to spend the rest of his life as a religious. When Tommasi objected to his father's plan, for it would require Tommasi's succeeding his father as head of the family holdings, his father relented and allowed his son to embark on his own career.

Tommasi became one of the great liturgists and scholars of his day. He studied languages, especially Greek and Hebrew, and developed liturgical works that were admired and used even by the Anglican Church. He was known as the "prince of liturgists." But his studies also produced essays on the Bible and a critical edition of the Psalms, which he published under a pseudonym.

Throughout his life Tommasi stepped back from honors and acknowledgments. Somewhat absentminded, he could spend hours involved in a task and then "wake up," not knowing exactly what he had been doing. His love of God captivated his attention and moved him through his daily work. He was a spiritual daydreamer. A humble man, he gave to the poor and helped those who came for support or advice. He fed the birds with as much sincerity and interest as he fed those who came for spiritual food.

The pope, Clement XI (who had reluctantly accepted the papacy under Tommasi's strong exhortation), decided to make Tommasi a cardinal, saying, "What Tommasi did for me, I will do for him." Tommasi balked at the idea. But the pope's wishes were not to be denied. Reluctantly Tommasi accepted, but added, "Well, it will only be for a few months." And he got his way. The new cardinal died within the year.

PRAYER

Joseph Mary, help me to "get lost in the spirit" now and then, especially when the hectic pace of modern life robs me of peace and calm. Show me ways to get involved in spiritual daydreaming and not take my duties so seriously that I forget the higher values of daily life.

DEVOTIONAL PRACTICE

It is often in the humblest activities that we can "get lost" with God—if our intentions and desires are to find God in those humble activities. Sometimes it just means being mindful that God can be found in the little distractions of our day.

As a devotional practice (as well as a contribution to the ecological health of your neighborhood), put out bird feeders or add another if you already have them. Watching birds feed in our yards can be mesmerizing and can provide a few moments or many hours of escape from the usual frets and worries that color our day. When you catch yourself watching the birds at the feeders, thank them for calling you away from your problems and difficulties. Be grateful to the Creator, who has given us such simple creatures to provide pleasure and distract us from the stressful duties of our lives.

ST. JOSEPH OF CUPERTINO

"Intentional laziness."

1603–1663

SEPTEMBER 18

As a child, Joseph Desa was known as "the Gaper" in the village where he lived. He walked around, often in a stupor, with his mouth hanging open. Forgetful, clumsy, distracted, he frequently missed meals. His impoverished carpenter father died when Joseph was young, and his mother mistreated him severely for his slovenly ways, his bad temper, and his laziness. About the only thing he had going for him was his deep interest in religion and spiritual practices.

After he failed as an apprentice to a shoemaker, when he was seventeen, Joseph applied for acceptance into the Franciscan order. They refused him. He then entered the Capuchins and lasted for about eight months before they asked him to leave. Finally, an uncle, who was a member of the Conventual Franciscans, arranged for Joseph to be admitted as a stable boy.

Joseph seemed to have found his niche. With the Franciscans, his religious devotion deepened and inspired the brothers, who decided he should be trained for the priesthood. He was ordained in 1628. But Joseph's ecstatic "distractions" persisted. He fell into trances, and supernatural events occurred around him. Miraculous happenings took place to the extent that some people accused him of being a publicity seeker. His most dramatic feat was his ability to levitate, which occurred seventy times in his life, usually before reputable witnesses. Because of the unpredictable nature of these bizarre events, he was not allowed to say Mass in public, go to the choir, eat with the community, or appear at public functions for thirty-five years. As if dealing with an embarrassing family member, the order wanted to keep him out of sight, where he could cause no major trouble.

The Inquisition investigated Joseph more than once, and he was sent from monastery to monastery. While at Assisi, he went through a period of spiritual dryness, typical of most mystics, when nothing consoled him and he was filled with doubt and despair. But his spiritual ardor returned, and devout Christians made pilgrimages to him when they discovered where he was. Eventually the Inquisition moved him to a remote Capuchin friary, where he was virtually imprisoned. He was not allowed to have visitors, write or receive letters, or leave the cloistered area of the monastery. Only a few approved members of the community had permission to be with him. But the supernatural phenomena continued on an almost daily basis until he died at age sixty.

PRAYER

Joseph, you were seldom understood or appreciated. God's manifestations in your life brought as much trouble socially as they brought happiness and consolation spiritually. Help me realize that to be favored by God's grace is not always easy, and that others may not understand or approve of my spiritual needs. Give me strength to live my life productively while I nurture my relationship with the divine.

DEVOTIONAL PRACTICE

Laziness usually interferes with both practical and spiritual duties. But in moments of "intentional laziness"—that is, moments of carefree reverie and relaxation—we can have some of our best thoughts and insights. As a spiritual practice, find time in your schedule to do nothing productive. Make the intention that you will spend a half hour just sitting, watching the world pass by, observing the changes in the sky, listening to sounds. You may find it hard not to think about important matters, but when you do, bring your attention back to the simple things going on around you. Do this exercise to acknowledge your need to be still, open, and accepting of whatever spiritual movements pass through you.

ST. JUDE THE APOSTLE

"Overcoming impossible odds."

FIRST CENTURY

OCTOBER 28

Jude is listed among the twelve apostles, but beyond that practically nothing about his life is known for certain. It is not clear when he was called to discipleship or exactly how he spent the years after Jesus' death and Ascension. Scholars believe that he is the same as Thaddeus, the brother of St. James the Lesser, and one of the canonical epistles is attributed to him.

And yet probably no saint has a greater following and devotion, particularly in times of trouble when people face seemingly impossible odds. Jude has become the Saint of the Impossible. People continue to pray to him for hopeless and difficult favors. It is not uncommon to find entries in the personal ads in local newspapers that say, "Thank you, St. Jude, for favors received." It is a longstanding tradition that if Jude answers your prayers, you should thank him formally.

How did Jude acquire this reputation?

Legends suggest that Jude preached the Gospel in Mesopotamia where he frequently ran afoul of local sorcerers and magicians and performed impressive miracles to establish his own power and authority, often against great odds. For example, he cured a local king of leprosy, tamed two wild tigers that had escaped, and influenced warring armies to make peace. On one occasion, sorcerers struck all the city's lawyers dumb so they could not speak (which may have pleased more citizens than we imagine!), but Jude restored their speech by holding up a crucifix before them. At another time, Jude sent serpents to bite wicked magicians, then ordered the serpents to suck out the poison so the magicians recovered in three days.

In spite of his successes, Jude, like many first-century Christians, was martyred with stones and clubs.

PRAYER

Jude, saint of the impossible, let me never lose hope in the face of overwhelming odds, even when circumstances look like they will never turn out for the best. Help me keep my faith in the Creator who has made all things, understands all things, and can do all things.

DEVOTIONAL PRACTICE

Jude's attributes that appear in artwork include: the ax, club, sword, halberd, stone, and stick. All can be used as defensive weapons in time of trouble. Buy or make a pendent that represents one of these attributes, bless it in honor of St. Jude, and wear it when living through difficult times or when facing opposition.

ST. JULIAN OF NORWICH

"All things will be well."

D. C. 1423

MAY 13

The mystic and holy woman known as Julian of Norwich was never formally be-atified by the Church, and yet to many people, from her own time to today, she is one of the holy ones among the ancestors. Nothing is known about her parents or family. The date of her death has been lost in time. And yet her writings, *Revelation of Divine Love,* based on the sixteen revelations she experienced in 1373, continue to be a classic in Christian mysticism.

Julian was an anchoress, or solitary, who lived in a small house attached to the church of St. Julian in Norwich, England. Early in life she asked God for three gifts: that she would have a deeper understanding of Jesus' sufferings, that she would have a life-threatening illness (what today we would call a near-death experience), and that she would be filled with contrition, compassion, and a "willful longing toward God." She received all three gifts.

Within the span of five hours on a spring morning in May, Julian received the "shewings," as she called them, most of which were related to Jesus' passion. The visions filled her with peace and joy, although she did not at first completely un-derstand the significance of these revelations. She meditated on them for fifteen years, and then one day she heard a "ghostly" voice explain the meaning to her. "Love was His meaning. Who showed them to you? Love. Why did He show them? For love." In this way, Julian learned that the meaning of Jesus' sufferings was nothing other than divine love.

Although Julian was illiterate in her younger days, she seems to have been familiar with other mystical writings. As an anchoress who never left her dwelling, she could speak through a window to visitors who probably included ordinary people as well as the religious and lay theological thinkers of her day. Her message to all her contemporaries was that God's love is eternal, all-embracing, and all-creating. Even the human condition that allows people to fall into sin and wickedness is part of this loving plan because through contrition a person's life can be transformed into even greater love.

One of Julian's messages of consolation, received from God and passed on to the worried and fearful people of her day, says simply, "I can make all things well; I will make all things well; I shall make all things well; and you shall see yourself that all manner of things shall be well."

From an ancient manuscript, thought to have been transcribed by one of Julian's contemporaries, we know that the English mystic lived into her seventies.

PRAYER

Julian, give me the optimism and confidence to believe that love is the meaning of suffering, and to believe that God can make—and does make—all things well.

DEVOTIONAL PRACTICE

It is often hard to stay optimistic in the stressful and troubled world we live in. Pessimists often seem to have a monopoly on reality. But it has been said that the pessimist is one who sees life only through the head, while the optimist sees life through the heart. Julian's sense of divine love and her confidence that "all manner of things will be well" are definitely perspectives of the heart. Use this devotional practice to find the love and wellness that dwell deep in your own heart.

Sit comfortably, close your eyes, and get into a meditative state of consciousness. Imagine Julian standing with you on the edge of a great plain filled with all the troubles of the world. She takes your hand and leads you into a cool, dark forest, along a mossy path to a clearing where there is a deep pool of fresh water fed by a spring bubbling up from the earth below. It is quiet and peaceful here. Shafts of sunlight filter through the leaves and disappear like jewels beneath the surface of the water.

You remove your clothes, wade into the crystal-clear water, bathe or swim, and swallow a few mouthfuls of it, letting it refresh your body and soul. Then walk back out, sit on the grassy bank, and imagine the holy woman Julian drying you off with a soft towel. She tells you that in the water and sunlight you can find the love that makes all things well. Sit here, contemplating this love and goodness, watching the sunlight from the sky sparkle through the water. Realize that the water and sunlight sparkle within you. When you feel like returning, come back to the place where you are meditating and repeat three times: "All manner of things will be well, for love is the meaning." Say this whenever you see sunlight shining on water.

ST. KEVIN

"All nature is here to help."

D. C. 618

JUNE 3

After studying with monks, Kevin (his Irish name, Coemgen, means "beautiful shining birth") retreated into the solitude of nature to find the glories of the Creator in creation itself. This was a common practice among the early Celtic Christians. Legends about Kevin tell us that the "branches and the leaves of the trees sang to him." Indeed, Kevin's rapport with nature was so strong that it seems his own spirit found kinship and fellowship with the birds and animals.

On one occasion, after an angel had led him to the Valley of Two Lakes, a beautiful glen in which he founded the now-famous monastery of Glendalough, Kevin was lying on the ground with his arms stretched out, praying and meditating. A blackbird perched on the palm of one hand and began to construct a nest. Kevin didn't move or disturb her. Next she laid her eggs, and Kevin continued to lie quietly. Throughout the nesting, hatching, and nurturing of her brood, Kevin allowed her to use the palm of his hand for a home. Only after the young birds flew off did Kevin get up and go about his business.

Stories abound of how animals and Kevin assisted each other and shared their environment. For instance, when Kevin's books of Psalms fell into the lake, an otter retrieved it so that no part of the delicate manuscript text was damaged by the water. Once a wild boar that was being pursued by a hunter and his dogs fled to Kevin for protection. Kevin cast a spell on the dogs so that their paws stuck to the ground. Then Kevin told the hunter that he would release the dogs if he and they promised to leave the boar alone, and so they did.

Kevin's relationship with animals benefitted other people as well. A neighbor's cow visited Kevin each day while the rest of the herd was in the fields. The cow would lick Kevin's feet, and when it returned home for milking, it gave as much milk as half the herd together. On one occasion, Kevin was fostering the son of an Irish chieftain, and a doe came and allowed itself to be milked so the young prince would be nourished. But one day a wolf ate the doe's fawn, and Kevin feared she would no longer come and share her milk with the baby, so he asked the wolf to take the fawn's place so the doe would continue to provide milk. Another time Kevin killed seven of his sheep to be food for a group of starving poor people. The next day the seven sheep were still among his flock.

It is reported that Kevin lived to be 129 years old.

PRAYER

Kevin, your fondness for nature, animals, birds, and other human beings continues to live in the stories about you. Show me ways to see other living creatures as children of the same Creator who made me. Most of all, let me appreciate the role that they play in the world, and how we humans and the more-than-human creatures must share this blessed Earth with each other, and help each other survive.

DEVOTIONAL PRACTICE

The stories about Kevin are similar to the accounts of shamans and mystics in every culture throughout the centuries. Only in our rational, literal, scientific culture do we find them hard to believe. Cultures that allow for many different kinds of reality have no difficulty in knowing that such things occur and that they occur for a purpose: usually to open our eyes to the marvels of the universe and the many supernatural influences that are part of everyday life.

Here is a spiritual practice to make you more aware of how the more-than-human elements of creation respond when we have some need. (The need here is to know that this can happen!) Choose some animal that does not live in your environment. Three times a day (morning, noon, and night) for three days, ask in a heartfelt way that the animal appear to you. Within a week you will see the animal, either physically or some representation of it (in a magazine, book, or movie, on television, in a store window, or on a billboard), or you may hear people talking about it. Then choose another animal, somewhat more exotic or unusual, so that it will seem more unlikely to appear. It too will appear. As you do these exercises, realize that you are beginning to see the universe as St. Kevin did: alive, responsive, communicative.

ST. LAWRENCE OF ROME

"The last laugh."

D. 258

AUGUST 10

During the oppressive reign of Emperor Valerian, the Spanish-born deacon Lawrence witnessed the death of the current pope, Sixtus II. Before he expired, the pope told Lawrence not to worry about him. "I am not leaving you," he said. "You will follow me in three days." Taking the pope's prophecy seriously, Lawrence commenced to sell off the Church's treasure and give the proceeds to the poor.

The prefect of Rome, on hearing of this mass disposal of Church valuables, rebuked Lawrence, saying that the Church's wealth should go to the government. He commanded that Lawrence reclaim the Church's treasures. Lawrence replied that he would do so, but that it would take three days.

Three days later, when Lawrence invited the Roman prefect to "come and see the treasures," the official discovered a disturbing site. Lawrence had gathered all the poor, crippled, orphaned, blind, ill, and dispossessed of Rome and presented them as the "Church's treasures." Infuriated, the authorities ordered that Lawrence be executed.

A large gridiron was prepared to roast Lawrence slowly over a fire. After he had suffered a long time over the coals, he joked with his executioner, saying, "You had better turn my body. I am already well done on one side." The executioner did so, and when Lawrence was near death, he quipped one more time, "I am cooked enough. It is time to eat." He then prayed for the city of Rome and died.

Lawrence was buried in a cemetery on the Via Tiburtina, on the site where the church of St. Lawrence-Outside-the-Walls now stands. His death inspired many Romans to join the Christian community, and later his famous martyrdom spread throughout the Church and encouraged others in times of persecution.

PRAYER

Lawrence, help me to find humor even in the most sorrowful situations, and to learn not to take myself and my troubles so seriously. Let me never lose the ability to make others smile, even those who oppose me and make life hard for me.

DEVOTIONAL PRACTICE

Commit yourself to smiling the next time things go wrong for you. Pause for a moment, recall Lawrence's composure in the face of torture, and make yourself smile. If possible, even make some wry comment, if only to yourself, that reminds you that frustration and disappointment will not last forever.

ST. LAWRENCE O'TOOLE

"Troubled negotiator."

1128–1180

NOVEMBER 14

In 1170 Lawrence O'Toole found himself in a messy situation. As archbishop of Dublin he was the chief negotiator with the English Earl of Pembroke, whom King Henry II had sent to assist the efforts of the Irish chieftain Dermot Mc-Murrogh to gain control of Ireland. Henry was delighted with the opportunity to gain a political footing in Ireland. The beginning of the English occupation in Ireland, and the "Troubles" that would continue to the present day, had begun.

Years earlier the same Dermot McMurrogh had taken the young O'Toole hostage in a dispute with his father. O'Toole suffered greatly during the two years' captivity under Dermot's notorious ruthlessness. Eventually that ruthlessness and barbarity would rally other Irish leaders to drive Dermot out of Ireland. Hence his request from the English king for military and political help.

While O'Toole was in meetings with Pembroke, Dermot's allies invaded Dublin, pillaged it, and raped and massacred large numbers of citizens. O'Toole broke off negotiations to return and care for the suffering and to defend what was left of the city. Then, unexpectedly, Dermot died, and Pembroke declared himself King of Leinster, on the shadowy claim that he was married to Dermot's daughter who, ironically, was O'Toole's niece!

The next step in the bizarre story is that Henry recalled Pembroke to England, but the Irish rallied around another popular chieftain, Rory O'Connor, and attacked Pembroke's forces that were now barricaded in Dublin. Again the archbishop stepped in to negotiate a settlement with Pembroke, but he failed. Pembroke's army went after O'Connor's Irish supporters, and they retreated. The following year King Henry himself came to Ireland, and many (but not all) of the Irish chieftains submitted to him.

O'Toole then became involved in trying to preserve some element of independence for the Irish church. He traveled to Rome to plead the Irish case before the pope, who supported him and appointed him the papal legate for Ireland. The new authority given O'Toole worried Henry for the next nine years. When O'Toole went to England in 1180 for the ongoing negotiations concerning Rory O'Connor, Henry forbade O'Toole to return to Ireland. Further discussions and another meeting ended with Henry giving the archbishop permission to go home, but O'Toole fell ill and died on the way.

PRAYER

Lawrence, being a negotiator can be a thankless task. Compromises leave everyone feeling that they have given up something important. Help me in disputes to realize that being civil and gracious is as necessary for my own peace of soul as winning all my points.

DEVOTIONAL PRACTICE

When you are in an ongoing dispute or argument with someone, light a votive candle that will last several days, with the intention that the light represent illumination and understanding for both you and your adversary. Also let it remind you to pray that both of you treat each other civilly and graciously.

ST. LOUIS, KING OF FRANCE

"A model Christian king."

1214–1270

AUGUST 25

Louis was the son of Louis VIII of France and Blanche, daughter of Alfonso of Castile and Eleanor of England. Louis's father died when the boy was twelve years old, and Blanche, a devout and compassionate mother and queen, became regent. Not only did she reign for Louis, but she taught him the protocols of statecraft and instilled in him the virtues of humility, fairness, diligence, courage, and mercy. When Louis was nineteen, he married Margaret, a daughter of the Count of Provence, and began a happy marriage that produced eleven children. In 1235, when Louis turned twenty-one, he became king, but he continued to rely on his mother's wise counsel for almost twenty years until her death.

In 1248 Louis launched a crusade to Egypt where his forces captured the city of Damietta. The king walked into it barefoot, accompanied by his family and attendants, to show that he was not coming as a vainglorious conqueror. Within a year, however, his fortunes turned, and he was taken prisoner by the Saracens. While in prison, he continued to recite the prayers of the Divine Office, as was his daily custom, and to refuse to lose his composure in the face of insults and abuse from his guards. Released on ransom, Louis then went to the Holy Land for four years, visiting famous sites. On receiving news of his mother's death, he returned to France.

In 1270 Louis once again left on a crusade, but he came down with typhus while en route. On his deathbed in Tunis, he lost his speech for three hours, but it returned sufficiently for him to recite a psalm and offer a short prayer before he passed on. His bones and heart were taken back to France.

Louis's reign was known for compassion toward his enemies, even as he boldly made peace with England and his European neighbors. He forbade lords to fight and oppress their vassals, and he opposed the injustices of local bishops. A man of his word, Louis became an astute and fair arbitrator in many disputes, improved the tax system, encouraged the practice of Roman law, and built France's first navy. He lived a deeply spiritual life, gave money to the poor, and encouraged the construction of hospitals, religious institutions, and centers of learning, such as the Sorbonne. He was the model Christian king of the Middle Ages.

PRAYER

Louis, give me the strength to exercise authority with restraint and compassion as you did. Let me not become egotistical or self-inflated over my own power and influence over others. When I am quick to disregard the feelings and dignity of others, remind me that we are all human beings and have common human needs.

DEVOTIONAL PRACTICE

Take a photograph or some symbol representing a person who inspired or mentored you as a child or when you were young, and hang it on a wall, or place it on your desk or dresser where you will see it. Honor it in some way, by acknowledging to yourself that, like Louis IX who valued his mother's advice well into adulthood, you will always need the counsel of someone older and wiser to prevent an inflated sense of self-importance that might cloud your decisions and keep you from acting for the good of all.

ST. LUCY

"See through your eyes, not just with them."

D. 304

DECEMBER 13

Lucy means "light," and the traditions that have grown up around St. Lucy concern our most valuable use of light: our eyes and our ability to see.

Lucy was born of noble parents in Syracuse, Sicily. A man who had been courting her asked her to marry him, but she refused. Out of spite, he denounced her to the authorities as a Christian. Lucy was a Christian, and during the severe persecution under the Emperor Diocletian, Christians were at great risk if they refused to take part in ceremonies to the traditional gods of the Empire.

Lucy refused to take part in the traditional ceremonies and was brought before the governor who sentenced her to be a prostitute in a brothel. The guards attempted to carry her away, but they could not move her. Her steadfastness in her faith manifested in her physical body, and the guards found her immovable. In retaliation, the governor ordered her to be burned. But when Lucy was put into the flames, they did her no harm. Finally Lucy was stabbed through the throat and died.

Two traditions developed concerning her eyes. In one, the judge tore her eyes out as part of her torture. In another, she herself pulled them out to give to a suitor who had admired them. In both stories her eyes were miraculously restored.

Lucy seems to have been impervious to suffering, and in one tradition she is remembered as saying, "God has granted that I should bear these things in order to free the faithful from the fear of suffering."

Lucy, help me to use the gift of sight wisely to see what is really important in life, and not be misled by transient fads and gratifications. May I be able to see the spiritual meaning behind life's events and to value this vision far more than a life of mindless distractions.

DEVOTIONAL PRACTICE

Practice "seeing" in a spiritual way. Sit quietly and look at a tree, flower, cloud, hillside, lake, or other feature in the landscape. Let your eye move along the edge of the object slowly so that you trace its entire outline. Then look directly at it, watching for movement of color, texture, or light. As you do this, ask that the divine power that fills this tree, lake, or object shift so that you will notice a change. You will become aware of changes in the physical form, color, or shape. These may be subtle or quite dramatic. See in them manifestations of the divine energy that lies within and behind all created things.

This practice will attune you to "seeing" spiritual realities in the physical world and to becoming sensitive to the impressions that these realities leave on your soul.

ST. LUKE

"A compassionate physician."

FIRST CENTURY

OCTOBER 18

St. Paul called him his "beloved physician," and when the apostle died, he wrote that "only Luke is with me." Luke, the writer of the third version of the Gospel, was probably a Greek physician from Antioch, although little is known about him prior to his becoming Paul's disciple, companion, and personal secretary and physician. He wrote in Greek for communities of Gentile Christians and so is one of the major voices speaking to non-Jews about Jesus' teachings.

Among Luke's stories about the Galilean are the ones, as we might expect, that concern illness and Jesus' powers as a healer. In Luke are the accounts of the crippled man let down through a roof so Jesus could cure him, the man with the withered hand, the woman who had suffered from a hemorrhage for twelve years, and the curing of Peter's mother-in-law. Luke also preserved the story of the Prodigal Son and other people rejected, despised, and outcast from society whom Jesus treated with compassion.

Luke's history of the growth of the early Church in the Acts of the Apostles is a truly mystical view of the working of the Spirit. He sees the Church as a community of Jesus' followers who were inflamed with courage and love by the influence of the Holy Spirit on Pentecost. From that Sunday morning, the early Christian community grew bolder, even in the face of persecution, and began to expand, spreading the teachings of Jesus beyond the Jewish world where he lived and died.

Luke's personal history is somewhat obscure. He traveled with Paul to Rome and was with him during both of his imprisonments. Legend says he visited Jesus' mother and painted several portraits of her. After Paul's death, Luke disappears from history, although he is thought to have died at age eighty-four in Boeotia. He is the patron of physicians and painters.

PRAYER

Luke, give me the vision to see my life as directed by the Spirit, just as the members of the early Christian community were so influenced on Pentecost. Sometimes it is difficult to remember that Jesus has sent the Spirit to be a friend, a companion, and a reminder of all that he taught, but if we can do so, we can live closer to his teachings. Indeed, we can live with and by his Spirit. Strengthen my belief in the workings of the Holy Spirit in my life.

DEVOTIONAL PRACTICE

Because Luke was trained in the medical arts of his day, he undoubtedly recognized the important spiritual component to physical health, as did traditional healers in most ancient societies. It is fitting, therefore, that the bull or ox is the animal associated with Luke, because it is recognized worldwide as having great physical strength and, in many religious traditions, as an animal of great spiritual power and mystery.

As a devotional practice, find a small representation of a bull and put it in a place of honor to witness to the union of body and spirit, the physical and the spiritual. Let it remind you that total health is a product of the spirit and the body working in harmony with each other and with the Divine Spirit in nature. As an animal of power, strength, and mystery, look upon the bull as a representation of the Divine Spirit, which exists in all things and which can manifest in your life in the form of a strong, powerful bull as well as a gentle dove.

ST. LUTGARDIS

"From fun-loving adolescent to bride and companion of Christ."

1182–1246

JUNE 16

Lutgardis, a young teenage member of a Benedictine convent in the Netherlands, was hardly living the life of a nun. She was put into the convent at age twelve by her father, who had lost her dowry money in a failed business deal. She herself had no desire to be a nun. Even though Lutgardis was pretty, vivacious, and intelligent, her father feared that no one suitable would want to marry her without the standard dowry expected in those days. Lutgardis retained her fondness for nice clothes, jewelry, and fun. She came and went in the convent as if she were a boarder, and even entertained men and women in the convent itself. In brief, she had an interesting but rather unorthodox social life.

Then one day while Lutgardis was entertaining a visitor, Jesus appeared to her and, in effect, told her to shape up. She saw his wounds and heard his request that she consider him to be her bridegroom and give her affections to no one but him. From that moment on, she gave up all thoughts about finding a husband and began to intensify her spiritual practices. The nuns thought it was a fad.

But Lutgardis stuck to her commitment. She continued to have visions of Jesus, and as if he were a kind of husband or constant companion, she spoke familiarly with him at prayer and when she was working around the convent. Lutgardis herself developed physical signs of her relationship with Jesus, such as blood appearing in her hair and on her forehead, similar to Jesus' wounds from the crown of thorns.

Twelve years later Lutgardis was still living a devout religious life. Her community, long convinced that her devotion was real, wanted to elect her abbess, but Lutgardis's plan was for an even stricter spiritual life. She hoped to join the

Cistercians. With the advice of her friend St. Christina the Astonishing, she entered a French-speaking abbey at Aywieres, where she never mastered the language and hence never had to worry about being elected to office. Still, Lutgardis's reputation spread, and she became a popular spiritual adviser, famous for her healing, prophecies, knowledge of Scripture, and ability to levitate.

Lutgardis lived at Aywieres for the next thirty years, suffering from blindness during the last eleven years of her life, but accepting it joyfully as God's will for her. She died on the day she had predicted: June 16, 1246.

PRAYER

Lutgardis, help me to see my relationship with Jesus, God, my guardian angel, or even a saint such as yourself in real-life terms. The "family of heaven" is not on some remote cloud, uninterested in the lives of those of us who are still on earth. Teach me how to talk with the saints, angels, and Jesus himself, knowing that they are constant companions if I am open to their influence.

DEVOTIONAL PRACTICE

Begin to put the sentiments of the above prayer into practice. Consider who among the "family of heaven" you have a special devotion to or who seems to take an interest in your life by appearing in dreams or making his or her presence known to you at various times of the day or night. Who in the spirit world of heaven is your special guardian or companion? If you cannot answer this question, pray over it and watch the movement of your soul for an answer. When you realize who your special guardian and companion is, be mindful of him or her during the day, share your thoughts, ask for advice, and most of all, say thanks and express your gratitude in words and deeds.

ST. MAEDOC

"Enduring friendships."

D. C. 626

JANUARY 31

Maedoc was born in Ireland but spent several years studying at St. David's school in Wales. When he returned to Ireland, he founded monasteries, the one most closely associated with him being at Ferns in County Wexford. Many legends about his friendships, miracles, and healings show him to have been a man of intense passion and love for both people and animals.

Early in life Maedoc and his close friend Molaise wondered if they would be together in their journeys and adventures until they died, or whether God planned for them to part and go their separate ways. On one occasion they were praying about this at the base of two trees. Suddenly the two trees fell, one toward the south, the other toward the north. They took this as a sign that they were to part. So Maedoc went south and built his monastery at Ferns; Molaise traveled north and founded a monastery on Devenish Island in Lough Erne.

Maedoc's love of wild animals was unlimited. One day when he was praying deep in the forest where he could be away from the talk and chatter of human company, a stag ran up, fleeing a pack of hounds. Maedoc threw his cloak over the stag's antlers, and magically the stag became invisible. Not only could the hounds not see their prey, but Maedoc's cloak also concealed the stag's scent. When the hounds left, greatly disappointed, Maedoc removed the cloak and the stag returned to its haunts in the forest.

Wolves were Maedoc's special companions. Once several wolves came into the monastery grounds and circled Maedoc, whimpering from their hunger. Rather than run in fear that the wolves would eat him, he rightly saw that they were asking for food. He gave them a calf to eat. One of the brothers objected to this, saying that the cow would not give milk without her calf. So Maedoc blessed the brother's head, and whenever the cow saw his head and licked it, she would give milk to him.

On another occasion a female wolf approached Maedoc on the road, hungry and weak. He asked a young boy who had been walking with him if he had any food. The boy had one loaf of bread and a fish. Maedoc fed these to the wolf, and the boy (as we might imagine) objected, saying that his master would punish him for not bringing the food back. Maedoc had the boy fetch leaves from the woods. Then he blessed the leaves and turned them into bread and fish for the boy.

After his death Maedoc appeared to a man who had been sick for thirty years. The saint appeared in a chariot with a young woman whom he said was St. Brigid. Maedoc told the man that he and Brigid were visiting Earth to celebrate their feast days, which are the last day of January and the first day of February. He predicted that the man would die on the following day, February 2, and so he did.

PRAYER

Maedoc, help me to appreciate the old friends God sent me at different times in my life. I pray that I may see all friends as gifts from the Creator of friendship, and that I may realize how rich my life has been because of the people with whom I have shared my joys, sorrow, hopes, dreams, disappointments, failures, and successes.

DEVOTIONAL PRACTICE

In the spirit of Maedoc and Molaise, who parted early in life, honor the friends from your earlier years with special rituals and prayers. Here is a way to do this. Select a friend you have not seen in years, possibly someone you may never see again in this life. (An old high school or college yearbook might help your memory.) Recall something the two of you did, shared, or used to say to each other. Light a votive candle for that person, and write his or her name on a piece of paper along with the memory of what you shared. Make the day a kind of "unofficial feast day" for the friend by keeping the image and thought of the person with you and saying short prayers for the person as you go about your tasks. At the end of the day, ritually burn the paper, sending the smoke out to bless the friend wherever he or she might be.

ST. MAGNUS OF ORKNEY

"A compassionate Viking."

D. 1115

APRIL 16

In the last two years of the eleventh century, a Viking ship commanded by the Norwegian leader Barelegs was ravishing the western coast of Britain. Two of his hostages were Magnus Erlendsson and Haakon, two cousins whose fathers, the joint rulers of the Orkney Islands, had been captured by Barelegs and sent back to Norway. The young Magnus had studied with monks and counted among his friends a bishop in Wales. He was not a traditional Viking warrior. As the ship approached the coastline of Wales, Magnus refused to take part in the raid.

"I have no quarrel with any man here," Magnus announced when Barelegs asked why he had come up on deck with no weapons. Barelegs thought Magnus was a coward who did not want to fight (even though he had taken part in previous raids that plundered the Western Islands of Scotland). Cowardice was not the issue, and so Magnus stood unarmed in the prow of the ship as it approached the shore. Welsh archers began to unleash their volleys of arrows. Magnus had stated his belief: "I shall not die if God wills that I should live." He sang psalms and prayed as the battle commenced. Miraculously he survived without a scratch.

Magnus was the product of two cultures: the warrior society of his family (descended from Thorfinn Skullsplitter) and the peaceable values learned from Christian monks. After the Welsh episode, he jumped ship off the Scottish coast, sought refuge with King Edgar, married a Scottish woman, and became the Earl of Caithness. In 1102 Barelegs was killed in Ireland, and Magnus's cousin Haakon returned to the Orkneys to take back his family's land. He also seized some of the territory belonging to Magnus.

Magnus consulted with the Norwegian council about his legal position in the

Orkneys, the Scottish islands that were ruled by Norway in those centuries. He returned with legal authority that Haakon agreed to respect, and the two cousins ruled the Orkneys on somewhat friendly terms for a few years. Magnus defended his territory from invaders and raiders much in the warrior spirit of his ancestors, but he refused to let his people join forces with Haakon who continued to operate as a raider and invader. Tension between the two men increased.

During a year-long visit to England, Magnus saw his territory, including part of Caithness, seized by Haakon. He returned and worked out a peace that was not to last. When relations broke down, they agreed to meet on a neutral island on Easter Monday, 1115, each bringing no more than two boatloads of men. Magnus arrived with his two boats. Haakon appeared with eight. Magnus knew he had been set up.

After a night in prayer Magnus promised his men, "I won't put your lives in danger. Our peace is to do God's will." Haakon's forces came on shore, and Magnus refused to fight or endanger his men. After a mock trial Haakon's cook executed Magnus. Magnus addressed his final words to his murderer: "Stand in front of me and strike me on the forehead with the ax, for it is not seemly to behead chiefs like thieves." The cook complied with his last request.

PRAYER

Magnus, help me to recognize the contradictions in myself and others. Pray that I may live more virtuously than the age demands and to resist the vices and faults that are considered normal. I pray that my ideals always be higher than the common denominator I see around me.

DEVOTIONAL PRACTICE

In Scotland Magnus is honored as a saint, martyred for his commitment to peace, compassion, and defense of the weak. And yet he lived in a violent society and was not averse to playing his "other" role as a warrior. Life is not black-and-white. No one is free from contradictions. Use this exercise to deepen your understanding of the polarities that color your own life.

Make a list of the cardinal virtues and their corresponding vices, or list the virtues expressed in the eight beatitudes and their opposites. Then examine your life for the past seven days. On what specific occasions did you act virtuously? On what occasions did you not? Is your "mix" of good and bad qualities acceptable to you, or do your standards require you to improve?

ST. MALACHY

"Prophecies and popes."

1095–1142

NOVEMBER 3

Malachy lived at a time when opposing groups within the Church waged armed combat against one another. In 1129 he was appointed to succeed Bishop Celsus as the head of Armagh, the political center of the Church in Ireland. But when Celsus died, his cousin claimed the right to be next bishop based on heredity. Malachy waited three years, armed conflict erupted, and two important relics— a sacred book and a crosier, both reputed to have belonged to St. Patrick—were stolen by his opponents. Malachy managed to recover them, however, make peace, and assume his position as Bishop of Armagh.

On a pilgrimage to Rome in 1139, Malachy met St. Bernard of Clairvaux and was so impressed with the Cistercian order that he asked to remain there instead of returning to Ireland. But the pope refused the request, and Malachy went home and founded Mellifont, the first Cistercian abbey in Ireland.

Malachy was asked once by his companions where he would like to die and be buried. He replied that if he died in Ireland, he would want to be buried at St. Patrick's tomb. But barring that, he would want to die and be buried at Clairvaux. Then they asked him when he would like to die, and he said on the Feast of All Souls.

Malachy died in 1142 on a trip to Rome. He had stopped off to visit Clairvaux and became ill, and he expired in Bernard's arms. The day was November 2, the Feast of All Souls.

Malachy is best remembered for his remarkable prophecy listing the next 112 popes, beginning with Celestine II who died in 1144. Each pope is described by a phrase, a symbol, or an image, and over the years, these have been uncannily accurate. Sometimes the description refers to the pope's background, his family's coat of arms, or key world events taking place during the pope's reign. An example is "de medietate lunae"—from the middle of the moon—to describe John Paul I (1978), who reigned for only a month (moon). John Paul II's description is "the eclipse of the sun," a prophecy that will be known only as the years go by. After him, Malachy tells us, there will be only two more popes. The last will be named Peter, and Rome will be destroyed.

PRAYER

Malachy, help me to go through life with an open heart and expansive spirit so that I might be aware of the signs and omens God sends. Most of all, I pray that I heed their messages and deepen their meanings for my spiritual growth.

DEVOTIONAL PRACTICE

An old traditional form of divination is to take a Bible, close your eyes, open it at random, and run your finger down the page, pausing whenever the Spirit moves you. The word, phrase, sentence, or passage you have picked will be either a literal or metaphorical answer to your question. This practice can be done to put a prophetic quality on your day.

Each morning ask for a passage that will give you some insight into the coming day, some advice on how to live the day, or some warning to be mindful of. At the end of each day, look back to see how the passage you picked manifested during the day. Do this regularly so that you become skilled in recognizing the biblical passage in the day's events and in interpreting its significance for your spiritual life.

ST. MARCIAN

"Unexpected miracles."

D. C. 387

NOVEMBER 2

A story about Marcian, a fourth-century hermit, reminds us that we cannot demand miracles, and yet they might happen anyway through mysterious avenues.

Marcian was born in Syria and retreated into a desert area between Antioch and the Euphrates River to live the life of a hermit. He sought solitude and anonymity to engage in the austerities that he believed were pleasing to God. For example, the hut that he built was so tiny there was no room in it to stand up or lie down without bending his body. The walls were narrow, the length short, the ceiling low. But it was what he wanted. Eventually word of his severe lifestyle spread, and others joined him. Soon Marcian became a well-known name in the area, and he had enough disciples to form a monastic community, although he appointed another to be the abbot.

When several miracles occurred through his intercession, people began coming to Marcian with their requests. On one occasion, a hermit from another area came with a bottle to request some healing oil to give to a man whose daughter was ill. In other words, if Marcian was to heal the girl, he would be doing it three steps removed! He told the hermit he would not give him the oil. Discouraged and offended, the hermit left. But the girl did get well, and her recovery began at the very hour that the hermit and Marcian were engaged in conversation.

As Marcian aged, well-wishers in the area began competing for the right to bury his body. They knew it would become a popular place of pilgrimage, and the directors of pilgrimage sites made money from visitors. Marcian hoped to outwit them by having his body secretly buried by a friend, who would tell no one where it was. So he was buried in some remote, undisclosed area. But fifty years later, the body was discovered and the remains were transferred to a more convenient place. As expected, it became a famous pilgrimage site.

PRAYER

Marcian, you wisely refused to do some miracles when you knew they would increase the fame and popularity that you never wanted in the first place. I can't do miracles, but I am susceptible to popularity. Remind me that in God's eyes I do not need to be popular and famous. My own life, even though it be as narrow as your cell, can please him.

DEVOTIONAL PRACTICE

It is quite likely that when the girl whom Marcian refused to heal recovered, many people did not realize the miracle involved. Skeptics could easily attribute the recovery to a coincidence. But believers would see the connection between her recovery and Marcian's words in the hour that the healing occurred.

As a spiritual practice, when something occurs that you are tempted to explain as a "mere coincidence," pause and consider the possibility that there was some divine intervention involved. We don't know everyone who prays for us, nor those who send us loving thoughts and wishes that impact our lives in dramatic ways. Rather than write events off as coincidences, keep an open mind that some saint, angel, friend, or relative is involved through prayer, sacrifice, or love.

ST. MARGARET CLITHEROW

"Divine laughter."

C. 1555–1586

APRIL 2

"Everyone loved her" was the frequent comment about Margaret Clitherow. She was attractive, witty, merry, a shrewd business woman, and a jokester. The daughter of a wealthy candlemaker, who had served as sheriff of York, Margaret married John Clitherow, an affluent cattle raiser and butcher who also held civic offices. They had happy, healthy children and a wide circle of devoted friends that included important people of the city as well as their own servants. Margaret Clitherow's life seemed ideal.

One cloud, however, hung over their happiness. Margaret had become a Catholic a few years after her marriage to John. The sixteenth century was a dangerous era for Catholics in an England still heady with the changes resulting from Henry VIII's break with Rome. John was easygoing, personable, and tolerant, and he claimed to have found only two faults with his wife: she fasted too much and she didn't accompany him to church. He didn't seem to mind paying the fines for Margaret's absence at church.

Margaret was imprisoned for two years for working for the Catholic cause. She remained in good spirits and looked upon it as a spiritual retreat, even though the prison atmosphere was dirty, foul, and dangerous. On another occasion, she was confined to her home for a year and a half as punishment for arranging an obviously Catholic education for her eldest son by sending him to study at Douai in France. At some point she began to make the home and space she rented a refuge for priests operating illegally in England. She also hid vestments, chalices, and missals and arranged for Mass to be said in her home. When

John was away, she made barefoot pilgrimages with other women at night to the place of execution outside the city where priests and Catholic sympathizers had met their deaths.

Eventually Margaret was betrayed by an eleven-year-old boy who was forced to disclose what he knew about illegal Catholic activity. The Clitherow premises were searched, and the incriminating evidence was confiscated. Margaret and Ann Tesh, a friend whom the boy also accused, were imprisoned together. Margaret joked with her in their cell that "we are so merry together that I fear, if they do not separate us, we will lose the merit of our imprisonment." As she was taken from her cell to appear before the authorities, she provided one last laugh for about thirty-five other prisoners: she made a gallows with her fingers and laughed defiantly at it.

Clitherow was pressured to ask for a trial by jury, but she refused. She knew she would be found guilty no matter what, and she did not want her family and friends to have to testify. Either they would perjure themselves and lie, or tell the truth about her subversive activities and then suffer the remorse of knowing they had brought about her death. She saw John only once during her imprisonment, and in the presence of a jailer.

Margaret's last requests before her execution were that her hat be sent to John to acknowledge him as "her head," and that her shoes and stockings be sent to her twelve-year-old daughter to encourage her to follow in her footsteps.

Margaret was pressed to death beneath over seven hundred pounds of stone. She was about thirty years old.

PRAYER

Margaret, help me see the humor even in the darkest times. A smile and a laugh, either for myself or others, can get us through the worst troubles. I pray that I may never lose my sense of humor, no matter what happens.

Laughter is good medicine for the soul. The next time you are in a public place, listen for the sounds of laughter. We often hear the voice of God in birdsong, the wind, falling water, the crash of waves on a beach, and other natural sounds, even in silence, but God's voice is equally present in the voices of people laughing and enjoying themselves. Thank God for the ability to laugh, and when you hear laughter, wish the laughers continued happiness.

ST. MARGARET MARY ALACOQUE

"Lost in the heart of Jesus."

1647–1690

OCTOBER 16

Two days after Christmas, 1673, Margaret Mary Alacoque had her first vision of Jesus. He told her that men and women must honor his heart, and that they were to see his heart as flesh. For the next eighteen months, Alacoque's visions filled out the program that Jesus was asking of her. And it was indeed a program. The devotion to the Sacred Heart was to include receiving Communion on the first Friday of each month for nine consecutive months, spending an hour every Thursday before the Blessed Sacrament (later called Holy Hour), and instituting a feast day to honor the Sacred Heart on the Friday after the Feast of Corpus Christi. Through Margaret Mary's undying devotion and insistence on the validity of her visions, all three practices became part of Catholic tradition.

But Alacoque's visions were not accepted by others very readily. At first the superior of the Visitation nuns to which she belonged scoffed at the visions, and the community was hostile toward her. A team of theologians reviewed her experiences and concluded she was deluded and probably should eat more. But Margaret Mary knew she was not hallucinating from lack of food. She kept her faith.

At one point when she fell ill, probably from the strain she was under, the mother superior told her that she would consider the visions to be true if God cured her. Margaret Mary prayed and got well immediately. Her superior then supported her. Later Jesus told her that a compassionate and understanding spiritual director would be sent to her. It turned out to be Claude La Colombière, a Jesuit priest who was appointed confessor to the nuns. He became convinced that Jesus was speaking through Margaret Mary.

Still Alacoque's visions were far from universally appreciated. She herself had doubts, depression, and illness and suffered great grief at Colombière's death. But in 1683, Alacoque eventually became assistant superior and then novice mistress. In 1685, the convent began private devotions to the Sacred Heart, and two years later, they built a special chapel to the Sacred Heart. Eventually sister convents began the devotions as Margaret Mary had outlined them, and in time the tradition spread throughout the Church.

On her deathbed, Alacoque received the sacraments and said, "I need nothing but God, and to lose myself in the heart of Jesus." She was fifty-three. In 1765, seventy-five years after her death, the pope officially approved the devotion to the Sacred Heart of Jesus.

PRAYER

Margaret Mary, help me to be single-minded and faithful to what I know is true. When I meet opposition from others, even within my spiritual circles, help me maintain unshaken confidence in my beliefs. Let me not, however, become close-minded or self-important, but accept criticism, reflect on it, and pray for the wisdom to see, know, and speak the truth.

DEVOTIONAL PRACTICE

Using the Nine First Fridays as a model, create an ongoing practice to honor a special saint, guardian angel, or representation of Jesus or the Creator. Go to Mass and Communion if possible, but also personalize the practice by adding some additional activity, such as spending an hour in prayer, taking a meditative hike through the woods or along a beach, or doing some charitable work. Select an activity that you can realistically maintain for one day a month (it need not be Friday) for nine months. Mark these days on your calendar. If circumstances prevent you from keeping your practice on the appointed day, do it on the same day of the following week.

ST. MARGARET OF CORTONA

"A teenage pleasure seeker."

1247–1297

FEBRUARY 22

Living with an abusive stepmother drove young Margaret to find ways to get out of the small Tuscan village that was her home. In her early teens, she fell head over heels for a dashing young nobleman and ran off to live with him in his castle as his lover. For nine years the two lived together, and Margaret enjoyed a luxurious life of fine clothes, jewelry, and her own horse, which she rode brazenly through the towns. Her life with the cavalier caused great scandal, but Margaret was loyal to him and they had a son. One day the young man's mutilated body was found beneath a pile of leaves—he had been murdered for political reasons.

Margaret saw this as an omen and repented of her life. She returned her possessions to her dead lover's family, took her young son, and returned to her father's house dressed as a penitent. He refused to accept her, however, so she went to Cortona and found refuge with two women. She made a public confession of her previous life and began serving as a nurse in the town. Eventually she moved to a small cottage where she lived on alms, gave most of her gifts to the poor, and for three years suffered great doubts about the spiritual life. Her thoughts continually turned to the life of luxury and celebrity that she had enjoyed with her lover.

But Margaret persisted in her spiritual practices and the doubts subsided. She became a member of the third order of St. Francis. She sent her son to school, and in time he too joined the Franciscans. Margaret herself became a visionary and channeled divine messages both for herself and others. Some visions were concerned with reforming the lax practices of religious and ecclesiastical life, others with averting political strife.

In the late 1280s, Margaret received official recognition for her work with the sick, founded a hospital, and organized a group of Franciscan women into a special order, the Poverelle, to run the hospital. Her own private life was nurtured by extreme ascetical practices: night vigils, prayer, sleeping on the ground, wearing coarse clothing, and eating only vegetables and bread. On the day she died at age fifty, she was publicly declared a saint.

PRAYER

Margaret, help me to remain true to my commitments even when my old way of life seems attractive and alluring. No matter how many years I may have spent mindlessly and selfishly living only for thrills and distractions, let me realize that they were part of my growth, part of my development to find the true meaning of my life. Let me build on them, and commit myself to a spiritual career that is rich and rewarding because of those years, not in spite of them.

DEVOTIONAL PRACTICE

Find an old photograph of yourself taken at a time when you were not concerned (or not as committed) about the spiritual life or a life of service to others as you are now. Place it where you will see it, and say the above prayer whenever you need to recharge your commitments.

ST. MARGARET OF SCOTLAND

"Spiritual spillover."

1045–1093

NOVEMBER 16

Margaret was born (probably in Hungary) to an English prince and a German princess. When she was twelve years old, the family went to live at the English court of King Edward the Confessor. Ten years later William the Conqueror invaded England, and the family fled to Scotland where they found refuge with King Malcolm III. Margaret was in her early twenties at the time. Four years later in 1070, she and Malcolm were married, and she became Queen Margaret of Scotland.

The new queen was deeply pious and followed a strict spiritual life made up of ascetical practices, prayer, good works, and service to individual churches and abbeys. Margaret's spiritual practices rubbed off on Malcolm. His fiery temper cooled, his slovenly manners improved, and he began to join his wife in her spiritual devotions. Margaret also worked for the welfare of her adoptive country by promoting the arts and education. She arranged to have the best teachers and priests come to Scotland, where she established schools and churches.

In addition to her public activities, Margaret had six sons and two daughters. Her daughter Matilda became Queen Maud of England when she married King Henry I. Three of her sons became kings of Scotland.

One of Margaret's spiritual practices was to observe two Lents. The common one before Easter, and her own, which consisted of the forty days before Christmas. During her Lenten seasons, she would rise at midnight to hear matins with the monks. Malcolm often rose to join her in these midnight devotions. The poor knew about her nightly vigils and would come to see her afterward, because before returning to bed, she would choose six of them, wash their feet, and give them alms.

In 1093 Margaret and Malcolm's castle was attacked by enemies. Malcolm and their son Edward were killed. Margaret herself was on her deathbed when she received news of their deaths. Four days later, at age forty-seven, Margaret of Scotland passed away.

PRAYER

Margaret, make me aware of the spiritual influence I have over those around me. Help me to never be self-righteous or overbearing about my spiritual beliefs or practices but to do them humbly and sincerely and let the benefits they bring me enrich the lives of others with whom I come into contact.

DEVOTIONAL PRACTICE

There is always spiritual spillover in our lives. Our spiritual practices can inspire others around us if we do them in ways that are appealing and avoid the self-righteousness that says, "I'm better than you are."

Many people carry a charm, wear a medal or a piece of jewelry, or keep some object with them to remind them of their beliefs and values. If you have such an object, you can use it for this ritual or find another specifically for the purpose. Take your talisman and bless it with water, fire, and incense. Make it a guardian token that will prevent you from alienating others with your religious views, spiritual practices, or ethical values. Dedicate it—and yourself—to witnessing to your beliefs and practices in ways that are gentle, humble, and inspiring, and never self-righteous or condemning and accusatory toward others.

ST. MARGARET WARD

"Trapped between Caesar and God."

D. 1588

AUGUST 30

Political and religious loyalties can often be at odds with each other. Fortunate are the people who live in a culture where their religious beliefs coincide with political beliefs and practices. But this has hardly been the case in the modern world, where so many religious and political opinions and theories have clashed and continue to clash. Sometimes a person like Margaret Ward is caught in the middle.

When the Spanish Armada sank in a storm off the coast of Ireland in July 1588, the English sighed with relief. Philip of Spain's crusade to defeat Elizabeth and restore Catholicism to England was temporarily foiled. Most English Catholics, no matter how much they hated the queen's laws against Catholicism, preferred to be ruled by an English monarch, not a Spanish one. But reeling in the aftermath of an imminent invasion by a foreign Catholic power, the English government stepped up its persecution of Catholics, and as a symbol of this, six additional gallows were constructed around the city of London.

Margaret Ward, a gentlewoman in service to a Londoner who sympathized with the Catholic cause, was caught in a plot to free William Watson, a priest who managed to get caught three times but always escaped with the help of outsiders like Ward. When Watson was caught the first time, Ward smuggled a rope in to him and he made his escape. An Irishman named John Roche assisted her and provided Watson with a boat and his own clothes to wear as a disguise. Roche, however, donned the priest's clothing and was mistaken for the fugitive and arrested. The rope eventually was traced back to Margaret Ward, and she, too, was taken into captivity.

Both were tortured but refused to reveal the priest's hiding place. Eight days after their arrest, they went to trial and were offered their freedom if they would petition Elizabeth for a royal pardon and thereafter attend Church of England services. Ward and Roche refused, and they were hanged, drawn, and quartered on the new gallows.

PRAYER

Margaret, Jesus said to give to Caesar what belongs to Caesar and to God what belongs to God. Some people cannot always do this without compromising their conscience. I pray for those who are caught in political circumstances like yours and must choose between obeying the government's law and obeying God's law as their consciences guide them. May I also learn to understand other people's positions, especially when they disagree with my own.

DEVOTIONAL PRACTICE

Get an old-fashioned set of scales, the kind with two plates hanging from chains on the end of a traverse arm. Then collect a handful of small pebbles. When you wish to pray for some political or social cause, take the pebbles and place them one by one on the scales so that the two arms balance, as you pray for or meditate on the cause. Notice how hard it is to achieve a balance. Ask that the energy, patience, time, and composure of mind that you put into this ritual become spiritual energy that will help ease the conflict around the cause.

When you have the two plates balanced, sit and reflect on how easy it would be to add one more pebble to either side and destroy the balance. Pray that those involved in the conflict acquire the same sense of how important balance is and how easily it can be lost.

ST. MARIA GORETTI

"Sex, violence, and forgiveness."

1890–1902

JULY 6

Maria Goretti was one of six children born to poor parents who were farmworkers in the Roman Campagna. Her father, Luigi, died of malaria when she was six, and Assunta, her mother, supported the family, encouraging her children to be frugal and hardworking. Maria, the oldest, was the most cheerful of the children and willingly took part in holding the family together.

One summer day when Maria was mending a shirt at the top of the stairs in their home, Alexander Serenelli, the son of her late father's partner, arrived at the house and pulled Maria into a bedroom. He ripped off her clothes and began forcing her to have sex with him. She resisted and called out, but the eighteen-year-old youth greatly overpowered the eleven-year-old girl. He pulled a knife and began to stab at her. She fell, and he thrust the blade deep into her back and ran off.

Maria's screams brought help, an ambulance arrived, and she was taken to a hospital where doctors diagnosed her as too weak to live. Her dying hours were an inspiration to those who were present. She forgave her attacker and hoped that the incident would not cause trouble for his family. She worried over how her mother would continue to live and support their own family without her help. A priest brought her Communion, and she died within twenty-four hours.

Serenelli was captured and sentenced to thirty years' hard labor in prison. He refused to express any sorrow for what he had done, until one night he had a dream that Maria picked him a bouquet of flowers and offered it to him. The dream changed his life, and when he was released, after twenty-seven years, he went immediately to Maria's mother and asked her to forgive him.

Maria was canonized in 1950. Her eighty-two-year-old mother, two sisters, and one brother were present at the ceremony. Still alive were many friends, relatives, acquaintances, and the man who murdered her.

PRAYER

Maria, we live in an era when more and more people want revenge for the harm that was done them. Everyone seems to be demanding justice and retribution for real or imagined abuse and assaults. Help us to remember the power of forgiveness, and that forgiving even our enemies is at the heart of being a Christian.

DEVOTIONAL PRACTICE

Buy a special vase and name it your "Forgiveness Vase." Whenever someone offends or insults you, buy or pick some flowers and place them in the vase. Every day that the flowers are still fresh, say a prayer of forgiveness for the person who hurt you. When the flowers have died, let your own desire for revenge die with them.

ST. MARINUS

"The fleeing husband."

FOURTH CENTURY

SEPTEMBER 4

Marinus was born on the Dalmatian coast (later Yugoslavia), across the Adriatic from the Italian peninsula. He was a stonemason by trade, and when he heard that the town of Rimini needed workers to rebuild its crumbling walls, he and a friend, Leo (later also a saint), set out to find employment there. Marinus was hired to square stone and perform other tasks in the large quarries of Monte Titano. Both men found satisfaction in their work and in the opportunity it gave them to serve other quarry workers who were sentenced to hard labor in the mines for being Christians. Many of these prison slaves were from upper-class families and not used to strenuous manual labor. Marinus helped them adjust to the rigorous schedule and encouraged them in their faith, which he and Leo also shared.

In time Leo was ordained a priest by the bishop of Rimini and left the quarries. Marinus became a deacon but continued to work as a mason and serve the Christians sentenced to labor in the mines. For twelve years he worked on the city, acquiring a well-deserved reputation as a worker and a comforter of souls.

Then trouble appeared. A woman from Dalmatia showed up one day claiming to be Marinus's wife, whom he had abandoned years before. Marinus, it is said, went crazy, and he fled for the hills. He hid in a cave on Monte Titano for a week, while the woman waited outside for him to emerge. It was a standoff. Eventually she got hungry and had to leave to find some food. Marinus took advantage of the situation, sneaked out of the cave, and escaped higher into the mountains where the terrain was even more impenetrable. The woman never found him.

Marinus stayed in the mountains, founded a hermitage, and lived there the rest of his life. Later the town of San Marino was built at the site of his hermitage. Today the town and the city-state are still named after this stonemason and, possibly, wife-deserting saint.

PRAYER

Marinus, pray for the husbands, wives, friends, and lovers who are having a hard time understanding and being kind to one another. Help those who are thinking of leaving their relationships to make their choices, either to remain or depart, from a position of strength, hope, and clarity.

DEVOTIONAL PRACTICE

We know nothing about the relationship betweem Marinus and the woman claiming to be his wife. Were they actually married? Did they have children? Were they only lovers? Was one or both of them abusive to the other? Who deserted whom, and why? Like many people we actually know, there are secrets about their private lives that will forever be unknown to us.

When we consider the couples we know who are having trouble with their relationships, we have to admit that although we may have strong feelings about the best outcome for their dilemmas, we really don't know what is best for them. Use this meditation to remind yourself that you cannot call the shots for others and that what you should really want is an outcome that will be for their greatest good.

Take a bowl of water and sprinkle salt and pepper on the top to represent both the positive and negative qualities of the couple's relationship. Gaze at the water for four or five minutes, while offering your prayers and best wishes for the couple. Remind yourself that you do not know whether the relationship needs more "salt or pepper," but your wishes are that the couple succeed in whatever is best for them to do. After a few minutes of gazing, close your eyes and imagine the couple swimming through water cluttered with objects and debris, trying to help each other reach the shore. Imagine yourself helping them as well and eventually reaching safety. End the visualization/meditation with another heartfelt prayer that whatever is in the best interests of all concerned will happen.

ST. MARTHA

"The practical seeker."

FIRST CENTURY

JULY 29

We know Martha because of her family. She was the sister to Mary and Lazarus, and their family held a special place in Jesus' affections, for he stayed there frequently. On one occasion when Jesus was with them, Martha was bustling about with the household duties, possibly preparing a meal for the guests. Jesus chided her for being so concerned with practical matters, and pointed out that her sister Mary, who was engaged attentively in the conversation, had "chosen the better part."

From that moment on, the two sisters have come to stand for the active and contemplative lifestyles. Jesus also threw out a challenge for anyone serious about the spiritual life: how to blend the two areas of life commonly thought of as the practical and the contemplative. Jesus called the reflective, meditative, contemplative work the "better part," or what some people think of as the "really important" areas of life. And yet without food, shelter, clothing, and the organizational skills that keep the practical side of life running smoothly, there is little time for the contemplative, "better" part.

Perhaps not everyone is called to be primarily contemplative in life. Or, put another way, working with practical matters may be some individuals' primary path for developing spiritually. It was Martha, concerned about family matters, who was the first to meet Jesus on the road and tell him that her brother Lazarus had died. When Jesus quizzed her about the continuation of life after death, she said that she believed it. She also stated her belief in Jesus' divine mission. "I have come to believe that you are the Messiah, the Son of God, the one who is to come into the world." Certainly by these words Martha proved that even a practical person like herself could be deeply involved in spiritual realities.

PRAYER

Martha, help me in the practical matters of life: home, work, family, friends. These are also things that make life worth living. Show me how to find spiritual comfort in committing myself to them and doing my best. Also, inspire me to find spiritual meaning within my family, caring for and being with the ones whose destiny is so intimately interwoven with my own.

DEVOTIONAL PRACTICE

As a spiritual practice, look for the Marthas and Marys in your life. You may find them within your own family, at work, in the neighborhood, anywhere. The people we know and meet can be carriers of spiritual knowledge for us. Look upon both types of individuals as important symbols of the spiritual life. Ask yourself, "What does this person, right here and now, teach me about myself, the purpose of life, the right balance of action and contemplation?"

ST. MARTIN DE PORRES

"Compassion for all sentient beings."

1579–1639

NOVEMBER 3

The lay brother Martin de Porres found more than enough opportunities to dedicate his time and energy to the needs of the poor people of Lima, Peru. De Porres brought to his mission not just a strong commitment to the less fortunate, but also an inner sense of what it meant to be among the downtrodden.

Martin de Porres was the illegitimate son of a Spanish knight and a freed slave woman from Panama. He was born in Lima, and to his father's credit, both Martin and his sister were acknowledged as his own children. Martin's dark skin and African features, however, were an embarrassment to the father, and eventually he abandoned his son to be raised by his mother.

At age twelve Martin learned the skills of a barber, and in those times barbers also performed surgical treatments for the sick. Caring for the sick became his primary role when he entered the Dominican priory at age fifteen. He was put in charge of dispensing food, blankets, medicine, clothes, and other necessities to the poor from the priory's storehouse.

De Porres founded an orphanage and a hospital for abandoned babies, remembering how but for the grace of God, he himself might have been abandoned and left to die on the streets of Lima. Seeing so many people from his own African heritage being put into slavery, he found time to work with recently arrived African slaves, providing them with the necessities that owners and overseers often did not make available.

De Porres is known as the saint of social justice (as well as barbers and hairdressers), but his concern for the better treatment of others did not end with the human species. He also had a fondness for animals, and he created a kennel at his sister's house for stray and sick cats and dogs. Ever mindful of the problems caused by hunger, he found a place in his heart even for mice, rats, reptiles, and other lowly, despised forms of animal life that he thought pestered human beings mainly because they were hungry and could not find enough to eat.

Martin was also a popular spiritual adviser, his acts of charity were praised far and wide, and stories of supernatural events that occurred around him included bilocation and the ability to fly. He was also known to dispense food that miraculously multiplied to meet the demand.

At the end of his life de Porres died in the priory where he had spent his entire adult life.

PRAYER

Martin, help me find compassion for all forms of life, not just the poor and suffering men and women whom our society so wrecklessly shuns, but for animals, plants, waterways, and all wildlife that are despised and abused. In whatever ways I can, let me put my compassion into practice and, as Buddhists say, strive to save all sentient beings.

DEVOTIONAL PRACTICE

The Buddhist practice of vowing to save all sentient beings is a noble sentiment, expressed in its loftiest ideal. Like the Christian concept of perfection, saving all sentient beings may not be realistically attainable in this life. But that is what makes it such a worthwhile spiritual practice—it forces us to extend our reach even beyond our grasp. As a devotional practice in the spirit of Martin de Porres and Buddhists everywhere, find some living being each day that you can feed, nurture, honor, or respect as a fellow sentient being. Strive to "save" it in some little way, and in so doing you will be saving yourself as well.

ST. MARTIN OF TOURS

"A conscientious objector for the faith."

C. 316–397

NOVEMBER 11

Martin, a young soldier, was not thrilled with military life. He had joined the army unwillingly when he was fifteen, mostly out of respect for his father who was an officer. The boy kept pretty much to himself, studying and learning what he could about Christianity, inspired by its message of peace and goodwill to others—not exactly the values conducive to being an effective Roman soldier.

While stationed at Amiens during a bitter winter, Martin stumbled on a poor man at the gate of the city, practically naked and freezing in the harsh weather. On an impulse he slipped out of his cloak and cut it in two with his sword and gave half to the beggar. That night in a dream he saw Jesus wearing that half of his cloak. So moved by the vision, Martin went immediately and asked to be baptized into the Christian faith.

Martin stayed in the army until he was twenty. Then when enemy tribes invaded Gaul, he refused his war bounty, claiming that as a "soldier of Christ" he could not fight against other men. "It is not lawful for me to fight," he announced. But when he was accused of cowardice, he offered to stand in the battle line unarmed. His superiors found this impudent and put him in prison, but he was soon released.

After living as a hermit on an island in the gulf of Genoa, Martin went to Poitiers and received from St. Hillary land on which to found his monastery at Ligugé. This was the first monastic community in Gaul, and Martin stayed there for ten years. Eventually he was made bishop of Tours, against his will, and he continued to live the unkempt life of a monk. Once a year he visited the parishes in his diocese.

Martin took a bold stand in the 380s when Priscillianism—an ecstatic, gnostic movement within Christianity that had begun in Spain—spread to Gaul. One of the bishops asked the state to intervene and put the heretics to death. Martin opposed the bishop, not because he agreed with the movement but because he believed that religious matters should be handled by the Church, not the secular authorities. Martin favored simple excommunication and exile for Christians who held unfavorable opinions. But his view did not prevail. The emperor beheaded Priscillian and his followers—the first known state execution for heresy.

Martin continued as bishop of Tours until 397, when he died from an illness.

PRAYER

Martin, help me take a stand for peace and nonviolence whenever I am confronted by hostile or angry conditions. Share with me your courage to stand in the midst of battle unarmed, a force for peace, protected only by my faith and the love of God.

DEVOTIONAL PRACTICE

Usually our closets and drawers contain articles of clothing we have not worn in years. As an ongoing spiritual practice, resolve to give one article of clothing to the poor every time you buy or receive a new one. In other words, consider all new clothes as replacements for older clothing. If you cannot commit yourself to this, then perhaps once each season (mark your calendar ahead of time), go through your closets and give something to the poor.

ST. MARY DI ROSA

"A forerunner to Florence Nightingale."

1813–1855

DECEMBER 15

Several years before Florence Nightingale became famous for creating military hospital units to treat soldiers right on the battlefield, Mary di Rosa was already on the battlefield with her companions nursing wounded soldiers. When revolutionary and political upheavals rocked Europe in 1848, di Rosa had had ten years of experience caring for the sick, disabled, and less fortunate people of northern Italy. In the wars that ensued, di Rosa and her religious companions worked in a military hospital, overcoming opposition by administrators and staff who preferred secular or military orderlies. The women proved themselves and moved out onto the battlefields to care for the wounded where they had fallen.

Born into a wealthy family, di Rosa was one of nine children. Her mother, a countess, died when di Rosa was eleven. When she was seventeen, her father had hoped to marry her off to some suitable partner, but Mary convinced him that she wanted to remain single. He agreed, and Mary began caring for the spiritual welfare of the young girls who worked in his textile mill. In time she arranged retreats and spiritual missions for them.

In the cholera epidemic of 1836, di Rosa volunteered to do hospital work, again focusing on the spiritual needs of patients, since she herself was not a trained nurse. For two years di Rosa supervised a workhouse for indigent and abandoned girls, and then set up her own boardinghouse for them when the owners of the present establishment did not want the girls staying there overnight. As if her involvement with the unfortunate members of society was not enough, her next project was to establish a school for girls who were deaf and dumb (she eventually turned it over to an order of nuns).

During di Rosa's ten years of social and spiritual work, she read theology and versed herself in sacred literature. By 1840 she had decided to found a congregation of religious women to carry on the type of activities she had found so rewarding for herself. Called the Handmaids of Charity, the group soon numbered thirty-two. Ten years later the order was officially approved, and two years after that, in 1852, Mary di Rosa and twenty-five sisters took their vows. Never in robust health, yet a woman of great energy and dedication, di Rosa died peacefully only three years after her profession, exhausted from her many commitments.

PRAYER

Mary di Rosa, help me find the energy to stay involved in the needs of those around me, supporting them whenever I can be of assistance. It is so easy to turn to my own affairs and ignore the suffering of others, but remind me of our obligations to be caretakers for one another, especially for those who are less fortunate. Give me the will to be of service.

DEVOTIONAL PRACTICE

There are people dying in military conflicts every day somewhere on the earth. Praying for war-torn areas is always a commendable practice, but you can add even more spiritual energy to their plight by simple devotions.

Pick one day a week to skip a meal or to reduce the amount of food you eat as a form of fasting for those dying in military conflicts.

Let a candle burn for several hours once a month for the same intention.

Do a meditation in which you see a street or battlefield where someone is dying. Observe the scene with all your senses. Ask to see the soul of the dying person leave the body in some shape or form, and then, in spirit, be there helping that soul move upward into the next life. Then return to the dying body, comfort it in some way, and bless it.

ST. MARY FRANCES

"Comforter of the dead."

1715–1791

OCTOBER 6

Mary Frances lived at home in Naples for twenty-two years after she became a member of the third order secular of Franciscans, a common practice in the eighteenth century. But life at home for a young woman (or man) can be a mixed blessing. As happens to many adult children living at home, Mary Frances was scolded by her family for coming home late. But in her case, her father and sisters were upset because she came home late from church. Even the neighbors gossiped about how often she went to Confession. What kinds of sins did Mary Frances commit that she should seek the sacrament of forgiveness so often?

Mary Frances was not a dissolute sinner but simply a devoted lay religious, spending as much time as possible in her spiritual practices. Even as a young child, she lived a deep interior life, and as she later said, her guardian angel instructed her in spiritual matters from when she was little. Her angel also helped her through the terrible period when she refused to marry the young man her father had selected for her, and she was beaten with a cord and locked in her room as punishment.

Mary Frances's relationships with angels continued into later life when the archangel Raphael brought her the blood of Christ from the altar while the Mass was still in progress. A local priest testified that after he consecrated the bread and wine, the archangel took the chalice from the altar, carried it to Mary Frances's home, and allowed her to drink a portion of it. When Raphael returned the chalice, there was less consecrated wine in it. On several occasions she also received the sacred bread in her mouth in miraculous ways that defy any physical explanation.

Mary Frances performed important psychopomp, or soul-escorting, work for the souls of the deceased. She willingly asked God to transfer to her the sufferings of the souls waiting in Purgatory so that they would gain admittance to heaven more quickly. Her spiritual adviser once remarked that there should be no souls left in Purgatory because of her vicarious help. Recently deceased spirits often appeared to her to ask for particular prayers and spiritual help. She always gave this willingly and considered it to be one of the most important aspects of her spiritual life.

At age thirty-eight Mary Frances moved out from her family home to become the housekeeper for a local priest. During the next thirty-eight years of her life she managed his household, while continuing her intense life of prayer and visionary experiences. Her special devotion to the Passion of Christ and to making the Stations of the Cross resulted in her receiving the five wounds on her own body.

When the French Revolution erupted, Mary Frances had visions of the general chaos that was to follow. "I see nothing but disasters. Troubles in the present, greater troubles in the future." She often prayed, "Dear God, do not let me live to witness these disasters." In answer to her prayers, Mary Frances died in October, 1791.

PRAYER

Mary Frances, continue to pray for the people dying today so they can make a quick and safe passage into the heavenly realms. Add my own prayers to yours for the souls of the departed who may be struggling to leave this world and to transform themselves into beings who are worthy of the divine presence.

DEVOTIONAL PRACTICE

A psychopomp is one who "conducts or escorts the soul." Most often, psychopomp work is done for the dying so that they make the transition into the next life more easily, but spiritual midwifery for babies is also a form of psychopomp services.

As a spiritual practice for someone you know who is dying or who has recently died, light a seven-day candle on your altar. As the flame takes hold of the wick, pray that its light will expand and encompass the soul of the departed friend. Offer prayers of reassurance to your friend that this small flame will join the heavenly light of great beauty that the dying see as they leave their bodies.

Pray that this combined light will quickly and smoothly escort the person's soul into the next realms. Each time you see the candle during the week, mentally and spiritually send the light from the flame to assist the soul in its journey.

ST. MARY MAGDALEN

"A most loyal friend."

FIRST CENTURY

JULY 22

There is actually no evidence that Mary Magdalen was a prostitute. Unsubstantiated assumptions have linked her with the sinful woman who anointed Jesus' feet at Simon's house, an incident described in the Gospel of Luke. But this woman is never identified. Unfortunately, Mary Magdalen has been stuck with that label, and it will no doubt persist. What we really know about Magdalen is that she was a follower of Jesus, and one of the most loyal of his friends. To her, he was a personal healer and teacher.

Mary was from Magdala, a town on the west shore of Galilee near Tiberias. When Jesus first encountered her, she was suffering from some kind of mental illness or emotional disorder. She probably was acting abusively and unpredictably, the kind of crazy behavior that makes most people cross to the other side of the street. Jesus, however, accepted her and cast out seven demons from her, and she recovered. Magdalen stayed with Jesus, ministered to him, and joined the company of disciples.

Magdalen went with Jesus' mother and other women to Calvary while most of his apostles and disciples kept their distance. She was one of the "three Marys" who came to anoint his body on Easter morning and discovered that the tomb was empty. An angel announced to the women that he had risen. Later, alone, Magdalen stumbled on the risen Jesus in the garden, and at first thought he was a gardener. But when he revealed himself to her as her former friend and teacher, she responded, "Rabboni! Teacher!" Her impulse was to run up and embrace him, but Jesus told her not to touch him for he had not yet returned to his

Father. Whereupon she went back to the other disciples to announce, "I have seen the Lord." She was the first to whom he appeared.

Legend says that after the Ascension, Magdalen accompanied the apostle John on his journeys, eventually going to Ephesus where she died. Of all Jesus' followers, she is one of the most admirable: a single woman, misunderstood, shunned, healed, redeemed, transformed, devoted, eager to learn, loyal, companionable, loving, and a strong, active mainstay in that first small community of Christians.

PRAYER

Mary, instill in me the same kind of loyal devotion that kept you close to Jesus. Help me to see him as a great teacher and to keep an open mind to his teachings, especially the ones that I find hard. Also, may I discover the courage to say to others, "I have seen the Lord," as you did on that first Easter morning.

DEVOTIONAL PRACTICE

Mary Magdalen's few recorded words include the remarkable statement "I have seen the Lord." At the end of the day, think back over the people you encountered and decide which person most clearly manifested Jesus' attributes and which person seemingly did not. Evaluate your own activity and behavior during the day, and determine where to place it along the continuum of Christlike qualities represented by those two people. Resolve that tomorrow you will live so that others might see the Christ in you.

ST. MARY OF EGYPT

"A prostitute with a divine purpose."

FIFTH CENTURY

APRIL 2

Mary, an Egyptian, went to Alexandria when she was twelve, and for the next seventeen years was one of the most famous actresses, singers, and prostitutes of that city at the crossroads of the world's commerce.

Eager to see Jerusalem and the Holy Land, Mary embarked on a pilgrimage. She paid for her voyage not with money but by offering the sailors sexual favors. Possibly because of this morally questionable means of financing a pilgrimage, some invisible power prevented her from entering the Church of the Holy Cross when she arrived in Jerusalem. But before an icon of the Madonna and Christ child, she had a sudden conversion, repented of her past life, and was then able to cross the threshold into the church.

Not long after, Mary heard the Virgin's voice command, "Go into the desert." She did so, and for the rest of her life she lived as a hermit in the Jordanian desert.

Around the year 430, the abbot Zosimas set out into the wilderness to look for a holy man he had heard about, and he stumbled upon Mary instead. She was alone, naked, and warding off temptations and self-doubts by continual prayer to the Virgin Mary. She asked Zosimas for his coat, which he gave her. Impressed by her sanctity and spiritual wisdom, the abbot returned a year later to visit her, but he found she was dead.

A divine message asked Zosimas to bury her in the desert, but the abbot had no tools. Miraculously a lion appeared, pawed a grave in the sand, and together man and animal laid Mary of Egypt's remains in her final resting place in the desert that had been her home for forty-seven years.

PRAYER

Mary, sometimes I am not able to do the spiritual practices that I know are necessary. It seems as if some invisible power prevents me, as you were prevented from entering the church in Jerusalem. Help me understand and make the changes in my life that will allow me to have a more devout spiritual practice, whether those changes be minor or major ones. Give me courage to be alone in my spiritual life and find consolation in God.

DEVOTIONAL PRACTICE

Buy a small figure of a lion or find a photograph of one. Place it somewhere that you will see it, and let it remind you of the harmony that exists between the natural and human worlds when we ourselves are in harmony with the divine.

MARY, THE MOTHER OF JESUS

"My soul magnifies the Lord."

FIRST CENTURY

MAY 31

When the angel Gabriel told Mary that she was to conceive and give birth to the Son of God, he also informed her that her cousin Elizabeth had also conceived six months previously, even though she was past childbearing age. Mary immediately went to visit Elizabeth in the hills of Judaea where she lived with her husband Zacharias.

On entering their home, Mary greeted Elizabeth, and the older woman felt the baby, later to be John the Baptist, stir in her womb. Then Elizabeth greeted Mary, "Blessed are you among woman, and blessed is your child." Then she told Mary that when she heard her voice, the child in her womb leaped for joy. At that moment Mary responded with her own canticle of joy.

"My soul magnifies the Lord, and my spirit rejoices in God my savior. He has deigned to notice me, his humble servant, and from now on, all generations will call me blessed. For he who is mighty has done great things to me, and holy is his name." Then Mary continued to recount how God shows mercy to those who are in awe of him, that he puts down the mighty and uplifts the humble, that he satisfies the hungry and sends the rich away empty.

Mary stayed with Elizabeth for the rest of her pregnancy and then returned home. In time she gave birth to Jesus, and soon after that she saved his life in Egypt where she and Joseph fled to escape Herod's soldiers who were sent to kill him. When Jesus began his own ministry, Mary encouraged the act of compassion that was his first miracle, the changing of water into wine for the marriage party at Cana. She accompanied John, the beloved apostle, to Calvary, and among Jesus' dying words was his desire that the two should look after each other as mother and son.

Scriptures tell us that Mary was part of the Christian community in Jerusalem after Jesus' Ascension, but her own death is not recorded. A strong popular tradition from the earliest times was that she was taken physically into heaven, and there she resides as Queen of Heaven and the Mother of All Living Things. She has many feasts days in the liturgical calendar. May 31 is the day honoring her song of joy, known by its Latin name, the Magnificat.

PRAYER

Mary, help me to sing songs of joy to God for what he does in my life. Whether they be great or small, easy or difficult, may I always see the workings of God and acknowledge them with heartfelt joy. Most of all help me to find some joy and meaning in the sorrowful occasions that are also teachings from God.

DEVOTIONAL PRACTICE

Mary's life, like most people's, included both joys and sorrows. Like all mothers, she experienced the joys and sorrows of her son. As a spiritual practice, notice the joys and sorrows of the people who are closest to you: family members, friends, and acquaintances. In the spirit of Mary's Magnificat, say to yourself a short silent prayer whenever you are aware that someone you love is experiencing joy or sorrow.

You could paraphrase the Magnificat: "My soul magnifies the Lord, and my spirit is joyful/is sorrowful in the joy/sorrow of [name the person close to you]." And then acknowledge that both the joy and the sorrow that you share with the loved one come from God. A short affirmation like this will help you to identify yourself with the emotions of those you love and to recall that all life's experiences, both joyful and sad, are part of our spiritual growth.

ST. MATTHEW THE APOSTLE

"A seeker of right livelihood."

FIRST CENTURY

SEPTEMBER 21

It would seem that Matthew was one of those people who are not really happy in their work. Immediately, when Jesus said, "Follow me," Matthew dropped everything, got up from his tax collector's station, and left. Actually, a man cut out to be one of the first apostles, as Matthew clearly was, is probably not the kind of individual that would find tax collecting for the Roman Empire a worthy form of livelihood.

Tax collectors were among the most despised government officials, especially in the far-flung reaches of the Roman Empire, such as Palestine, where corruption was rampant. The profession was known for attracting greedy, cheating, dishonest individuals more interested in lining their own pockets than in being fair. To compound matters, Matthew was a Jew from the tribe of Levi, born in Galilee, and was seen as a collaborator with the Roman armies of occupation. He was working for the enemy.

Little wonder then that Matthew may have been waiting for a reason to quit. Later when Jesus ate at Matthew's house, neighbors raised the cry that Jesus was eating with sinners and tax collectors, two groups who were not allowed in the synagogue. But the occasion sparked Jesus' reply which has become one of the hallmarks of true Christianity: "Those who are well do not need a doctor; the sick do." Throughout Jesus' career he made a practice of eating meals with the rejected and the outcasts from polite society.

Somewhere between A.D. 60 and 90, Matthew wrote his version of the Gospel—probably in Aramaic, since he was writing for Christianized Jews. The original has never been found, and the oldest extant copy is in Greek. Legend says that Matthew preached in Judaea and was martyred either in Ethiopia or Persia. Today he is the patron saint of bookkeepers and bankers.

Matthew, give me strength to be honest in my line of work, even when others are not. Help me also to find enjoyment and worthiness in what I do, either in the work itself or in my treatment of coworkers, clients, and customers. Most of all, pray that I find the strength to leave my work and change jobs if I realize that what I am doing is not the right livelihood.

DEVOTIONAL PRACTICE

Our daily work should be part of our spiritual practice. Consider the many tasks you are involved in each day at work, and choose one to be a reminder of your commitment to lead a spiritual life and serve others. Get in the habit of being mindful when you begin that task, saying a short prayer or affirmation about your desire to do the job well. While you work at that task, practice being more aware that you are a witness to the kind of life that treats all people decently and fairly. Eventually, this attitude should spill over into your other tasks, not only at work but also at home.

ST. MAXIMILIAN

"I cannot do evil."

D. 295

MARCH 12

Because Maximilian was the son of a veteran, he was expected to serve in the Roman army, but he refused on the grounds that he was a Christian. He was then ordered to appear before a tribunal to present his case.

Maximilian had basically two reasons for refusing military service as a Christian: pacificism and opposition to idolatry. As a soldier he would be expected to sacrifice and pray to the god of war, Mars, and to wear the emperor's insignia around his neck. Neither Mars nor the emperors who claimed to be divine were the God that Maximilian wanted to worship. He told the authorities that he already wore the badge of Christ. When it was pointed out to him that other Christians served in the army as soldiers, Maximilian replied, "That is their business."

During the thirty-odd years when the persecutions against Christians subsided (between the reigns of Valerian and Diocletian, from 260 to about 295), many people in the Empire were baptized into the new faith. Roman authorities viewed this as a threat to the empire, because celibacy was a primary Christian virtue, and they viewed Christians as not committed to the Roman concept of marriage that produced the children needed for military and political service. Also, they would not worship the state and the emperor as divine. To Christians, the Roman Empire was not eternal.

Maximilian also had misgivings about the so-called Pax Romana, the Peace of Rome. His view of the Roman Peace seems to have been similar to what a Celtic chieftain in Britain said about it: "They make a desert, and call it 'peace.'" Maximilian was asked at his trial, "What harm do soldiers do?," and he replied,

"You know well enough!" The Roman Peace was founded on violence, coercion, intimidation, terror, and slavery. Even though Christians could serve in the military (and in time the Church would devise the concept of the "just war" to sanction military service by Christians), Maximilian took a pacifist stand. He was, however, not executed for pacificism but for "impiety"—he would not worship the emperor, Mars, or the Roman state.

Although Maximilian could probably have escaped and saved his life, he chose to appear at his hearing and witness to his faith. He stated boldly, "I cannot serve. I cannot do evil. I am a Christian." Before he died, he told his fellow Christians who had come to be with him not to worry. "I will welcome you into heaven," he promised.

PRAYER

Maximilian, help me view the activities of the government under which I live with the eyes of faith. I pray that what I know as God's truth will always motivate my actions, even if it contradicts what politicians currently expect from citizens.

DEVOTIONAL PRACTICE

Roman citizens thought their empire was eternal. But it fell. Do you view American civilization as eternal? Do you expect it to fall someday? Can you imagine what life would be like, or who you would be, if American civilization came to an end?

Consider the things that make up the American lifestyle as you live it. Do they contribute to the welfare of your soul? Are you growing spiritually by the activities, work, and pastimes that make up your current life? Is your way of living soul-destructive? Reflect on these questions honestly, and ask God and the spirit of Maximilian to help you stand up, say no, and change whatever is currently poisoning your interior life. American civilization is only temporary; it will not last forever. But our souls are eternal.

ST. MAXIMILIAN KOLBE

"Laying down one's life for another."

1894–1941

AUGUST 14

In 1941 Nazi prison guards rounded up ten prisoners chosen to be executed from Block 14 of the concentration camp at Auschwitz, Poland. They planned to make the ten men an example of what would continue to happen if any more prisoners tried to escape. A group of men had successfully escaped the death camp, and the ten victims slated for execution were selected at random. Maximilian Kolbe, a Catholic priest whom the Nazis had arrested once and freed, but then rearrested in 1941, watched the ten prisoners being selected.

Kolbe had been born near Lodz, Poland, and at age ten had had a vision of the Virgin Mary. She offered the young boy two crowns, one red and one white, and asked him to choose. Knowing he wanted everything that she had to offer, he took both. He entered the Conventual Franciscans at age thirteen, took his vows in 1911, and was ordained seven years later. About that time he began developing his concept of the "Militia of Mary Immaculate," a movement within the Church to train people to think of themselves as soldiers for the Mother of God. His newsletter, *The Knight of the Immaculate,* was published in the millions and translated into many languages.

In 1927 Kolbe founded the first "City of the Immaculate," a bold undertaking to create cities populated solely by religious friars. The first city, located in Poland, was home to eight hundred friars when World War II broke out. Kolbe was superior of the community. Another city was planned for Japan. But when German troops invaded Poland in 1939, Kolbe was arrested for the first time for subversive activities. In 1941 he was arrested again and sent to Auschwitz.

Among the ten prisoners selected for execution in Block 14 was a Polish sergeant who was the father of a family. Boldly, Kolbe stepped forward and asked to be executed in place of the married man. The Nazis granted his request, and Kolbe was executed by an injection of carbolic acid.

PRAYER

It is hard to step forward and take the place of someone about to die. Maximilian, help me to do this in the "little deaths" that occur each day when we deny ourselves in order to serve others. Show me how to be more selfless and how to volunteer to do things for others, especially unpleasant tasks or jobs that will get no public recognition. Strengthen my belief that we are meant to lay down our lives for others in both major and minor ways, and help me to do so.

DEVOTIONAL PRACTICE

Choose someone in your life whom you live with or work with on a daily basis. Each morning for three days say the following affirmation:

"Today in some way I will 'lay down my life' for him/her." Speaking metaphorically, you are asking to find some way to deny your own interests and put that person first. You may discover a way to do it each day, but if not the first two days, on the third day you will have an opportunity to do so.

ST. MECHTILDIS OF EDELSTETTEN

"The voice of an iron angel."

D. 1160

MAY 31

Mechtildis was a twenty-eight-year-old nun when the Bishop of Augsberg asked her to assume directorship of a convent of nuns in dire need of reform. At first she declined the offer, thinking she was too young in both age and wisdom to head such a serious undertaking. With pressure from the pope, however, she acquiesced. In some ways she was right for the job. She had both political and religious clout. Her noble parents had founded a double monastery on their estate at Diessen, to which they sent young Mechtildis when she was only five. She also numbered among her influential kinfolk the Emperor Frederick I.

On assuming the office of abbess, Mechtildis cracked down on the lax manner in which enclosure was being practiced. Too many lay visitors were invading the cloister, bringing with them too much news of the world, with its wars, scandals, gossip, and other distractions which prevented the nuns from leading a life of silence and prayer. Mechtildis herself had gained a reputation for silence— just one of her many austerities. A Cistercian monk who knew her claimed that when she did speak, however, it was like listening to an angel, so full of wisdom and insight were her words.

When some of the nuns balked at her reforms, Mechtildis brought pressure from the bishop to have them expelled from the order. Like a latter-day corporate manager, she fired them, rather than allow them to continue disrupting the harmony of the convent. Ruthless though it might seem, Mechtildis put her sense of religious life and her commitment to the good of the community above the welfare of individual nuns who felt cramped by the reforms.

Mechtildis also had a great reputation as a healer. She healed the sick, restored speech to the dumb, and brought the eyesight back to one of her nuns. Her life of prayer and asceticism made her a worthy channel of God's healing power. Her psychic sense alerted her when her death was near. Knowing that she was not long for this world, she resigned her office at Edelstetten, went home to Diessen, and died.

PRAYER

Mechtildis, give me the courage to stand up for the rules when I know they are fair and just. Also help me in difficult tasks involving human relations, such as hiring, firing, promoting, and reprimanding those for whom I am responsible. Let me never be vindictive in these decisions, but let me carry them out with grace, good humor, and love.

DEVOTIONAL PRACTICE

Before you have to reprimand someone at home or work, or fire a troublesome employee, or criticize a coworker for his or her performance, take the time (assuming there is time) to do the following ritual: Light a candle to give you clarity and wisdom. Burn a stick of incense to sweeten the words that you will need to use. Then sit for ten or fifteen minutes, visualizing or imagining the person's higher self or guardian angel before you. Practice what you will say to the individual by speaking it out loud to the higher self or angel. Then ask the person's spirit to give you the patience and charity to do the job well. Recall this ritual when you are actually confronting the person.

ST. MONICA

"A mother of many prayers and tears."

C. 331–387

AUGUST 27

A priest told Monica that "it is not possible that the son of so many tears should perish." Her son was Augustine, who would become one of the major thinkers in the early Church. The tears were Monica's, the mother who patiently and sorrowfully prayed for him to reform his dissolute life.

As a young woman in North Africa, Monica married a man named Patricius, who had a reputation for violence, bad temper, and reckless living. She had three children with him and dedicated her life to bringing them up as Christians. She also hoped that her husband and his mother would become Christians, and through her prayers and good example, they did convert to Christianity in 370. Patricius, however, died the next year.

Augustine caused Monica great grief. A brilliant student, he studied in Carthage and threw himself into the diversity of the urban culture, which distracted him from the life of piety that Monica hoped for. Augustine enjoyed the many philosophies and religious ideas competing with one another, and he experimented with them. He also had a mistress by whom he had a son.

Eventually Monica's prayers—and tears—paid off. Augustine reformed his ways and announced he would go to Rome to study, and the family left in 383: Monica, Augustine, and his son. A few years later they moved to Milan where Augustine was baptized on Easter in 387.

While waiting at the seaport of Ostia to return to North Africa, Monica died, but not before she could tell her son how much he pleased her. "All my hopes have been fulfilled. . . . All I wished to live for was that I might see you a child of heaven." Knowing that her son was indeed a child of heaven and eager to give his life to God, Monica died happily.

Monica, may I share your patience and long-suffering. When my own children or family members seem to be wasting their lives, keep me from despair, and help me to pray, set a good example, and gently and compassionately encourage them to improve themselves. But most of all, help me see that their lives are their own and that God's plans for them may not be the same as mine.

DEVOTIONAL PRACTICE

Monica's phrase "a child of heaven" can inspire us to look at our own family members and friends in a more spiritual way. We are all children of heaven. Heaven is our birthright, even if we forget it or lose it for a time. If there is someone you are praying for, put a photograph or some symbol of the person on an altar if possible, or in some place in your home where it would not seem unusual in any way. When you pray for the person, sit before the photo or symbol, light incense, and let the smoke and sweetness that envelop the person's image remind you of the heavenly realms that are the person's true home. Pray that the individual comes to realize this in whatever way God has planned for him or her.

ST. MOSES THE BLACK

"A saintly outlaw."

C. 330–C. 405

AUGUST 28

Moses was born into slavery in Ethiopia and became a servant for an official in the Egyptian government. Like many slaves before and after him, Moses had two choices. He could be humble, hardworking, and obsequious, and in this way hope to get along well with his masters. Or he could be obnoxious, uncooperative, hateful, temperamental, threatening, and hope to get dismissed or moved to some better situation. (Of course, he would also risk punishment.) Moses chose the latter, and it paid off. He stole from his masters, insulted them, and in general developed a bad attitude that got him kicked out.

Once on his own, Moses became the ringleader of a band of outlaws who ravaged the countryside, terrorized the community, and created havoc for everyone in the vicinity. At some point lost in history, Moses reformed his ways and began to live a respectable Christian life. It is thought that hermits in the Skete Desert found him and converted him. At any rate, Moses became a monk at the monastery at Petra and gained a reputation for his severe ascetical practices. He was ordained a priest and lived as a hermit.

Moses lost his life in a way reminiscent of his early days. A band of looting Berber tribesmen killed him, along with six other monks. But in this his last confrontation, Moses was a different man. He was killed because he refused to defend himself. He had laid down his sword years before and saw no reason to pick it up again.

Moses, there are times when I want to get revenge for the insults and injuries that have been inflicted on me. It seems so easy to justify being hateful to those who are hateful to me. Even in little ways, I often want to trade an insult for an insult, or a snide remark for a snide remark. Help me to get over this and to see how foolish it really is.

DEVOTIONAL PRACTICE

During the course of a day we often find opportunities to insult others or make life unpleasant for them by gossip or cruel remarks. Here is a practice to counteract this: At the end of the day reflect back over the comments you made that may have hurt someone, or even the ones you *could* have made when you held your tongue. Write out the comment on a piece of paper. Beneath it, write a counter comment that would have been supportive, kind, encouraging, or forgiving. Then burn the slip of paper, as you say a prayer for the person involved. As the paper goes up in flames, ask that the hurtful words be destroyed and that the kind words be carried out into the universe where they will create peace and harmony.

ST. MUCIAN MARY WIAUX

"Pray always."

1841–1917

JANUARY 30

The Christian Brother with the strange name was well loved by the boys at the school where he taught. But teaching wasn't why he was loved. In fact he was not a good teacher at all, and when the administration discovered this, they quickly moved Wiaux onto the fringe of the academic program.

Born in Belgium and christened Louis Joseph, Wiaux took the name of a little-known Roman martyr when he was professed as a Christian Brother. In 1858 he was assigned to the Brothers' college at Malonne, where he remained the rest of his life. When it became evident that teaching was not his forte, he was given odd jobs around the school, such as ringing the bell, supervising the playground, running the dormitories, organizing walks, and overseeing the daily music and drawing periods. Wiaux did these well.

Wiaux's concern for and dedication to the students was evident to everyone. People saw in him the compassion and holiness that is expected in a man living a life of service to others and inspired by the love of God. Pupils called him "the brother who is always praying." Boys trusted Wiaux, and he was able to encourage and inspire many to make the most of their talents even if they were not top academic performers.

After his death, when the canonization process had begun, Wiaux's true accomplishments became known, accomplishments that often don't get recognized or appreciated during one's lifetime. As one colleague put it, Wiaux was "a man of prayer," who performed "his daily tasks with holiness . . . hurting none and forgiving all."

Mucian Mary, give me the self-assurance to do small tasks well and not hunger after fame and glory. Help me understand that it doesn't take accolades and public awards to realize my self-worth. If I do my daily work in the spirit of holiness and in the presence of God, I know that, like you, I will be rewarded someday.

DEVOTIONAL PRACTICE

Wiaux made a practice to go about his day in a gentle and forgiving way that would not hurt others. Often we do hurt others because we are unthinking, preoccupied, or distracted. We are simply not aware that what we do—even if it is morally right—may hurt someone else in some way or other.

As a spiritual practice, remind yourself during the course of the day that everyone you see is struggling with some inner battle, self-doubt, worry, or physical pain, whether it shows or not. Whenever someone around you expresses his or her suffering in some way, say a brief prayer for the person, and visualize him or her in a peaceful state of happiness or contentment. Make the visual image very graphic; for example, see the person lying on a sunny beach, eating ice cream, laughing at a good joke, being embraced by a loved one, or just running through a meadow of flowers singing a favorite song. The energy you put into this practice will make an impact on the person, often immediately. Watch for it.

ST. NICHOLAS

"The anonymous gift giver."

D. C. 350

DECEMBER 6

What is truly remarkable about St. Nicholas is how famous he has become considering so little is known about the man. He was the bishop of Myra in Asia Minor, was imprisoned for his faith during the persecution by the emperor Diocletian, was present at the Council of Nicaea, and died in Myra, where he was buried in the cathedral. That is about the extent of the historical data. And yet there are more depictions of Nicholas by Christian artists than any other saint, with the exception of the Virgin Mary. In the Middle Ages, almost four hundred churches were dedicated to him in England alone. His feast day has inspired the winter holidays, with traditions that would become what we now know as Christmas.

Nicholas takes his place alongside the other "solstice fathers" of Santa Claus, Old Nick, and Father Christmas because of one story. A rich man in Myra went bankrupt during Nicholas's tenure as bishop, and having three daughters and no money for dowries, despaired of their ever marrying. Incredibly, he decided they should become prostitutes. When Nicholas heard of this, he devised a way to save the girls. He surreptitiously tossed a bag of gold through their window one night. In the morning, the father was amazed by the miracle and used the money as a dowry for his eldest daughter. A second time, Nicholas left a bag of gold so that the next daughter could marry. On the third occasion, when Nicholas sneaked up to the house at night to leave his anonymous gift, the father caught him so he could thank him for changing their lives. And thus Nicholas became a patron of anonymous gift givers.

In 1087, when the Saracens conquered Myra, Nicholas's relics were moved to the west. Two Italian cities, Venice and Bari, vied for the honor of being the location where the relics would be interred. Bari won, and the city became a famous pilgrimage site in the Middle Ages for people who wanted to honor the man who was remembered for rescuing children, prisoners, sailors, famine victims, and many others through his compassion, generosity, and miracles.

PRAYER

Nicholas, give me the spirit of giving. Teach me that it really is more blessed to give than to receive, and that to whom much has been given much will be expected. Help me to overcome my fears that if I give generously I will suffer want.

DEVOTIONAL PRACTICE

In the spirit of St. Nicholas, give an anonymous gift to someone who really needs it. It might be a parent, child, sibling, cousin, niece, or nephew—or someone who is not related to you at all. The gift could be tickets to a movie, a book, an article of clothing, a tool or appliance you know the person needs, or some silly item that will make the person smile and brighten up his or her day. Enclose a card that simply tells the person to enjoy the gift; sign it "A Friend." The gift will bring an element of mystery and miracle into someone's life.

ST. NICHOLAS OF TOLENTINO

"Street preacher to street people."

1245–1305

SEPTEMBER 10

The towns of northern Italy were rocked in the thirteenth century by civil war erupting from powerful families locked in a struggle for control of local politics and religious offices. The feuds between the Guelfs and the Ghibellines created chaos in many places and for many people. A humble Augustinian friar named Nicholas helped ease that chaos in one town, Tolentino.

Nicholas had been invited to stay at a monastery near Fermo, and one day he heard a strong voice calling to him while he was praying. The voice said, "To Tolentino, to Tolentino. Persevere there." Immediately, Nicholas knew where he must go.

When he arrived, Nicholas knew that to ease people's pain he would have to go directly to them: to the homeless, the poor, the dispossessed, the sick, and the dying. He began a campaign of street preaching, working his way through the slums of the town and seeking out the "street people" where they lived. He served adults, children, the aged, even the criminals and scoundrels who thrive wherever law and order break down. Nicholas was a great success as a street-corner preacher, and his mission in the alleys and gutters of Tolentino brought great relief to many people.

Nicholas was blessed with healing powers and cured the blind and the sick. He also had a natural, and possibly supernatural, talent at composing quarrels and playing the peacemaker between enemies. Even married couples on the verge of violence and separation found in Nicholas a skillful mediator. At his canonization process, a woman testified that Nicholas had reformed her husband who had abused her and beaten her throughout their years together.

Nicholas died after a year-long illness. But his life was a testament to the moment of his conversion as a young boy, when he heard another Augustinian friar preach on the scriptural passage: "Love not the world, nor the things which are in the world. . . . The world passes away." When Nicholas himself passed away, Tolentino lost a saint who had made the world a slightly better place.

PRAYER

Nicholas, I may not be a street preacher, but I can use your example to be willing to go where I am needed, or to where people need help. At home, at work, at play with friends, I pray that I will be sensitive to how I might be of service to others and do whatever I can to make their lives a little better.

DEVOTIONAL PRACTICE

To get in the practice of watching out for others, write on separate slips of paper the names of the people you routinely come in contact with over the course of a week. Put the slips in a bowl and place it on your altar. Think of this as your "service bowl." At the beginning of each week draw a name from the bowl, offer a prayer for that person, and ask Nicholas's help to find a way to be of special service to that person sometime during the coming week. Be especially willing to go out of your way to meet the person on his or her own turf to perform your service.

ST. NON OF WALES

"The pregnant nun."

SIXTH CENTURY

MARCH 3

Non was one of the Irish missionaries who crossed the sea to spread the message of the Gospel to other lands. Her journeys took her to Wales. One day the young and beautiful nun was walking through the Welsh countryside when Sant, chieftain of Ceredigion, saw her and was overcome with desire for her. He raped her in the fields. Tradition says that at the moment Non conceived a child, in spite of the violent act in which it took place, two white stones rose up from the earth, one at Non's head, the other at her feet, to signify the importance of this event. The son she conceived was to become the patron saint of Wales.

Non gave birth to St. David nine months later under equally auspicious circumstances. Druids had predicted to a local chieftain that the son of the pregnant nun would have power over the entire region. The ruler vowed to kill the boy when it was born, and he learned from the druids where the birth would take place. On the day of David's birth, both Non and the ruler approached the meadow that was destined to be the site of David's entry into this life. The man waited with a drawn sword. The mother came to deliver her child. But then a ferocious storm arose that was so threatening that the ruler (along with everyone else) fled for shelter.

Non, however, lay in the meadow surrounded by warm sunlight. During her delivery the stone that she grasped for support received the imprint of her hands and split open. Years later the stone was revered for the sacredness of the occasion, and when a church was built on the spot, the stone was concealed in its foundation.

Non raised David alone. The fatherless boy and his mother eventually became the two most beloved saints of Wales. Non herself continued her work as a missionary and died in Brittany near Finistère.

PRAYER

Non, give me the same faith that you must have had to see even in an act as despicable as rape the working out of the divine plan. May your example inspire me to know that from violence and cruelty can come holiness and inspiration.

DEVOTIONAL PRACTICE

Many people today identify themselves as victims and/or survivors of various kinds of abuse. Sometimes doing so allows the painful events of the past to continue to cause misery in the present. Although each person must find his or her own way to healing, here is a ritual based on the events in St. Non's life that may help some people:

Get a stone about the size of a football. Wet your hands and grasp the stone firmly with both hands while you place the memories and the pain you suffered in the past into the stone. As you let go, your wet handprints will remain on the stone for a few moments as they dry. Then take the stone to a place in nature where it will be inconspicuous. Leave it there, expressing your gratitude to it for accepting your pain. Whenever you are inclined to think of yourself as a victim or survivor, recall that the stone sits before God as a witness to your desire to change that way of thinking about yourself.

ST. NOTBURGA OF RATTENBURG

"A wise but disobedient servant."

D. C. 1313

SEPTEMBER 14

Notburga was a peasant girl who entered the service of Count Henry of Rattenburg when she was eighteen years old. The count took her on as a kitchen maid and serving girl, which appealed to the young Notburga. The kitchen of this prosperous castle often had great quantities of leftover food which Notburga gave to the poor who came daily to the door for handouts. Not content to give them only the scraps, she often saved some of her own meal to add to what she dispensed. Henry's mother approved of the practice, and Notburga was admired for her charity.

But when the count's mother died, Henry's wife, Ottila, found the practice unbecoming and wanted to put an end to it. She ordered that all leftovers be given to the pigs. Notburga, an obedient servant, did as she was ordered for a time, but then resumed her practice of distributing scraps to the poor. She felt charity superseded obeying a law that caused great hardship. She was dismissed for her impertinence.

Count Henry, however, being caught in local wars and skirmishes, suffered a reversal of fortune. As his bad luck increased, he blamed it on his wife's stinginess and her dismissing Notburga. After she died, he remarried, and reinstated Notburga as his chief housekeeper. His fortunes soon took a turn for the better. Notburga was overjoyed at her own good fortune and lived the rest of her life in the castle, fulfilling her duties faithfully and acquiring the reputation of being a holy and happy woman.

Before she died, Notburga asked the count that he place her body on a cart drawn by oxen and allow them to wander until they came to a stop, and then bury her wherever that might be. Count Henry fulfilled her wishes, and the oxen halted at the church of St. Rupert at Eben, where Notburga, now patron of servants, was buried.

PRAYER

Notburga, help me find happiness and spiritual fulfillment in doing the humblest chores. Household tasks can be irksome, but pray that I do them well and find God's presence even in sweeping the floor, washing dishes, or cleaning the bathroom.

DEVOTIONAL PRACTICE

Decide that two days from now you will perform your household chores mindfully and prayerfully. Think about this over the intervening forty-eight hours, so that when the day arrives you have prepared yourself. Then do the normal daily tasks as you would on any other day, but do them watching yourself, as if part of you had stepped back to observe the other part that is doing the work. Be mindful of all your ancestors, including the saints, who did similar tasks, and realize that this work is not useless or a waste of time but can be an expression of your gratitude for life.

ST. ODO OF CLUNY

"Two-fisted troubleshooter."

C. 879–942

NOVEMBER 18

Odo was born near Le Mans, France, and raised in two noble households, one belonging to the Duke of Aquitaine, who founded the abbey of Cluny. He studied in Paris, received the tonsure when he was nineteen, and became a cannon in St. Martin's church at Tours. Odo enjoyed studying and playing music, and he lived a rather comfortable life. Then one day he read the rules that St. Benedict had written for the monastic life and was embarrassed to realize that even though he was not a monk, his own life fell far short of Benedict's ideal. Odo decided to become a monk.

When he was forty-eight, Odo was appointed abbot of Cluny. His biographers say that he ruled with "a rod of iron," threatening and intimidating wayward monks with severe punishments. They shaped up. Over the course of his life, other abbots invited him to reform their own communities, and Odo seems to have been an excellent troubleshooter, moving in, checking out the problems, then making suggestions that were probably more in the nature of "take it or leave it." Odo was equally successful in persuading lay nobles who had control of monasteries to turn them over to ecclesiastical authorities.

Odo was also involved in political disputes. The pope asked him to make peace between Hugh of Provence, who was claiming to be king of Italy, and Alberic, the Patrician of the Romans, who also claimed authority in Rome. Odo arranged a marriage between Alberic and Hugh's daughter that kept things quiet for a while. But twice more during his lifetime, Odo was called in by the distraught pope to iron out difficulties that arose between the two contenders for political power in Italy.

On the return from his last visit to Rome in 942, Odo stopped at a monastery at Tours where he died in bed.

Odo, I pray for the insight to reform my own life where it falls short of what I know I should be doing. Do not let me become too severe in what I expect of myself, though. I ask simply that I be able to map out a plan of improvement that is reasonable and within the scope of my capabilities.

Sometimes we can be too severe in what we expect of ourselves and others. Being able to overlook minor infractions of the rules and wink at small failures is a mark of compassion and understanding. Think of the people in your life (including yourself) whom you live or work with and your current criticisms of them. Spend a few moments visualizing them struggling with the many problems of their lives. Everyone is engaged in a great struggle of some kind. Be kind and forgiving.

ST. OSITH

"Trusting the times apart."

C. 700

OCTOBER 7

Osith, the daughter of a British chieftain, had not planned to marry the East Saxon king Sighere. She preferred to stay in the nunnery where she had been educated. But her parents arranged the alliance, the wedding was set, and Osith complied.

Shortly afterward, her husband tried to force Osith to have sex with him against her will. As she struggled to fend him off, a stag ran by and caught his attention. Sighere was a compulsive hunter and could not resist the prey. He left Osith, called for his horse, and rode off. Osith used the occasion to get out of what looked like a very abusive relationship. She fled to East Anglia and asked the local bishop to give her the religious habit.

Sighere complied with her requests, deciding that an unwilling wife was not to his liking. In an exceptional show of goodwill, he even gave Osith a tract of land near a creek, where she built her monastery. Other women joined her, and she proved to be an admirable administrator.

Trouble arrived, however, when the monastery was attacked by a band of marauders. The raiders tried to carry off Osith, but she fought them bravely and successfully. Finally they killed her by cutting off her head.

PRAYER

Osith, give me the wisdom to deal appropriately with my spouse's/partner's hobbies and interests that do not include me. On those occasions when he/she is away, help me use the time profitably and not harbor unwarranted fears that I am being abandoned. Help me keep perspective on our need to have friends and pastimes that do not include each other.

Sometimes in relationships it is hard to allow our partners the freedom to pursue interests that do not include us, such as hunting, watching football, or playing bridge. Yet it is often best to have time apart, as well as other friends, as long as they are not detrimental to your relationship. Such time away and other companions can actually strengthen relationships.

If your partner has a regular "night out with the boys or girls" and you have no other obligations, use the time to engage in some ongoing devotional practice, such as spiritual reading, writing in your journal, attending services at church, or dropping by a chapel or church just to escape the ordinary world for a few moments. Choose something that you enjoy and can look forward to. In this way you will be able to use the time alone profitably and develop a spiritual practice that will not take even more time away from your relationship.

ST. PATERNUS

"An unrelenting prophet of doom."

D. 1058

APRIL 10

Paternus's birth and origins are obscure, but his ending is as certain as it is shocking and dramatic. Possibly Paternus came from Ireland, following what was a centuries-old tradition in his day: the wandering Irish monk spreading the Gospel message throughout Europe. Paternus eventually reached Westphalia and settled in the monastery at Paderborn, where he met his tragic fate.

Not content with life in the community, Paternus asked permission to live as a recluse. The abbot agreed to his request, and Paternus was walled up in a cell attached to the abbey wall. There he lived, cut off from human contact, brooding on life, death, sinners, and the fate of the world. In a vision, he foresaw the fate of the city, and he announced it as if he were an Old Testament prophet. In no uncertain terms, he warned that unless the citizens renounced their sinful ways, did penance, and reformed their lives, the entire city would be destroyed by fire within thirty days.

As might be expected, most people in the city thought Paternus had gone off his rocker, and they ignored the dire warning. He was crazy, they thought, nothing but an old fool and an alarmist. But on the Friday before Palm Sunday in 1058, fires broke out mysteriously and simultaneously in seven different sections of the city. The flames caught hold, and strong winds whipped and carried them throughout the town. The monastery itself caught fire and, like the entire city, was completely destroyed, leaving nothing but the charred earthen foundation. Fortunately the monks were able to flee at the last minute, and no one died in the conflagration.

Except Paternus. Feisty to the very end, Paternus refused to break his vow of solitude by joining the fleeing monks. He remained walled up in his cell, even though other monks encouraged him to get out. He either burned to death or suffocated in the small smoke-filled room. It is recorded that his death "seems to have left a deep impression on his contemporaries."

PRAYER

Paternus, I pray that I may understand people like you who take a rigid view of vows and commitments, as well as people who have a more flexible attitude. I also wish that I may be able to balance the many commitments in my own life to achieve the greatest good for the greatest number of people.

DEVOTIONAL PRACTICE

When is it wise to go down with a sinking ship, and when is it better to jump to safety? What point did Paternus prove by staying in his burning cell? Would leaving it have broken his vow of enclosure and offended God?

While it might seem to us that had he lived, Paternus could have continued to serve the community as a model of inspiration and a wise voice calling people to lead a better life, we may never know how it looked to Paternus or to God. Perhaps that is the lesson about his death that impressed his contemporaries.

Reflect on the various moral or ethical positions you hold, then ask yourself the following three questions:

- Would you be willing to die rather than violate them?
- Could a violation of one or more of them be justified, especially to save your life (or someone else's), so that you (or they) might continue to serve others and witness to other equally important divine truths?
- Can you imagine other people of sincerity and integrity answering these questions differently?

ST. PATRICK

"Following the advice of one's soul friend."

C. 389—C. 461

MARCH 17

At age sixteen Patrick, the son of a Roman-Celtic family living in Britain, was kidnapped by Irish pirates and carried across the Irish sea. For the next six years he tended sheep as a slave in western Ireland. During that time he had visions in which an angel or helping spirit, whom he called Victor, appeared to comfort him. Patrick later recalled that Victor visited him thirty times during the six years of captivity. The two talked, carrying on conversations as one would with a trusted friend. In fact Victor was part of a strong tradition in Celtic spirituality, going back even into pre-Christian times: the practice of having a soul friend.

Victor was Patrick's soul friend, a person either alive in the body, deceased and appearing as a spirit, an angelic being, or even a friendly animal, like the stag that followed St. Ciaran wherever he went. A soul friend encourages and advises you on the most important matters of your spiritual life. With Victor's encouragement, the young Patrick decided to escape, and he simply walked across Ireland to the eastern coast, where he found a ship's captain who offered to take him on board. He eventually reached home, became a priest, and later responded to another vision: that of the Irish people calling to him, "Come back and walk with us once more."

Patrick returned to Ireland and spent the rest of his life teaching and organizing Christian communities along the Roman model, primarily in the north. In the south and west, Christian communities followed the older hermetic model organized as monasteries and abbeys led by monks and nuns, rather than the episcopal model run by bishops. Many of Patrick's churches did not survive much beyond his life, since Ireland at that time lacked the town structures needed to support the Roman Catholic Church, and Celtic Christianity seemed more natural to the Irish than Roman Catholic Christianity. But his influence with the Irish people did survive, and the land of his captivity became one of the most Christian and eventually Roman Catholic countries in western Europe.

Victor advised Patrick right up to his death. Patrick loved the place called Armagh and wanted to die there, but Victor sent another angel to admonish him: "Why do you journey to Armagh without Victor's guidance?" He then told Patrick, "Victor calls you," and Patrick changed his direction, and so he did not die in Armagh. But Victor promised that Patrick's memory and influence would always be centered at Armagh, "the deep hamlet, the dear hill, that I love, the fortress which my soul haunts." Today Armagh is the center of Catholic Ireland.

PRAYER

Patrick, teach me how to know and trust the angelic and heavenly friendship that is all around me. If I do not know my guardian spirits, help me to discover them. If I do, show me how to deepen my relationship with them and listen to their wise advice about leading a spiritual life and loving God.

DEVOTIONAL PRACTICE

In the ancient Celtic tradition, a soul friend could be male or female, older or younger than you, a priest, nun, or layperson. What was important was the person's sincere interest in your spiritual life and your trust and friendship with that person.

Consider who among your family or friends has the potential of becoming your soul friend. Pray over this, and ask for guidance from God. Then present the idea to the person, saying that you respect his or her wisdom and would like to meet periodically to talk about spiritual matters that are important to you. If the person agrees, set up times to get together, and begin this practice. Remember that the soul friendship does not have to be reciprocal, although it is stronger if it is. What matters is that you seek advice from your soul friend, and let that person decide whether or not you will function as a soul friend for him or her.

ST. PAUL OF TARSUS

"From blindness to tolerance."

D. C. 67

JANUARY 25

On his way to Damascus to arrest Christians, Saul of Tarsus was struck by a blinding light. Lying on the road, he heard a voice ask, "Saul, Saul, why do you persecute me?" The stricken Saul asked who was speaking, and the voice answered, "Jesus of Nazareth, whom you persecute." The voice then told him to go on into Damascus where he would learn what to do next. The encounter left Saul blind.

Meanwhile, Ananias, a wise leader in the Christian community at Damascus, was troubled by the effect Saul's presence might have there. He was at first worried because he knew that Saul had arrived to make trouble for the Christian community there, as he had in Jerusalem. Saul was one of the notorious persecutors of Christians, a severe and narrow-minded Pharisee, a former student of the famous teacher Gamaliel, and well versed in the Mosaic law. Saul was trouble. He despised the influence that Jesus of Nazareth had on many Jews, particularly the loosening up of the strict Jewish code that governed so many areas of daily life and that he personally found inspiring and fulfilling.

But a divine prompting quelled Ananias's fears, and he knew that he was to go to Saul and heal him. So Ananias sought out Saul, placed his hands on him, and said, "Brother Saul, the Lord Jesus, who appeared to you on your journey, has sent me that you may receive your sight and be filled with the Holy Spirit." Then the blindness that had tormented Saul, probably both physically and mentally, fell from his eyes. Not only did he see again, but he understood the truth of what he had been doing.

Saul was baptized, took the name Paul, and immediately preached that

Jesus was the divine Son of God. People were astounded at his remarkable conversion.

Then the former enemy and persecutor of Christians became one of their foremost promoters. Paul's travels, letters, and theological insights helped shape the early Christian communities in the Mediterranean. Perhaps his most lasting legacy was his convincing arguments that Jesus' path should be open to everyone, not just Jews. When circumcision and other Jewish law requirements were dropped, the Gospel message was open to anyone, and Christian communities could be formed by people of any cultural or racial background.

Paul was executed in Rome in the year 67.

PRAYER

Paul, make me aware of the blind spots in my own vision. Just as you were narrow-minded, looking at everything from a strict Jewish perspective, so are we sometimes blind to the diversity of truth by looking at everything from a too-narrow Christian perspective. This can be especially true in circumstances where holding that perspective disrupts the peace and friendship of others whose beliefs are different from our own. Help me learn tolerance.

DEVOTIONAL PRACTICE

This healing meditation is intended to remove blind spots in your own vision concerning people in your life whom you see as antagonistic toward you. It requires a strong belief in the value of tolerance and a desire to be more tolerant toward those people in your life who bother you.

Sit in your usual place of meditation, close your eyes, and ask the divine presence to be near so that you are palpably aware of it. Then ask that your inner eyes be opened and that you will become more tolerant of someone in your life who currently antagonizes you. Next hear the words and sentiments of Ananias: "I am here to heal you. Receive your full sight, and be filled with the Holy

Spirit." Then feel the hands of Jesus or a saint or angel touch your head or shoulders. Sit there hearing these words over and over again, and feel the hands on your body. When the words and the presence of the divine have filled you, offer a prayer of thanks, and resolve to go about your day with a greater tolerance for the person who has been bothering you.

ST. PAULA FRASSINETTI

"A time to be born, and a time to die."

1809–1882

JUNE 12

Paula Frassinetti's oldest brother was a priest in a seaside parish near Quinto, Italy. Being in poor health, Paula went to live with him when she was twenty-one. Parish life stimulated her, and she became active in working with parishioners along with her brother. She was particularly attracted to the plight of poor children who seemed to have no future. The nineteenth century witnessed the spread of educational opportunities for children of all classes, and Paula decided to work for this goal. She set up an institute in conjunction with the parish to teach the children of the poor.

Paula gathered other women to join her, and in 1834, she established a new order which eventually she named Sisters of St. Dorothy when she discovered there was another organization similar to her own and dedicated to that saint. The work spread, and in thirty years, the sisters were invited to set up schools in Portugual and Brazil.

Paula's own life was nurtured on a solid practice of prayer. Her favorite time for praying was at night, when the cares of the day subsided and the stillness and quiet of the midnight hours made it easy to be in the presence of God. She often spent most of the night in prayer. Her intensely spiritual life gave her great insight into the needs and desires of others, and she became a much sought-after adviser on personal matters.

Paula's advice to people who longed for an early death in order to be rid of the troubles and challenges of this world was quite simple. God did not ask us when we wished to be born, she reminded them, so he does not need our suggestions about when we should die. We should trust in his wisdom to take us when the time is right.

Paula suffered several strokes and died a quiet death in the motherhouse she had established years before.

PRAYER

Paula, give me the strength to push on and not long to leave this world before my time is up. Quicken my faith in the rightness of all things, especially death, both my own and the deaths of others who are dear to me.

DEVOTIONAL PRACTICE

Occasionally set your alarm to wake you in the early hours after midnight so that you can get up to pray for at least fifteen minutes. Or decide that the next time you wake up in the night, you will get up and pray. You will probably find this difficult at first, but determine that you will do this at least three times in the spirit of a night vigil. You may grow to value these hours of prayer more than any others in the day.

STS. PERPETUA AND FELICITA

"The martyred mothers."

D. 203

MARCH 7

Persecution of Christians under Roman emperors produced some of the most dramatic and inspiring episodes of martyrdom in the early Church. Perpetua, a noblewoman of Carthage, and Felicita, a slave, were martyred along with several others during the persecutions under the emperor Severus. Perpetua was the mother of an infant son, and Felicita was pregnant when they were arrested and imprisoned in a private home. Both women were studying the teachings of the Church and preparing for baptism. During their imprisonment, they were baptized by their instructor, who was among them. Then the group was moved to a real prison.

As they awaited their fate, Felicita gave birth to a daughter. Two days later Felicita would die in a Roman circus, and her daughter would be given to one of her sisters to raise. Perpetua and her companions spent their last days with such composure and confidence in their ultimate fate that the prison warden was converted by their example. Eventually they were sentenced to death at the public games, which included an animal circus as a birthday present for the emperor's son, Septimius Severus. The Christians were to be thrown to wild animals.

When the day of execution arrived and Perpetua and Felicita were put into the arena, the wild animals failed to play their part. The two women were unharmed. Not to be denied his judgment, Severus had them put to the sword.

The example of the two women and their companions so inspired early Christians that accounts of their ordeal, written by eyewitnesses, along with Perpetua's own description of their imprisonment, became standard reading for ecclesiastical services. The story of their fate was read right along with the Scriptures.

I ask for the faith and composure to follow my beliefs even to death if need be, but certainly through the lesser persecutions that can occur daily in a society that does not place high value on the spiritual life. Perpetua and Felicita, help me to live and die committed to God and the service of others.

DEVOTIONAL PRACTICE

It seems that the wild animals knew that to harm the two holy women would be an outrage. So often we think that our spiritual life and aspirations are solely human, and that the animals, plants, and elements around us do not share or understand our values. But in Celtic Christianity it is believed that the flowers, animals, birds, and elements sing praises to God every day. Should we be silent? As a spiritual practice, go out into nature, by a tree, river, rock, or flower garden, and sing any song you choose to praise God. Before you begin, however, ask the elements near you to join you (even in their silence), or to listen to you—or even more wonderfully, to teach you *their* songs so that you can sing with them.

ST. PETER THE APOSTLE

"Say yes and mean it."

FIRST CENTURY

JUNE 29

"You are the Christ, the son of the living God." With these words, Peter the apostle, mentioned more frequently than any other in the Gospel, announced his faith in the man from Nazareth who had changed his life forever. Peter, a fisherman from Bethsaida, in Galilee, and his brother Andrew were among the first people called to follow Jesus. Peter always made his boat available for the itinerant teacher and healer, as well as his home—on at least one occasion, Jesus stayed there and healed Peter's mother-in-law.

Originally named Simon, he was called Cephas by Jesus, which means rock, later translated into English (from the Greek) as Peter. He was to be the rock on which the new spiritual community would be based. The fisherman played a leading role in the early Church—both in Jesus' lifetime and after the Ascension. Amidst the squabbles among Jesus' followers in that first century, Peter headed the faction that eventually came to power in Rome. It was Peter who baptized the Roman centurion Cornelius and established the precedent of bringing non-Jews into the Christian fold without circumcision. Peter also loosened other rules to allow non-Jews to join without taking on the many regulations derived from Judaism.

A spontaneous, impulsive man, Peter reached out enthusiastically to whatever life presented. He jumped from the boat to walk on water with Jesus, he cut off the ear of an enemy with his sword, he swore to Jesus that he would die for him, he baptized Gentiles. He declared his love for Jesus three times. And yet Peter was the one who denied his friendship with Jesus three times, endearing himself to countless generations as a simple human being with the best intentions but subject to the normal fears and insecurities of human life.

Tradition states that Peter went to Rome, was imprisoned, and was crucified head downward about the year A.D. 64, during the reign of the emperor Nero.

PRAYER

Peter, give me the courage to respond to life spontaneously and with great enthusiasm. Help me overcome the doubtful, worried, or reluctant ways that keep me from throwing myself into my activities, especially new challenges that come my way. May I acquire your passion for life and be ready to hear new truths and to declare my love for those I truly love.

DEVOTIONAL PRACTICE

If you are a person who is slow to say yes to life, or to express yourself openly and spontaneously, try this practice: Each day for a week, find some place to write the word "yes." It might be on the back of envelopes that come in the mail, on the newspaper, at the top of a diary or journal entry, in the dust you find somewhere, on the frost of a windowpane. It doesn't matter where. Get in the habit for seven days to write "yes" wherever you can, and do so with the intention that you will also try to say the word to the challenges that life presents to you.

ST. PETER CANISIUS

"Spiritual work and spiritual loafing."

1521–1597

DECEMBER 21

Peter Canisius came from a family where achievement was highly prized. Nine times his father served as burgomaster of Nijmegen in Holland where Peter was born. Prior to that, his father had been a tutor to the sons of the Duke of Lorraine. Years later Canisius would berate himself for having wasted a lot of time as a child. Perhaps this is what his father told him, for in whatever ways he may have thought he squandered youthful hours, he nevertheless studied hard enough to receive a master's degree at the University of Cologne when he was only nineteen. He then studied law at the Louvain for a few months to please his father. But he realized that he did not have the temperament for it, and he went back to the university to study theology.

Back in Cologne, Canisius took part in a spiritual retreat from one of the first disciples of Ignatius Loyola and was strongly drawn to this new company of religious men. He joined the Jesuits in 1543 and was ordained three years later. In the course of a busy career as a Jesuit, Canisius traveled all over Germany teaching, preaching, fighting against the Protestant movement, and working to win people back to the Roman Catholic Church. But his outstanding accomplishments were in the fields of writing and publishing.

Johannes Gutenberg invented the process of movable type in the mid-1400s, and the resulting printing press launched a revolution that would forever change Western culture. Books (and people who could read and write them) became the primary sources of information, power, and influence. Canisius realized this and created what would become the Catholic press. He threw himself into the fray of battle between Protestants and Catholics and the various reform movements sweeping Europe both inside and outside the Church.

He published his catechism, *A Summary of Christian Doctrine,* in 1555, a work that went through hundreds of printings and was translated into fifteen languages. He edited the works of Cyril of Alexandria and Leo the Great, as well as the letters of St. Jerome. Among his works were a martyrology, a manual for Catholics, and a breviary of prayers. Canisius also began a series of books that were intended to refute the anti-Catholic histories of Christianity that were being written in Protestant circles. His busy schedule of writing, editing, teaching, and preaching still gave him time to found what would become the University of Fribourg in Switzerland.

Canisius suffered a stroke in 1591 but lived another six years. With secretarial help, he managed to write and edit until his death, a few days before Christmas in 1597.

PRAYER

Peter, help me keep a healthy balance between work, play, and loafing. Share with me the wisdom you acquired from an extremely busy life, and teach me the importance of resting and doing nothing.

DEVOTIONAL PRACTICE

Like the young Peter Canisius, we may not appreciate how much we actually accomplish each day, week, or month. There is a tendency in every age to think that life is speeding up and that there is not enough time to do all that needs to be done. We could all use more "downtime" to loaf, smell flowers, and daydream— activities that let us appreciate the goodness of Creation. Even God rested on the sixth day to appreciate what he had made.

Look over the coming week and pick an hour when you can just relax and do nothing but enjoy the fact that you are doing nothing but relaxing. If you can find no hour, but you have time for spiritual activities scheduled, cancel one of them. It is better now and then to take time out even from spiritual work to prevent becoming a spiritual workaholic.

ST. PETER CLAVER

"A slave of slaves forever."

1580–1654

SEPTEMBER 9

In the sixteenth and seventeenth centuries, about a thousand African slaves passed through the South American city of Cartagena each month. Cartagena was a major depot in the slave trade, the site of the yards and pens where newly arrived men and women would be "broken"—that is, prepared for the mines and plantations where they would work the rest of their lives. The slave yards were also the site where the Jesuit priest Peter Claver chose to work. His mission was, in his words, to be "the slave of the blacks forever."

Born near Barcelona, Claver entered the Society of Jesus when he was twenty and volunteered to work in the New World. He came to New Granada, now Colombia, in 1610 and was ordained a priest five years later. His work in the community of African slaves involved providing medicine, food, clothing, encouragement, and the message of the Gospel. He became a forceful advocate for the enslaved population, continuously seeking better treatment from the authorities. Claver also pleaded with slave owners to alleviate the cruel suffering that was inescapable in the slave system.

Claver's strategy was to visit and minister to enslaved Christians at the mines and plantations where they lived. Although the owners of the operations would offer the Jesuit priest a comfortable room in the hacienda, Claver chose to spend his visits in the slave quarters themselves. In doing so he could observe whether the laws for the protection of slaves were being enforced or to what extent they were being ignored. He could then report to the civil authorities on his findings.

Peter Claver also worked among lepers and prisoners and preached in the main plaza of the city. His sermons were powerful and hard-hitting. In a century when the appreciation of indigenous peoples was far from enlightened and the treatment of non-Christians was cruel and inhumane, Claver's voice was a ray of hope to many people.

In 1650 the plague broke out, and Claver was stricken and never fully recovered. He died in his cell four years later, having cut back his public work and being virtually neglected by everyone.

PRAYER

Peter, help me to understand the common humanity of all God's people, no matter what race, religion, class, or condition of life. Give me the courage not to shrink from contact with people who are different from me, but to reach out to them in whatever ways I can to alleviate their suffering and hopelessness.

DEVOTIONAL PRACTICE

Sometimes we are prejudiced against people who are different from us or live in very different cultures from our own simply because we know practically nothing about them. Or what is worse, we have heard myths and misconceptions about them, so-called facts that are not true. As a form of spiritual reading, choose a book that presents fairly and compassionately the people and customs of some part of the world with which you are not familiar, or of which you have a dim view based on what you think you know about them. An informed librarian can help you select a reputable book. Read the book to become more enlightened about the values and mores of other cultures.

ST. PETER JULIAN EYMARD
"Haunted by a blessed idea."

1811–1868

AUGUST 1

When Peter Julian Eymard, a Marist priest, was forty, he made a pilgrimage to Notre-Dame de Fourvières, where he realized that he was being haunted by an idea that would not leave him alone. He later said, "What hours I spent there," obsessing about his innovative plan. It was a plan to remedy a major gap in Catholic devotional practices. As he put it, "Jesus in the Blessed Sacrament had no religious institute to glorify his mystery of love." Eymard admitted that the idea was very vague at that time, but his goal was to somehow establish an order of priests whose "only object was entire consecration to the service of the Blessed Sacrament."

Five years later in 1856, Eymard left the Marists amid much criticism and submitted his plan for an order of priests who would maintain perpetual adoration of the Blessed Sacrament displayed on their chapel's altar. The archbishop of Paris approved, and Peter and one companion were given a house where they could begin their new vocation. The Blessed Sacrament was displayed three times a week, and Eymard preached to people who came for the service. The Congregation of Priests of the Most Blessed Sacrament had begun.

But it was slow going at first. Not many young men or priests were interested in joining. There were many critics who spoke against the enterprise. In 1858 Eymard founded the Servants of the Blessed Sacrament, an order of nuns whose lives would also center on continual adoration of the Blessed Sacrament. Eymard, along with his priests and nuns, continued to work to spread devotion to the Blessed Sacrament. In 1861 they had three houses. The religious also worked with lay adults, preparing those who had never received Communion to do so. In the meantime, Peter wrote several popular books on the Blessed Sacrament.

Although his congregation received papal approval, it was not until 1895, nearly thirty years after Eymard's death, that it received total confirmation. Eymard's final years were difficult, for he suffered from gout, insomnia, and a nervous breakdown, and was finally weakened by a stroke. He died at age fifty-seven.

PRAYER

Peter, I pray that I might take the spiritual ideas that haunt me seriously. The plans that I make to deepen my spiritual life may require dedication, commitment, and changes in my life, but help me to stick to them.

DEVOTIONAL PRACTICE

The idea that disturbed Peter Eymard was that God resided in a small wafer of bread and no one paid sufficient attention. In a way, this is true in other areas as well. God is in everything, yet how many people take time to notice? As a spiritual practice place a stone, branch, flower, seashell, or other natural object on your altar, and sit before it, being mindful of God's creative spirit that keeps that object in existence. Then when you sit before the Blessed Sacrament in a church or chapel, your ability to focus more intently and prayerfully should be stronger for the practice you have had in honoring God in other areas of his creation.

ST. PETER ORSEOLO

"Pirate fighter, doge, hermit."

928–987

JANUARY 10

Peter Orseolo's life would have made a good action movie. At age twenty the young nobleman was put in command of the Venetian fleet and personally led the successful campaign against the pirates that infested the Adriatic Sea. His comfortable life as a wealthy, influential Venetian was interrupted in 976, when he was forty-eight, by a popular uprising that deposed and killed the current doge, the ruler of Venice. Orseolo may have been personally involved in the outbreak. Certainly his interests were involved, since he was elected doge to succeed the murdered ruler. Orseolo's reign lasted only two years, but it seems that he administered the city decently and efficiently.

Then one night in 978, Orseolo disappeared. His wife of thirty-two years and their one grown son had no idea where he went. For quite some time, Orseolo's whereabouts were a mystery, but then word came back to Venice that he was living in a Benedictine monastery at Cuxa, on the border of France and Spain. Orseolo apparently had had a sudden desire to be a monk. Or did he?

There is evidence that Peter and his wife ceased having sexual relations after the birth of their son, an arrangement adopted by many couples who chose to live a spiritual life based on chastity in those earlier years. Also, Orseolo wrote a letter when he was forty indicating that he was attracted to the monastic life even then. So perhaps the fifty-year-old disappearing doge had planned his escape from the world, politics, and family responsibilities for some time.

Orseolo lived at the monastery for a while but then requested permission to withdraw deeper into the wild to build a hermitage so that he could have even greater solitude and time for prayer and meditation. Orseolo died in his late fifties, and his tomb became a place of pilgrimage and miracles.

PRAYER

Peter, I pray that when I think about the future I, like you, will have spiritual plans to work toward. Keep me from falling into the rut of thinking that the rest of my life will be only what I now know. Give me the spirit of freedom to always look for new spiritual adventures.

DEVOTIONAL PRACTICE

Let's assume Orseolo had planned to become a monk early in life and that his entry into the monastic life was not a sudden, midlife crisis (as we would say today). It is good to plan ahead in regard to our spiritual lives as well as our secular lives. If we plan for retirement, buy life insurance policies, invest money for our children's education, and make other arrangements for our later years, shouldn't we also have some "plan" for our spiritual elderhood?

As a spiritual exercise, plot out a time line for the rest of your life (be generous!). Mark on it major turning points, such as graduation, your children leaving home, turning forty or fifty, retirement, and so forth. Then consider major spiritual activities that you would like to engage in, such as a pilgrimage, a long retreat, creating sacred artwork (music, painting, poetry), and volunteer work in a charitable organization. Put these on the time line where you might reasonably expect to be able to accomplish them. As the years go by, renew your commitment to the activities you have marked out, add new ones that occur to you, and make adjustments wherever necessary. The important point is to be actively engaged in planning for your spiritual future.

ST. PHILIP THE APOSTLE

"Seeing and believing."

B. C. 67

JANUARY 25

Philip was from Galilee and possibly a follower of John the Baptist, for when Jesus invited Philip to follow him, Philip seemed ready to embark on a more spiritual journey. Philip then went immediately to Nathaniel and told him, "We have found him whom Moses, in the law and the prophets, have written about." Nathaniel then made his now-famous remark, "Can anything good come out of Nazareth?" To which Philip simply said, "Come and see."

Philip's practical response to Nathaniel was typical of this apostle for whom we have such little recorded evidence. The three synoptic versions of the Gospel don't even mention him. But in John's version of the Gospel, Philip takes center stage now and then, always demonstrating a practical, matter-of-fact approach to the teachings and mission of Jesus. For example, when a crowd gathered to hear Jesus teach and there was nothing to feed them, Philip asked, "Where can we buy bread for so many to eat?"

On another occasion, a party of Greeks came to see Jesus and approached Philip with their request. Philip followed what was probably the accepted protocol. He went to Andrew, and the two together announced the Greeks to Jesus.

It was Philip who responded to Jesus' remark that no one could go to the Father except through him with the simple request, "Show us the Father, and it is enough for us." Again the practical-minded Philip thought that seeing would be believing. But Jesus rebuked Philip, "Have I been with you so long and you do not know me? Philip, whoever sees me sees the Father."

Philip was with the apostles on Pentecost Sunday and received the Holy Spirit. Where he went from there, to whom he preached, how he died—all is

377

speculation. We never hear of him again. One tradition says, however, that he went to Greece to teach and preach, and was crucified upside down, like Peter, in the year 67.

Philip, there is a place to be practical and sober-minded in religious matters, just as there is a place for mysticism, visions, and ecstasy. Help me to look for the spirit in the concrete matters of daily life, but also save me from being blind to the invisible workings of the spirit. Pray that I may learn that I do not need to see in order to believe, but that I need to believe in order to see.

DEVOTIONAL PRACTICE

Jesus told Philip that whoever sees him sees the Father. Today Jesus is no longer physically with us, so we might continue to wonder and ask, How can we see the Father? Or see Jesus? Following Jesus' teaching that whatever we do for one another we do for him, plan to do some practical, sensible favor for someone in the next couple days. Pray about it, know exactly what it will be, and prepare yourself so that when you do it, you are conscious that you are doing it for Jesus, and that by seeing Jesus in your act, you are also seeing the Father.

ST. PHILIP EVANS

"A game of tennis, a harp, and death."

1645–1679

JULY 22

In 1678 a priest hunter in Wales put a bounty on the head of Philip Evans to the sum of 200 pounds. The rebel Jesuit refused to be intimidated and stayed in the country, administering to his people. The next month he was arrested and imprisoned, as part of the general crackdown on Catholic priests in a century rocked by religious turmoil throughout England and Wales. Evans had joined the Society of Jesus when he was twenty, and had been ordained in France in 1675. He had taken an oath to return to his native Wales as a missionary.

Evans was put in a dungeon in Cardiff where he met John Lloyd, another priest-prisoner, with whom he struck up a friendship. When Evans's trial came up, only two witnesses came forth to testify that he had indeed said Mass, proof that he was a priest. He was sentenced to death but was allowed a bit more leniency while he awaited execution. Lloyd also was condemned to death.

On July 21, 1679, official word came that the two men would be executed on the following day. When Evans received the news, he was playing tennis in the prison yard. When the guard ordered him back to his cell, he refused until he had finished his game. After all, it was to be his last.

On the final day, Evans spent the remaining hours of his life playing the harp and talking to visitors who had come to say good-bye. When he stepped up to the place of execution, he looked at his friend and said, "Adieu, Mr. Lloyd, though for a little time, for we shall shortly meet again." Evans died after serving as a priest for scarcely four years.

Philip, you met your death calmly and serenely, enjoying the few pleasures you had right up to the end. Help me to be equally composed in the face of death, and give me the same assurance that we will meet our friends in the next life.

DEVOTIONAL PRACTICE

Consider the hobbies and pastimes you enjoy. Occasionally, when you begin to work or play at them, pause to reflect on the possibility that since we don't know the time of our deaths, this might be the last time that you will have the opportunity to do them in this life. When we make death an "ally" in this way, we begin to appreciate life more fully and find greater pleasure and commitment in the things we do.

ST. PHILIP OF HERACLEA

"Where does God really dwell?"

C. 304

OCTOBER 22

Philip, the bishop of Heraclea, witnessed to the true nature of spiritual faith when confronted by Roman officials. During the emperor Diocletian's persecution of Christians, the local governor ordered the church doors sealed so that Christians could not enter for services. Philip confronted the officer who came to close down the church with the question: "Do you imagine that God dwells within walls, and not rather in the hearts of men and women?" Undaunted, Philip held services outdoors.

Later, officials returned to seize the sacred vessels that the community used for celebrating their faith. Again Philip countered the orders by stating that they would gladly surrender the sacred objects. "The vessels we will give you, for it is not by precious metal, but by charity that God is honored." Still later, in a confrontation over the sacred writings that were forcibly taken from the community, Hermes, one of Philip's deacons, stated that the government could never destroy the word of God, for it was not written on parchment but in the minds and hearts of believers.

Eventually Philip and his assistants were captured, imprisoned, and cruelly tortured. Officials burned the church and the sacred writings. When asked to offer sacrifices to statues of the Roman gods, they refused. When asked to sacrifice to the emperor, they refused. Equally adamant about not honoring human displays of power, they also refused to sacrifice for the welfare of the city.

At this point, Philip was dragged through the streets, which left his feet so mutilated that he had to be carried to the stake, where he and his companions were martyred. After the fire burned itself out, the martyrs' bodies were still whole, so the judge ordered them thrown into the river. Friends retrieved the bodies, however, and gave them a decent burial.

Philip, enlighten my understanding so that I realize that my faith does not reside in buildings, sacred objects, or spiritual writings but in my mind and heart. May I carry in my heart the same fervor and devotion that I experience in church or reading sacred literature. Help me remember during the day that my faith is always alive, even when I am distracted or forgetful of my spiritual practices.

DEVOTIONAL PRACTICE

If you have an altar or a special place where you keep your Bible, candle, statue, or crucifix, dismantle the spot for one week. Remove the sacred objects and store them away where you will not see them. Leave the place empty. As you see the empty place during the week, be reminded that your faith does not depend on the missing objects. Your faith is alive and well in your mind and heart.

ST. PHILIPPINE DUCHESNE

"Coping with life's disappointments."

1769–1852

NOVEMBER 17

In 1841 Philippine Duchesne, a nun in the Society of the Sacred Heart, was given permission to work directly with native people in Kansas, a dream she had had for over thirty years. Duchesne had been interested in teaching Native Americans since 1805, a year after she joined the order in France. Originally she had been a Visitation nun, but convent life was destroyed by the Reign of Terror during the French Revolution. When Napoleon made peace with the Church, Duchesne was unable to draw her community back together, so she eventually joined the new Society of the Sacred Heart.

Madeleine-Sophie Barat, the founder, agreed with Philippine that a mission to native people in North America was worthwhile, but not until 1818 did the opportunity arise. That year, Bishop Dubourg of Louisiana asked Barat for a small number of nuns to begin a school on the Missouri River just north of St. Louis.

Duchesne and four companions arrived at the small cabin that Dubourg had given them to be the first free school west of the Mississippi. Duchesne was fifty years old, had never really learned English, and found the native people in the area different from what she had imagined and difficult to deal with. By 1828 the nuns had six houses in the Mississippi Valley. It was frustrating work, travel was hard on the frontier, yellow fever broke out, and Philippine caught it.

In 1840 Duchesne resigned as superior in Missouri, and the following year she went to Sugar Creek, Kansas, at the request of Jesuit father Peter De Smet. At age seventy-one, she was finally going to realize her dream of working directly in a native community. But her advanced age, poor health, and continuing frustration in trying to learn Indian languages forced her back to Missouri. Her final years were involved in keeping the order's first house in St. Charles open, along with another house in a nearby town, but the latter was closed to focus money and energy on the major school in St. Louis.

To increase the disappointments and difficulties of those years, Duchesne's correspondence with Barat in France had been intercepted by her superior for over two years after she returned from Sugar Creek. Both women were dismayed and puzzled over the lack of communication, but eventually Barat sent Duchesne's niece to America to find out what had happened, and the truth came out. The two old friends once again continued their correspondence.

Philippine Duchesne died at St. Charles, Missouri, in 1852.

PRAYER

Philippine, so many turning points in your life were filled with frustration. Help me to deal with disappointments and frustrations in my own life. I pray that I will be able to see the bright side of things, even when my dreams don't turn out the way I had planned.

DEVOTIONAL PRACTICE

Philippine Duchesne kept up a correspondence with her friend and mentor Madeleine-Sophie Barat and used letter writing to think, reflect on, and express the disappointments of her life. As a spiritual practice when life's disappointments seem to be too much to bear, sit down and write a letter to some person who inspired or comforted you earlier in life, such as a parent, grandparent, teacher, or older friend. You need not send the letter. Just the act of writing it will help put things in perspective and help you deal with the frustration. As you write the letter, comment on how the disappointments are affecting both your ordinary life and your spiritual life. Use the act of writing as an exercise to see how the outer events in life reflect the inner circumstances of your soul.

ST. RHIPSIME

"Beauty and strength."

D. C. 312

SEPTEMBER 29

A portrait painter in Rome arrived at the community of consecrated virgins headed by Gaiana. He announced that he was painting the portraits of eligible women from whom the Emperor Diocletian planned to select a wife. Among the Christians in the community was Rhipsime, a woman widely admired for her astounding beauty. Her portrait pleased Diocletian, and he decided to marry her. Rhipsime, however, had no interest in Diocletian or in any man for that matter, since she was dedicated to the celibate life. Gaiana realized that trouble was afoot by Rhipsime's refusal, so she took the entire community, left Rome, and sailed to Alexandria, Egypt.

From Alexandria the women went to the Holy Land and then to Armenia, where they became weavers in the capital city, an occupation that provided an income for them so they could continue their lives as dedicated virgins. But word soon spread about the exceptionally beautiful Rhipsime who lived with the community, and Diocletian eventually learned about the women's whereabouts. He sent orders to King Tiridates to kill Gaiana and send Rhipsime back to Rome, unless Tiridates wanted to keep her for himself.

The king decided to look into this more closely. So he ordered a contingent of his men to invade the women's quarters and bring Rhipsime back to his palace. Rhipsime prayed for help. A thunderstorm broke out that so terrified the men's horses that they scattered in all directions. Tiridates was not to be foiled, and he sent soldiers to bring Rhipsime to him by force.

When Rhipsime stood before the king, he immediately fell under her enchantment and, losing control, grabbed her to force a kiss on her. Much to his embarrassment, he discovered that Rhipsime was not only beautiful but also strong. She seized him and overpowered him, tossing him to the floor in what was probably an astonishing display of martial skill. Outraged by being humiliated, Tiridates ordered Rhipsime to be imprisoned. Again, she outmaneuvered him by escaping at night and returning to her community of women.

The following morning Tiridates sent yet another contingent of soldiers to the women's home, who seized Rhipsime and burned her until she was almost dead. Then they tore her arms and legs off. Gaiana and her thirty-five companions were all murdered.

PRAYER

Physical looks and strength are important in many situations, but interior beauty and strength are what will count in the long run. Rhipsime, help me keep a balanced outlook when it comes to outward appearance and physical strength. Whether in myself or in others, help me not become too obsessed by physical qualities. Show me how to look for and strengthen the inner beauty in myself and in others.

DEVOTIONAL PRACTICE

Dedicate your usual exercise routine or workouts to Rhipsime or any saint whose physical prowess you admire. So often we forget that the saints were women and men who had the same needs for physical health and stamina that we have. Although the saints are admired for their interior lives and their search for God, many took the ordinary needs of daily life seriously as well. Make your exercise time a spiritual workout by being mindful of the importance of good health in carrying out your ordinary tasks as well as your spiritual practices.

ST. RICHARD PAMPURI

"The healing touch."

1897–1930

MAY 1

When Erminio Filippo Pampuri was three years old, his mother died. Seven years later, his father was killed in an accident on the road. Young Erminio learned early in life what it was like not to have the strong support of loving parents, but he continued to study hard in school and prepare himself for adulthood. Pampuri served in the Italian military during World War I and later, when he was eighteen, entered the University of Pavia to study medicine. In six years he had completed the course and graduated as a doctor of medicine. He worked as a physician in Milan.

Although Pampuri's professional schedule was busy, he was devoted to parish life and founded a Catholic Action group to inspire service among his fellow parishioners. In a few years, he knew that he wanted to dedicate his life more fully to the Church's work, so he entered the order of the Hospitallers of St. John of God, a religious community that ran hospitals and cared for the sick. His religious name was Richard.

Richard's work among the sick became well known, not only for his skill as a doctor but also because of the sanctity that he brought to it. Mothers brought their babies and young children to him just to be touched. Richard's blessing contributed to healing both the body and spirit. Children calmed down and became more manageable after contact with him.

As was so often the case, the healer was himself a wounded man. During his World War I days, Pampuri contracted a disease that affected his lungs, an ailment that never completely left him. He was frequently in poor health, and at age thirty-three he died in a hospital run by his own order.

Richard, help me to appreciate how the simplest glance, smile, or touch can enlighten another's day. As I go about my daily rounds, may I find ways to bring healing into others' lives.

DEVOTIONAL PRACTICE

Although not everyone is blessed with a healing touch, our touch can be a source of healing and blessing for others, especially when accompanied by a brief prayer. In the course of the day we touch others physically, sometimes intentionally, sometimes not—an inadvertent touch of hands with a checkout clerk when paying for groceries, picking up a child who has fallen on the sidewalk, a friendly pat on the back to a colleague who has done a good job, as well as the hugs, kisses, and pats we bestow on family members. Think of these as being moments of grace. Let them be reminders of prayers, blessings, and good wishes that can be said silently at the moment.

ST. ROBERT BELLARMINE

"The reasonable critic."

1542–1621

SEPTEMBER 17

In 1610 Robert Bellarmine, a cardinal and a Jesuit theologian, suggested an interesting ruse to his friend Galileo, who had become entangled with the Church over his scientific findings. Galileo used a telescope to explore the night sky to test Copernicus's theories that the Earth and the planets circled the sun, rather than following the older theory that the sun and planets circled the Earth. It was a simple ruse. Bellarmine told Galileo to tell the Church authorities that what he had discovered was a *hypothesis* rather than a fully proven theory. Galileo took the advice and got the Church off his back. Somewhat. It wasn't until late in the twentieth century that the Church officially acknowledged that Galileo had been right.

Robert Bellarmine was known for his shrewdness, his intellect, and the brilliant reasoning that he brought to every discussion and debate. He lived in a time teeming with controversy. In fact, he taught controversial theology at the new Roman College for eleven years. A dominant voice in the Church's Counter-Reformation policies, he refuted Protestantism with logic and reason, rather than with dogma, rhetoric, and general denouncing of Protestant views.

Bellarmine also brought his rational approach to political and ecclesiastical issues. He wrote a paper denying the divine right of kings, a theory of kingship that held sway in Christian Europe at the time. James I of England was personally criticized. The Paris *parlement* publicly burned a copy to show its disapproval. But even the papacy was not outside Bellarmine's scrutiny. He wrote another treatise criticizing the pope's authority over secular rulers. Bellarmine maintained that the papacy had only indirect rather than direct jurisdiction over temporal governments. This position so alienated the current pope that he threatened to have Bellarmine's work put on the Index, the official list of forbidden books. Fortunately for Bellarmine, the pope died before he could accomplish it.

The brilliant theologian who had been at the hub of so much intellectual and academic controversy for most of his life spent his last ten years writing about spiritual matters. He published a commentary on the Psalms and a handbook for the faithful entitled *Art of Dying Well*. Bellarmine himself died well at a Jesuit novitiate in Rome where he spent his last days.

PRAYER

Robert, show me ways to bring reason and logic to my life. When I am prone to reacting emotionally to crises, help me respond with clear thinking, to reason things out rather than fly off the handle. Reasoning is one of God's gifts. Grant that I may use it well.

DEVOTIONAL PRACTICE

There is a difference between reacting and responding. The former is usually quick and immediate and includes emotional motivation and not a lot of thought. The latter is slower and more deliberate, and can be based on reason and logic. It can be hard to respond, rather than react.

As a spiritual practice, make journal entries each day reflecting on how you handled crises or troubling situations. As you look back on these incidents, you will see a fuller perspective, something our emotional reactions at the time often don't let us do. Consider how you might have responded if you took the time to think more clearly—as you do when you write about the events in a journal. Use the prayer above to acquire more skill at distinguishing between reaction and response, and to become better at responding.

ST. ROQUE GONZÁLEZ

"God understands all languages."

1576–1628

NOVEMBER 17

The Spanish government was committed, in theory, to the welfare of the native peoples of the Americas. In practice, however, conquistadors, soldiers of fortune, and colonial settlers rode roughshod over the lives and rights of indigenous communities. For all intents and purposes, the natives of the New World were enslaved to work the mines, farms, and ranches of wealthy landowning colonists. Spain was an ocean and many months away.

The thirty-three-year-old Jesuit priest Roque González came from a noble Spanish family living in Paraguay, but he understood the need for traditional people to survive, possibly because he himself was of mixed blood. Trained as an architect, mason, and carpenter, González joined the Jesuit mission to create sustainable towns for native people, based on the colonial town plans developed by the Spanish. He built a central plaza surrounded by Indian dwellings on three sides, with the church and the priests' quarters constituting the fourth. Native families were taught skills and social customs similar to those of Spanish colonials, so they would be independent, self-sustaining communities. Part of the land was held in common and part was owned by individual families who worked for themselves to acquire the tribute demanded by the government, similar to that expected from Spanish colonists. Within the villages, authority was in the hands of native leaders.

González realized the need to preserve the native language, Guarani, and created schools to teach and develop it so that it could compete with Spanish and the European practices that were encroaching on indigenous cultures. Today Paraguay is the only South American country that is fully bilingual.

The work of the Jesuits would eventually get them expelled from Paraguay, and González, perhaps sensing that, continually distanced himself from the Spanish authorities, moving deeper into the territory to have greater freedom to work with native people. González felt that he did not need the protection of Spanish soldiers to protect his work. He wrote his brother, who was an acting governor of the district, that if he were to be successful, he must preach love and trust, not military power. "Our faith was preached to them [the natives] as in the preaching of the Apostles—not with the sword."

As might be expected, not all native leaders appreciated González's concerns, nor his vision, nor his faith. The Jesuit activities competed with those of some native leaders, both political and spiritual, who did not perceive the difference between these priests and the Spanish conquerors who had destroyed their culture. González's last settlement was in territory still controlled by traditional leaders who resented the Christian intrusion. Along with two Jesuit companions, Alonso Rodríguez and Juan de Castillo, González was killed by tribal factions embittered by the destruction of their traditional ways of life.

PRAYER

Roque, share with me your vision of the need for every man and woman to live an independent life. Help me to learn respect for all people and to understand them as fully human beings worthy of God's love.

DEVOTIONAL PRACTICE

A great deal of what we know and understand is colored by the language we speak. People who speak other languages have different understandings based on the connotations and nuances of the words they use. As an exercise to enrich your appreciation for the ways that people of other cultures think and speak about God, go to a library or bookstore with a good selection of foreign-language dictionaries, Bibles, or textbooks and learn the phrases used to refer to God, both those that are similar to your own and especially those that are different from yours.

Memorize these phrases and occasionally use them in your prayers and meditations. They will give you different insights into our common Creator, and expand your own spiritual life as you identify with other human beings who call upon the same Divine Spirit but with different expressions and phrases.

ST. ROSE OF LIMA

"The soul's beauty is not skin deep."

1586–1617

AUGUST 23

Rose was one of the most beautiful young women in Lima, Peru. Born of Spanish parents, she grew up with many admirers, who complimented her on her extraordinary beauty and the quality of her skin. Over the years, she grew tired of the compliments and began to view them as temptations to indulge herself and think more highly of herself than was warranted. To counteract this, she rubbed pepper on her face to create blotches. Then when someone complimented her fine hands, she put lime on them, causing such severe pain that for a while she could not dress herself. In these ways and others, Rose hoped to prevent losing herself in a sensuous life based on inflated images of her physical beauty.

Rose's parents urged her to marry, but she argued with them about this for ten years. Finally, she took a vow of virginity and became a member of the third order of St. Dominic. She continued to live in a shack in her parents' garden. Sewing and gardening helped support the family when they fell on hard times, and Rose grew to like the peace and quiet of the small hut.

When word spread of Rose's way of life, the family garden became the spiritual center of Lima. Visitors came to talk with her, ask her to pray for them, and benefit from her healing work. Many friends, however, pestered her to give up the life of a recluse and return to normal society, but she refused, and continued to live a life of prayer and penance for fifteen years. Many people accredited her prayers for saving Lima from earthquakes that struck nearby.

Rose eventually became sick and moved in with a local official and his wife, who cared for her for the last three years of her life until she died at age thirty-one. She is the patron of all South America.

Rose, help me to keep a balanced attitude about physical beauty. Physical good looks are not an indication of the soul's true beauty. Only when the soul's interior light radiates the skin, eyes, smile, and voice are we whole and beautiful. Pray that I might nurture my inner beauty and always look for the soul's beauty in others, regardless of outward appearances.

DEVOTIONAL PRACTICE

Consider some area in which you recognize personal vanity to some degree. It might be your skin, eyes, hair, beard, clothes, jewelry, or scent. Choose some day to forgo your usual grooming habits regarding this vanity, and go about your day less glamorous than usual. For example, don't trim your beard, tie your hair back simply, don't wear cologne or perfume, forget about makeup, don't wear your usual jewelry. In whatever way you choose, eliminate some physical adornment in the spirit of honoring the beauty of your soul within that needs no outer enhancements. During the day, if you "feel naked," recall that your inner beauty can substitute for the missing element.

ST. ROSE OF VITERBO

"A teenage revolutionary."

1235–1252

SEPTEMBER 4

The twelve-year-old girl preaching revolution in the streets of Viterbo caused great alarm for other villagers as well as her own family. But the young Rose would not be stopped. When she was eight, she had fallen seriously ill and had had a vision of the Virgin Mary. In the vision, she was told to wear the clothes of a Franciscan but to continue living at home to witness to the blessings of God in her own neighborhood. When she recovered, Rose donned the habit of a lay penitent and did just as the vision commanded her.

But Rose was not content to live solely as an inspiring example of a saintly life. Political controversy also inspired her. The town was occupied by the forces of Emperor Frederick II, who, recently excommunicated for the second time, decided to wage war against the papal states in Italy. Rose took to the streets denouncing her fellow villagers for tolerating the presence of Frederick's troops. She called them cowards.

Crowds gathered at Rose's home, some people coming out of curiosity, others out of fear that she was antagonizing the soldiers and should be kept quiet. The situation grew tense and continued for several years. Finally, some citizens demanded she be put to death. To settle the matter, Rose and her family were banished from Viterbo. Exiled in a nearby town, Rose predicted the imminent death of the emperor. Just as she foretold, Frederick died within a few weeks.

When the papal supporters returned to power in Viterbo, Rose and her family came home. But her life of controversy was not over. She petitioned to join the local convent and was turned down because her father was not affluent enough to provide a dowry. In time the parish priest gave Rose and a few companions a house and a chapel near a convent of nuns, who protested to the pope that they had exclusive rights to be the only order of nuns in the area. Legally, they were right, so Rose and her companions had to leave.

Rose returned to live with her parents and died shortly thereafter at age seventeen.

Rose, it is hard to be a prophet in your own town or neighborhood. Help me to not be afraid of standing up for my spiritual values and practices before my family and friends. Give me strength to withstand the daily criticism or misunderstanding that may occur if the people I live with do not approve of my devotion or fail to support me.

DEVOTIONAL PRACTICE

Children often see the truth and speak it. Recall the kids in the folktale who knew the emperor was naked and didn't hesitate to say so. Notice the next time you disagree with the accepted opinions being voiced. Imagine yourself as a young child, disagreeing openly with the adults present, and decide whether you could safely state your disagreement. Sometimes you might decide that the child's spirit within you can object to what others are saying. At other times, you might decide to hold your tongue. The point of this practice is to look at situations from the point of view of a child and rediscover the wisdom that can come from not always being trapped in an adult's frame of reference.

ST. SABAS THE ABBOT

"Basket weaver and runaway."

439–532

DECEMBER 5

Sabas's father was an officer in the Roman army stationed in Cappadocia when Sabas was born. When Sabas's father was transferred to Egypt, he took his wife with him and left Sabas with an aunt and uncle. The aunt treated him abusively, so the eight-year-old boy ran away to live with another uncle. In time, the two uncles began to fight over who should control Sabas's property. The dispute ended up in the law courts. Sabas, wisely, ran away again, this time to a monastery.

After living the monastic life for twelve years, Sabas requested permission from his superior to retire into the desert to live a more solitary life, but he was told that he was still too young. He may have toyed with the idea of just running off (once again), but he stayed in the community until he was thirty. Then he received permission to spend five days a week in a cave far from the monastery so that he would have more time alone with God but still be able to take part in the common life.

Each Sunday evening Sabas left the monastery grounds and headed for the cave with a bundle of dried palm leaves. During the week, as part of his spiritual practice, he made fifty baskets. The goal he set for himself was ten baskets a day. On Saturday morning he returned to the monastery with the baskets for the weekend services.

Over time, other people came to be part of Sabas's life. He acquired disciples and was pressured into being ordained a priest in 491. His own mother joined him in Palestine and founded hospitals and places of refuge for pilgrims. Sabas was still hungering for more solitude, and even though he was abbot of the community, he managed to run away every Lent. He simply disappeared for the forty days of prayer and fasting. His disciples did not approve of this behavior, they complained, and some broke away and founded their own community.

At the end of his life, when he was in his nineties, Sabas was still trying to run away. When he realized his end was close, he asked to be left alone. He lay quietly for four days, seeing no one, talking to no one, just preparing himself to meet God. Then he died.

PRAYER

Sabas, may I find the courage to run away now and then, if only for an hour, just to be alone with God and consider how my life is going. When others accuse me of wasting time, help me be firm in knowing that this kind of solitude is as important as other activities.

DEVOTIONAL PRACTICE

Sometimes people find meditating difficult because they cannot sit quietly without some kind of activity. They fidget. A simple, repetitious activity like basket weaving can occupy your hands while your mind engages in contemplation. Find some craft or activity to do as part of your meditational practice. Knitting, weaving, mending, embroidery, tying fishing lures, or some similar activity will work. The key is to let the activity mesmerize you so that you drift into a visionary or dreamy state of consciousness in which you can contemplate spiritual matters.

ST. SAFAN

"Pray everywhere."

D. 739

DECEMBER 19

Like many Irishwomen who became monastics and saints, Safan was raised in important political circles in ancient Ireland. She was the foster daughter of a chieftain or local king in Ulster. She was married briefly before becoming a nun, and traditions link her with the founding of the monastery at Clonbroney, where she served as abbess.

Many stories attest to Safan's generosity and hospitality, always important values in Celtic society, and the wisdom with which she guided the spiritual development of those who sought her advice. It is reported that a heavenly light shone around her, usually when she was at prayer or meditation. The following two encounters provide insight into Safan's spiritual views.

On one occasion, a monk asked Safan which is the best way to pray—that is, if there are postures more conducive to prayer and meditation than others. "Should we stand, sit, kneel, or lie down when we pray?" he asked. Safan replied, "We should pray in every position."

Another time, a teacher approached Safan with his plans to give up study and devote his entire time to prayer. She pointed out, "If you refrain from all study, then you will also neglect spiritual study." The same teacher told her that he wanted to go on a pilgrimage to deepen his spiritual life and find God. Again she answered along the same lines: "If you cannot find God on this side of the sea, by all means journey overseas. But since God is near to all those who call on him, you have no need to cross the sea." Then she said, "The kingdom of heaven can be reached from every land."

The night Safan died, the abbot Laserian saw two moons in the sky. One of them descended and shone right before him. Then he recalled that he had asked Safan to give him a sign when she passed on into the next life. He knew she had passed on.

PRAYER

Safan, I pray that I might share your insights regarding the presence of God. May I pray in every position, no matter what I am doing. May I find God in all activities and places.

DEVOTIONAL PRACTICE

Try praying in positions different from the one you usually use. Lie down on your back as well as stomach. Sit. Sit in different places. Stand. Kneel. Try a walking meditation through a quiet park or meadow. Whatever your favorite position and place are, vary them from time to time. Not only will you discover that the power of prayer and the presence of God are everywhere, you will also keep your spiritual practice from becoming routine.

ST. SEBASTIAN

"A physical and spiritual athlete."

D. C. 288

JANUARY 20

About five years before he died, Sebastian, born at Narbonne in Gaul, entered the Roman army at Rome. Evidently a brilliant and professional soldier and natural athlete, Sebastian rose quickly through the ranks. He was appointed captain in the praetorian guards by the emperor Diocletian and reconfirmed by the emperor Maximian. What neither ruler knew about Sebastian was that he was a secret Christian.

But not too secret. While in the army, Sebastian shared his faith in Jesus' teachings with those he met and converted rather influential people, among them the master of the rolls, Nicostratus, who administered prisoners, and Zoe, his wife, whom Sebastian cured of deafness and an inability to speak. He cured Chromatius, the prefect of Rome, of gout, and the prefect then became a Christian along with his son. Moved by his new faith, Chromatius freed prisoners and his own personal slaves and resigned his position. Through Sebastian's example and secret preaching, many people such as these were converted.

Eventually Sebastian was discovered by Roman authorities, captured, and sentenced to be executed by Roman archers. The former Roman soldier was shot with arrows and left to die. But he was discovered by a holy woman who nursed him back to health. Once recovered, Sebastian confronted the emperor Maximian and rebuked him for his persecution of Christians, whereupon the emperor ordered Sebastian to be beaten to death. Although his career as a soldier lasted only a few years, his fame spread widely, and Sebastian became the patron of soldiers, athletes, and, ironically, archers.

I know that physical strength and skill can be important to the spiritual life and that all God's gifts are opportunities to celebrate his goodness. Sebastian, help me find moments to exercise, play, and enjoy the physical exertions that can be channels of divine grace. Show me ways to find God and his wisdom in athletic activities.

DEVOTIONAL PRACTICE

A spiritual practice can include what we might call a "body practice"—that is, some physical activity you do mindfully, prayerfully, and with the intention of celebrating your physical health and skills as gifts from God. In the spirit of Sebastian, turn your sport or exercise activities into periods of spiritual deepening. Before you begin, say a prayer, offering your workout to the Divine Spirit. Be aware of your skill, strength, wins, and losses, and find in them spiritual teachings. Transform your physical energy into spiritual energy, and offer thanks for your body, your health, and the enjoyment you derive from athletic activities.

ST. SOLANGE

"Star watcher and star-watched."

D. 880

MAY 10

Solange was the daughter of vinedressers in rural France. The family also owned some sheep, and Solange's task was to tend the sheep out in the fields. She was known as a pious young girl, as well as for being quite beautiful. Her reputation for holiness and beauty spread throughout the district. Solange had a guiding star that constantly shone down upon her, even during the day. Neighbors noticed that it grew brighter and more brilliant when Solange was lost in prayer or meditation.

The young shepherd girl was able to heal illness and advise others about the spiritual life. She also had an intimate rapport with animals, both domestic and free, and they would come when she called and give her company.

One day, Bernard, one of the sons of the Count of Poitiers, came to see her as she tended her flocks. He made sexual advances toward her, which she resisted. The young count then overpowered her and placed her up on his horse, with the idea that he would carry her off. She continued to fight him, and slipped from the saddle, seriously injuring herself in the fall. Bernard then drew his sword and killed her.

There is still a field near her home where she liked to pray called "The Field of St. Solange."

PRAYER

Solange, help me be more in tune with the natural world, especially the stars in the night sky. Teach me how to find my special star and use it as a symbol that links me with the Creator, who made all of the natural world.

Many people believe they have a guiding star or a lucky star. The general belief that some divine protection and help resides in the stars is universal and has brought great comfort to people throughout the ages. There is an old folk custom to make a wish on the first star you see at night.

Go outside on a clear night and notice which star (or cluster of stars) attracts your attention. Look at it and get to know it. Later, find out which constellation it is in and learn when in the year that constellation appears in the night sky. Think of this star as a special friend that the Creator has placed in the sky to watch over you. Even during the months when it is not visible at night, it still crosses the heavens during the day, so no day passes without its presence being in your life.

Develop the practice of going out at night and praying beneath that star or letting it carry your thoughts up into the greater cosmos. Be aware of this star during times of trouble or whenever you need a physical sign that the spirit continues to operate in your life.

ST. STEPHEN

"Be open to the Holy Spirit."

D. C. 35

DECEMBER 26

In the first community of Christians in Jerusalem, the need arose to appoint deacons to care for the practical needs of the members in order to allow the elders more time each day for preaching and prayer. Among the seven deacons first selected was Stephen, a Hellenistic Jew most likely from the Diaspora, then living in Jerusalem. In the Acts of the Apostles he is described as "a man of faith and the Holy Spirit."

Soon the leaders of some synagogues, still uncertain what to make of the Jews who now followed the teachings of Jesus, argued with Stephen over his beliefs. They challenged him to disputations, debated with him, and lost. So sharp and filled with the Spirit was Stephen, that time and again the elders in the synagogues failed to outargue him about his faith and his teachings. Eventually they accused him of blasphemy against the law of Moses and against God, and they hauled him before the Sanhedrin to be judged.

Stephen stood by his message. He said the Temple would be destroyed, that the Mosaic law was only temporary, and that God had sent Jesus as the Messiah to lay out a new order of holiness. "You are stiff-necked," he accused his accusers. "You resist the Holy Spirit as your fathers did." Then, before the congregation of Jewish elders, Stephen had a vision and described it courageously. "Look, I see the heavens opened and the Son of Man standing on the right hand of God."

This was too much for the authorities. They forced Stephen from the temple, dragged him outside the city walls, and stoned him to death. As he died, he prayed, "Jesus, receive my spirit," and he forgave his attackers, asking God not to attribute what they were doing to him as a sin. Stephen was the first martyr.

PRAYER

Stephen, I need to see and feel the workings of the Spirit in my life. I need to be more fully convinced that my daily activities are filled with the holiness of the Spirit of God. Help me to deepen my faith and find the influence of heaven right here on earth.

DEVOTIONAL PRACTICE

Often the Spirit is described as flowing through us, or pouring forth, or showering upon us—all images of water. Jesus spoke of "Water and the Spirit." Use the following water ritual to deepen your appreciation of the Spirit's activity in your life.

Get a special bowl and place it on your altar or shrine. Fill the bowl with water from a spring or a swiftly flowing stream, or with rainwater. As the water evaporates and you collect more to replenish the bowl, be mindful of how lavish the gifts of the Spirit are, how they flow and shower upon us every day. Think of specific blessings that have come into your life. Give thanks for them, and understand that you must make some effort to use those gifts and appreciate them, just as you must make an effort to gather water and keep the bowl full.

ST. STEPHEN HARDING

"A chance encounter and a changed life."

D. 1134

APRIL 17

Stephen Harding and a friend were traveling back to England from Rome. As they journeyed through a forest in the French province of Burgundy, they came across a settlement of monks living in ramshackle huts, far from civilized society. The hermits spent their days engaged in hard physical work and prayer. Their asceticism impressed Harding. He asked if he could stay. The monks said yes, and Harding bade his friend farewell. In the spirit of the moment, Harding seized his destiny and became a monk. He would remain one the rest of his life.

Nothing is known about Harding's parents and very little about his early life, except that he was educated in the abbey of Sherborne in Dorset. When he left, he traveled to Scotland and Paris, perhaps to study or just to knock around. He does not seem to have been interested in the monastic life until by chance he stumbled on the hermits in the Burgundian forest.

In 1098, the abbot and about twenty other monks, including Harding, left the community and founded another house at Cîteaux, deep in a forbidding forest and quite distant from the nearest town. In time Harding became prior. His rule was quite severe, and he seemed intent on policies that were headed for failure. He refused to allow the local courts to meet at the abbey, which alienated the local nobles. Furthermore, he would not allow any elegant and costly equipment or clothing for services and church decor. Since monasteries could attract visitors and patrons by the wealth and luxury that they displayed, the community at Cîteaux soon acquired a reputation for being a dull place. Even the number of novices began to diminish. As if to top off their misfortunes, many monks died from some mysterious disease. Harding was about to question whether it was possible to continue.

Then out of the blue, a troop of thirty-one wealthy men appeared, headed by a twenty-two-year-old man named Bernard. He asked admittance as monks for all his company, which included his four brothers and an uncle. Harding agreed, and soon the monastery's fortunes turned around. New recruits appeared, and other houses were founded, one at Clairvaux. Harding appointed the then twenty-four-year-old Bernard to be abbot. By 1119, nine other monasteries had spun off from Cîteaux and Clairvaux.

Then Harding drew up the statutes for his communities, which today are known as the Cistercian order. In 1133 he stepped down from leadership, blind and weakening from old age. He died at Cîteaux.

PRAYER

Stephen, I wish I could be more spontaneous in my spiritual life, as you were on that spur of the moment when you stayed in France to be a monk. So often I am leary of acting spontaneously. Help me to be less controlling, less fearful, and to take reasonable risks for the sake of my spiritual growth.

DEVOTIONAL PRACTICE

On a weekend or a day off, when you have some free time, take the Gospel and open randomly to a page with your eyes closed. Run your finger down the page, stop, open your eyes, and read the two or three lines you are pointing at. Ask yourself what they suggest as an activity that you could reasonably perform that day. Then if it's possible, do it. If you can't, ask yourself why not. What does it say to you about the spontaneity in your life?

ST. STEPHEN OF PERM

"Ethnic art and language in the service of God."

D. 1396

APRIL 26

The Permiaks were an indigenous people living in southern Russia, east of the Volga River and southwest of the Urals. They spoke their own language and were cut off from the mainstream culture of Russia. When Stephen, a Russian who had been born in Perm, returned from Rostov years later as a monk, he realized that it would be a travesty to undermine the Permiaks' language and native forms of expression to teach them the Christian faith in Russian or Latin.

Stephen believed that all languages had their source in the mind of God and that each language was valuable in God's ear. Furthermore, it made more sense, he thought, for people to worship God with the words and phrases that came naturally to them. So his first undertaking was to translate parts of the Scripture and liturgy into the Permiaks' native language. But Stephen did not want to foist the Russian alphabet upon a people who found it alien, so he created a new alphabet explicitly for the Permiaks. He painstakingly crafted each letter from designs and patterns that were native to Permiak art, embroidery, and wood carving. Teaching the Permiaks the alphabet and how to use it was harder than Stephen had imagined, so he developed schools where people could be educated to literacy and learn the teachings and practices of the Christian faith.

Stephen became the first bishop of Perm in recognition for the almost superhuman task of bringing literacy, an alphabet, a school system, and the Christian faith to this remote area of the world.

Stephen, help me develop a love of language like you had. So often we take words and literacy for granted. Even the alphabet seems so common that we hardly notice the shapes and designs in the letters we use every day. Teach me to watch how I speak and write, to take time to use language well, and to appreciate my language and those of other peoples as gifts from God.

DEVOTIONAL PRACTICE

Writing out meditations as you do them in a journal or diary accomplishes two things. First, it helps keep your mind focused and prevents distractions. Second, you have a written transcript of your spiritual thoughts and feelings so you can go back and reread them—a good practice in itself especially for those times when you do not feel like meditating, because you are either too tired or too distracted. You also have a record of your soul's journey through the seasons, and you can go back to a particular time and recall what was important then and perhaps recapture the spirit of previous meditations.

ST. STURMI
"The problem of mixed messages."

D. C. 779

DECEMBER 17

When he was a young boy, Sturmi was entrusted to St. Boniface by his parents and was raised in an abbey. He preached for a few years after becoming a monk, then asked to retire to the more isolated life of a hermit. In 744 he founded a monastery at Fulda, in an area that was one of Boniface's favorites, and the patron saint of Germany hoped to make it a model for other institutions.

One of the primary goals of the early German Christians at this time was the conversion of the Saxon tribes who still followed their ancient spiritual traditions and were hostile toward Christianity. Sturmi and his monks took up the cause of preaching to the Saxons, but the tense and always potentially violent relations between the various groups in that area made it dangerous. To compound matters, Sturmi found himself caught in a bind: The people he hoped to convert were getting mixed messages about Christianity from the Christian military powers.

Charlemagne and his son Pepin were engaged in political wars with the Saxons. At first, the wars were punitive, aimed primarily at punishing and intimidating the Saxons so they would not cause trouble for Charlemagne's realm. But then the wars became a matter of conquest. The goal was to conquer, subdue, and rule over the Saxons. None of this was conducive to the Saxons' becoming Christians, since they correctly saw the strong mutual interests between the Church and the Crown.

When Charlemagne took his army into Spain to launch offensives against the Moors, the Saxons took the opportunity to attack. They drove the monks out of the area and threatened Fulda itself. Sturmi and his companions bided their time, and when Charlemagne returned, they accompanied his military expedition

412

against the Saxons. Sturmi still hoped to bring the Christian message to the tribes even as they fell to Charlemagne's forces. But Sturmi became ill and died at Fulda before he could see whether the Saxons would accept Christianity in the wake of war.

PRAYER

Sturmi, show me the way to stay true to my spiritual values even when the government is pursuing policies that contradict them. Help me realize my dual citizenship in both the secular and sacred worlds and learn how to function with integrity and decency in both.

DEVOTIONAL PRACTICE

Sometimes we find our spiritual values and goals at odds with government policies. When someone is a citizen of both the secular and sacred worlds, it can be hard to have a foot in each. But if we are mindful of the dual character of our lives, we can deal more successfully with the tension this dualism creates.

Find a small stone that you can carry in your pocket or coin purse. Let the coins represent "the things that are Caesar's" and the stone "the things that are God's." Whenever you go to pay for something, let the stone remind you of the need to hold fast to the spirit, even though the political culture you live in might be at odds with the life of the spirit and what you pray for.

ST. TERESA OF AVILA

"The interior castle of the soul."

1515–1582

OCTOBER 15

As young children, Teresa and her brother Rodrigo were so impressed by the lives and deaths of the martyrs that they ran away from home, hoping to get out of Spain and into Moorish territory in Africa, where they planned to be put to death for their Christian faith. An uncle stopped them before they got too far. Still determined to live intensely spiritual lives, the two children returned home and built a hut of stones in their garden. Now they planned to be hermits, but they never finished the project. Only later, as an adult, did Teresa get the chance to put into practice the deep love of God she felt so early on.

As a Carmelite nun, Teresa was personally responsible for founding seventeen monasteries and introducing reforms to make the monastic life a truly spiritual refuge from society. In her day, many monasteries were like social centers for the wealthy men and women of their towns and nearby countryside. Nuns left the cloistered areas and skipped their religious devotions on the weakest excuses to take part in the frivolity occurring within the monastery walls. Teresa's reforms won great support from some, but incurred the wrath of others, including superiors within the order.

In 1562 Teresa's sister and her husband built a new monastery for her at Avila under the pretext that it was to be the couple's new home. The town was outraged, the governors feared it would become a financial drain on the town's resources, and there were threats to tear it down. But eventually, the opposition subsided when other Church officials backed the project. The monastery was there to stay.

Like that of her friend and coreformer John of the Cross, Teresa's life was plagued with opposition, slander, and ill will from people within her own order who preferred the more relaxed regulations. On occasion, nuns refused to follow her reforms and become hysterical over them. In time King Philip II and other influential people, both in government and in the Church, recognized the importance of her way of life, and a separate province was created for the reformed order, called Discalced, to indicate the order's practice of not wearing shoes.

No matter the controversy surrounding her, Teresa continued her life of prayer and penance. She had visions and heard angelic voices. She experienced mystical raptures, even involving physical levitation, which she explained as God's need to draw not only our souls to him, but our bodies as well. Her writings continue to inspire spiritual seekers. Her *Autobiography*, *The Way of Perfection*, and *Interior Castle* are classics in the literature of mysticism.

In spite of the austerities she advocated and the mystical intensity that characterized her life, Teresa was charming, gracious, witty, generous, intelligent, and sensible. When she died at age sixty-five, her last words were, "O my Lord, now it is time that we may see each other."

PRAYER

Give me the courage to persevere in my spiritual practices even when others think I am foolish and wasting my time. Help me, Teresa, to find refuge in prayer and devotions, especially when I feel out of step with the fads and trends that others think are so important. May I find inspiration in your life and keep my sense of humor no matter what.

DEVOTIONAL PRACTICE

Using Teresa's metaphor of an "interior castle," put a photograph of a castle that you find appealing in some place where you will see it regularly. Let it be a reminder of the richness of your interior life, which cannot be assailed or threatened from without. When you look at the castle, recall how God's love for you protects you and keeps you safe.

ST. TERESA OF LISIEUX

"The story of a soul."

1873–1897

OCTOBER 1

Teresa of the Child Jesus, the name taken by Marie-Françoise-Thérèse when she was professed as a Carmelite nun in 1890, had a great devotion to the Virgin Mary but always hated to say the Rosary. She also fell asleep during prayers. In many ways, she was an ordinary young woman, and yet in others she was quite extraordinary.

When Teresa was fifteen, she and her father, a watchmaker, were part of a pilgrimage to Rome. At an audience with Pope Leo XIII, the teenage girl told him boldly that she wanted to be a nun at Carmel but had been denied because she was too young. She wanted a special dispensation to join the order. The pope upheld the order's decision and told Teresa that she would have to wait. On returning to France, however, Teresa continued to apply, and the local bishop gave his consent. At fifteen, Teresa joined her two older sisters as a Carmelite nun.

In 1894 the prioress, her sister Pauline, suggested that Teresa write a history of her childhood to show the workings of God in her early life. She finished it two years later, and was then asked to write about life in the convent. The two works, combined and titled *The Story of a Soul*, became a widely read, spiritual biography of a nun whose life, joys, and sufferings (she had tuberculosis) continue to inspire many people. Her writing is filled with spiritual truths, self-revelations, and remarkable sensitivity to the role of grace in daily life. Because of her devotion to doing little things well and for love of God, Teresa became known as the Saint of the Little Way.

In 1888 Teresa's father suffered two strokes, which left him mentally impaired. His daughter Celine cared for him until he died in 1894 (and then became the fourth daughter to enter Carmel). Teresa called these years "our father's martyrdom" and considered them "the dearest and most fruitful of our lives." In 1893 she became novice mistress. A few years later, during Passion week, Teresa began to hemorrhage at the mouth. She called it "a far-off murmur announcing the coming of the Bridegroom." Eighteen months later, she died.

PRAYER

Teresa, your life was short, but you saw in it the workings of the Divine Spirit. Always attentive to God's grace, you responded no matter what the implication, no matter whether you were called to great joy or great sorrow. Help me to be equally sensitive to the Spirit working in my life and to be able to respond as I am called.

DEVOTIONAL PRACTICE

Keeping a daily journal is a widespread practice for people living a spiritual life. But writing a spiritual autobiography can help you see the role that the Divine Spirit has been playing in your life from your earliest years to the present. It is also a good way to get a sense of your own destiny, what God is calling you to do or be, and how well you have followed the path.

Buy a book of blank pages and begin to write your spiritual autobiography. Begin in your childhood with your earliest memories. You can make each entry cover a period or phase in your life, such as a year or several years. Include the important things that were going on in your family, at school, with friends, on your first job, and in important relationships. Include the things you did for hobbies, entertainment, travel, and self-improvement. Approach these as the background to your spiritual growth and development. Pay particular attention to and reflect on the important decisions you made, the turning points in your life, your successes and failures, what you are proud of and what you regret. Reflect on your entries from the point of view of someone who is witnessing the progress of a soul or, as Teresa would say, "the story of a soul." What can you learn from this story?

ST. THAIS

"A prostitute startled by inconsistency."

D. C. 348

OCTOBER 8

Thais was a famous prostitute in Egypt. She had been brought up by Christian parents, so St. Paphnutius, an elderly hermit, decided to visit her one day to see what had become of her faith. Disguised as a regular citizen (rather than wearing the crude clothing of a hermit), he made an appointment with Thais as if he were just another man seeking her company. When he was taken into her boudoir, he asked Thais if they might retreat to an even more secluded place.

"Why?" she asked. "What are you ashamed of? If you fear other men seeing you, be assured that no one will come in on us. If you are worried about God seeing you, then no place we go is safe, for he can see us anywhere." Paphnutius was surprised to hear such talk from a prostitute. "Do you believe in God?" he asked. "Of course," she replied. "I know that God will reward the good with eternal happiness and punish the wicked with eternal sorrow."

Paphnutius was flabbergasted. He asked her, "How can you know these truths and yet live so sinfully, and what is more, lead others into sin with you?" The words, as he spoke them, were inspired by the Holy Spirit, and God's grace entered Thais's heart. She saw the inconsistency of her life, and she was moved to repent. Then Paphnutius revealed to her his identity, and she begged, "Father, tell me what I should do." He told her that she should return with him to live a life of prayer and penance.

Thais asked the hermit for three hours to settle her affairs. She collected the clothing, jewels, and valuable gifts that her customers had given her and burned them publicly. Next, she called upon all the men who had ever come to her and told them to repent their lustful ways and turn to God. Then Thais went with Paphnutius to the monastery.

Thais asked Paphnutius how she should pray after living such a dissolute life for so many years. He told her to turn toward the east and repeat these words, "You who created me, have pity on me." For three years this was her prayer and ritual. When the time of her penance was up, the hermits released her and told her she could live with the other nuns in the monastery. But fifteen days later, Thais died.

PRAYER

Thais, wake me up to the inconsistencies in my life. Especially, show me how my work, friends, entertainments, purchases, and use of time may be at odds with the spiritual values that I say are important to me. Help me to live rightly according to the spirit.

DEVOTIONAL PRACTICE

It is interesting that Paphnutius asked Thais to face east while saying her prayer of repentance. In early Celtic monasteries, the monks faced each of the four directions and the center to offer their prayers. Honoring the four directions and the center is a worldwide spiritual custom.

Meditate on each of the four directions and the center, considering what each symbolizes for you. For example, many people see the east as representing births, beginnings, new life, freshness, youth; the south as fullness, passion, enthusiasm, creativity, commitment; the west as experience, wisdom, memory, and death; the north as rest, dreams, visions, and waiting; and the center as the heart of creation.

Decide which spiritual blessings or powers you find appropriate for each direction. Then compose a short prayer or affirmation of two or three lines that asks for the blessing or power of each direction. As a daily practice, face each direction and recite these prayers. During the day be aware that the directions and the spiritual powers are a sacred horizon, always encompassing you with divine protection.

STS. THEODORE AND THEOPHANES

"Tattoo torture."

775–841 AND 778–845

DECEMBER 27

The brothers Theodore and Theophanes are sometimes known by their Greek surname, Graptoi. They were not born with this name, however. The Greek word means "written on," and the story of how they acquired the name is one of the more gruesome stories in the history of Christian conflict.

Theodore and Theophanes were born near the Dead Sea in the biblical land of the Moabites. When they were still young boys, they became monks in an established monastery. During these years, the Christian communities were racked by the controversy over whether pictures, statues, and other graphic images should be part of Christian practice or whether this constituted a form of idolatry. The side of the controversy against the images was called iconoclasm, which means "the smashing of images or icons." Theodore and Theophanes sided with the position that images of Jesus, Mary, the apostles, and other religious figures should be allowed because they enhanced spiritual devotion.

The Christian emperor, Leo, who was an iconoclast, had the outspoken Theodore whipped and, together with his brother, banished to an island at the mouth of the Black Sea. The two men suffered greatly in the cold weather and could not find enough food to stave off hunger. When Leo died, the two returned to Constantinople.

The next emperor, Theophilus, came to power in 829. Like Leo, he was a committed iconoclast and ordered the two monks to be scourged and banished once again. The exile lasted two years, and the men returned to their monastery at Constantinople. They had not been broken, however, and continued to defend the use of images and to attack those who would outlaw them, including the Christian emperor.

This time, Theophilus resorted to more drastic measures to subdue the two brothers. He ordered a court poet to compose twelve lines of verse concerning the issue. Then the monks were bound and tied to a bench on their backs, while torturers slowly and brutally inscribed the twelve lines of poetry on their foreheads by cutting, pricking, and puncturing the letters into their skin. When night came, the task had not been finished, so the two brothers remained there until morning when the lines were completed. Then for a third time Theodore and Theophanes were banished.

Theodore died in exile in 841. Shortly after that, the emperor died. Then the following year, St. Methodius, who favored images, was made patriarch, and Theophanes returned in triumph. He was made bishop of Nicaea but died about three years later.

PRAYER

Theodore and Theophanes, you spent your entire lives caught in a dispute over which of two opposing opinions would prevail. While you courageously defended your position, you suffered greatly from those opposed to you. Help me to live up to my own beliefs as you did.

DEVOTIONAL PRACTICE

It may seem odd that people would be willing to lay down their lives over the issue of whether or not to allow religious pictures and statues to be part of someone's spiritual practice. Today we would probably tolerate both positions, knowing people of good will could be found in each camp. This issue, which was such a burning controversy a thousand years ago, would probably be a nonissue. In fact, some contemporary Christian churches and meetinghouses are bare of religious artwork, while others, such as Catholic churches, are filled with it.

As a devotional practice to help you understand other people's religious practices, get a book or encyclopedia on the world's religions (both major religions, such as Judaism and Buddhism, as well as local tribal traditions, such as Native American and African religions). Then look over the many varied practices that have been part of the human effort to find and honor the sacred. Some may inspire you, while others disgust you or make you laugh. The great diversity of creation includes many unique ways to worship the Creator.

Find ones that appeal to you and that can be incorporated into your own beliefs, and try them. You might do them just once to see what they are like, or you might make them regular practices if they enrich and deepen your own spiritual life.

ST. THERESE COUDERC

"A pioneer in the women's retreat movement."

1805–1885

SEPTEMBER 26

The Vivarais is an ancient rural section in southeastern France, a mountainous area remote and unfriendly in the winter storms that move through the area. Therese Couderc, a young nun, and two other nuns arrived in the region in 1827 to run a retreat center for women pilgrims who came there to visit the shrine of St. John Francis Regis. At age twenty-three, Couderc was appointed superior of the community. She was well adapted to the harsh, rural environment, having grown up in a farming family. Under her care and the inspirational work of John Terme, the priest who had founded the order and requested its assistance in the mountain refuge, the center underwent considerable growth.

The following year, 1828, Terme came to a decision about the enterprise that was astonishing for its day: nuns, not priests, should conduct retreats for the women who came to visit the pilgrim site. Nowhere did nuns give retreats. But the concept caught on, and, under Mother Therese's supervision, its appropriateness was immediately evident. The Society of the Cenacle was born, and in time its retreat houses spread worldwide. Although they followed the format of Jesuit retreats, Cenacle retreats were conducted by women.

Therese Couderc launched the program at La Louvesc, and soon a new convent and church were needed. But eventually the financial backing failed, large debts piled up, and the center fell on hard times. Couderc blamed herself for mismanagement and resigned in 1838. Internal dissension in the movement caused her great suffering, and there was disagreement and conflict over who was the true founder. For most of the rest of her life, Couderc lived in relative obscurity as a simple nun. Twenty years later, by decree of a local bishop, Therese Couderc was officially recognized as the cofounder of the Cenacle retreat movement, along with John Terme. Her prayers and penances for its success became her major work in later life, and she died after a long illness at the age of eighty.

Therese, you were a groundbreaker in a movement that was avant-garde for your times. Help me to be innovative and not run away from trying something new. Show me how to persevere when there are no rules to guide me, when I am called upon to pioneer an untried enterprise.

DEVOTIONAL PRACTICE

Typically retreats are three, six, or eight days long. Some are longer. While you may not be able to take time off from work or family obligations to go on a formal retreat, you can always do a "private, hidden" retreat known only to you and God. Choose the days that will constitute your retreat, and mark them on your calendar in advance. Try to clear your schedule as much as possible during this time, or choose days when you know you will have extra free time.

Decide what spiritual practices you will engage in, or which ones you will deepen. For example, plan to meditate or increase the number of periods of meditation or the length of time you meditate. Schedule time for spiritual reading. Take quiet reflective walks in nature. To whatever extent you are able, fast or abstain from favorite foods. Write in your journal. Stay up in the stillness of the night and just be aware of the presence of God. Do not watch television, listen to the radio, or read newspapers or magazines. Turn off the phone, if possible. Do some personal ritual to begin and end the retreat.

While you may not be able to do all these things, select some of these activities or even just one that you can realistically perform for the number of days you choose. Whatever you do will make these days sacred.

ST. THOMAS THE APOSTLE

"Creative doubt."

FIRST CENTURY

JULY 3

Thomas was one of the apostles, but we do not know much about him before he threw in his lot with Jesus of Galilee. His surname means "Twin," and the appellation that has come down through the centuries is "the Doubter." Thomas's doubt or skepticism, however, has provided many lessons for people over the years, for out of doubt can come great faith.

Like the other apostles, Thomas appears to be a man of contradictions and human imperfections. He said to the others, "Let us go with Jesus so that we may die with him." But like most of the apostles, he fled into the night and hid safely while Jesus was arrested. For some reason not recorded (and a source of continual speculation), Thomas was not with the other apostles when Jesus appeared to them after he returned from the dead. Thomas refused to believe that their teacher was back and made his famous challenge about not believing until he could put his hand into the spear wound in Jesus' side and his fingers into the holes left by the nails in his hands and feet.

Eight days later, when the apostles were gathered together again and Thomas was with them, Jesus appeared and gave Thomas the proof that he had requested. He showed him the wounds from the Crucifixion. At that point the skeptic in Thomas was overcome by the believer, and he said, "My Lord and my God." Jesus then encouraged not only Thomas but all those who would come later, "Blessed are they who have not seen, and yet believe."

Tradition says that Thomas ended up preaching the Gospel message in India. The Gospel according to Thomas relates the miracles and teachings of this period. On one occasion, he presented himself to a local ruler as a carpenter and architect. The ruler gave Thomas money to build a palace, but he gave the money to the poor. When the ruler complained and threatened him, Thomas rebuked him with words that possibly came from his own earlier bouts with unbelief: "You cannot see the palace now, but you will someday, when you leave this world."

PRAYER

Thomas, I too am a person of contradictions. Some days I am filled with great doubt; on others I have great faith. Help me to use my unbelief to strengthen my faith rather than to weaken it.

DEVOTIONAL PRACTICE

It has been said that every spiritual practice requires three things: great faith, great doubt, and great commitment. We cannot escape any of these three if we are truly living a spiritual life. We must learn how to use all three. Make a bracelet from cord or fiber and tie three knots in it. One knot is for faith, one for doubt, and one for commitment. Wear it on days when you feel more filled with doubt than faith and when the doubts seem to be undermining your commitment. In the spirit of the apostle Thomas, use your doubt to look for the evidence that will strengthen your faith and commitment.

ST. THOMAS AQUINAS

"The lightweight straw of scholarship."

C. 1225–1274

JANUARY 28

At the beginning of Thomas Aquinas's brilliant career as a thinker and writer, he was called a "dumb ox." At the end of his career, he considered everything he had written as "so much straw." Who was the scholar who shaped Catholic theology for over seven centuries and is associated with these barnyard images?

Aquinas was born in the family castle in northern Italy. When he was five, he was sent to the monastery school at Monte Casino, a few miles away, to begin his studies. He was shy and reserved, and rather bulky in form, so other students called him a "dumb ox." But his slowness masked a brilliant intellect. In 1239 he went to the University of Naples where he joined the Dominican order. His family was upset over this, not because they did not want Thomas to be a monk, but because they did not want him to be a poor, mendicant monk. His mother had her sights on the Benedictines, possibly hoping he would become abbot of Monte Casino. His older brothers, leading a company of soldiers, captured him on the road and hauled him home, and he was confined in a castle for two years to get over his idea of being a poor monk. Eventually the family relented, and their twenty-year-old son rejoined the Dominicans.

Aquinas later held a chair of theology at the University of Paris and spent his life as a teacher, writer, and preacher there and in other centers of learning. About 1266 he began the work that would make him famous and shape Catholic theology for the next seven centuries, the *Summa Theologiae*. In it, he carefully distinguished between faith and reason, and he marshaled arguments from reason to prove the existence of God, as well as his eternal nature and goodness. Aquinas also wrote prayers and hymns that are still used in Catholic liturgy.

In 1272, while saying Mass, Aquinas had a vision that made all his learning and writing pale before the truths of what was revealed to him. The ecstatic experience convinced him that all he had written to date was "so much straw," and he left the *Summa Theologiae* unfinished. Two years later at about age fifty, he died.

PRAYER

Thomas, help me keep a balance between my head and my heart. While formal learning and intellectual development are important, I pray that I never consider visionary and heartfelt experiences to be second-best. God reveals himself in both ways, and I ask that both my head and my heart will be open to divine truths.

DEVOTIONAL PRACTICE

Here is a ritual to express the importance of the heart's knowledge to complement the knowledge of the head:

Gather a handful of straw or dried grass and carry it to a hilltop or up a mountain on a windy day. Consider how the vital life force has disappeared from the dried stalks of grass. They are now just husks, empty of the energy that once made them green. Reflect on how the same can happen to us if the inner greenness and warmth of the heart dry up. Realize how necessary it is for the heart to warm the intellect to keep it from becoming dry and brittle with cold, lifeless thoughts. Then wait for the wind to pick up as it acknowledges your sentiments (it will!), and then toss the straw into the air and let the wind carry it off.

ST. THOMAS BECKET

"Murder in the cathedral."

1118–1170

DECEMBER 29

Thomas Becket's parents were both of Norman descent. His father was the sheriff of London. After studying at the University of Paris and becoming a lawyer in London, Becket joined the household staff working for the Archbishop of Canterbury. In 1154 he became a deacon, and then the same year archdeacon of Canterbury. A bright young man, Becket was quickly climbing the political ladder in medieval England. The following year, Henry II appointed him chancellor. He was now the most powerful man in England next to the king. He enjoyed the lavish lifestyle, entertained sumptuously, and led his own troops on a campaign in France. Becket seemed to fit the powerful, aristocratic structure perfectly. Most important of all, he enjoyed the confidence of Henry.

In 1162 Becket became Archbishop of Canterbury (after a quick ordination to the priesthood), and at once changed his manner of living. He dispensed with the lavish entertainments and contented himself with simplicity and austerity. He also began to fall out of favor with Henry when they clashed over the Constitution of Clarendon, a statement giving the king rights and privileges over the clergy, essentially depriving them of their own courts and the right to petition Rome when disputes arose between the Church and the government. In effect, the clergy would be answerable to the king, rather than to the pope.

As the controversy heated up, Becket escaped to France in 1164 and stayed in a Cistercian monastery. In 1170 Louis VII of France mediated a reconcilation between the two men, and Becket returned to England. But the peace was short-lived. Soon the two were at odds again over privileges Becket demanded as Archbishop of Canterbury. Then, in one of his famous outbursts of rage, Henry made the comment that he wished someone would rid him of this troublesome cleric. Four knights took him up on his word, waited for Becket in the cathedral, and bludgeoned him brutally with swords, spilling his blood and brains over the floor.

The murder shocked people all over Europe. In 1173 the pope declared Thomas Becket a saint, and the following year Henry II did public penance for the archbishop's death.

PRAYER

Thomas, give me the courage to stand up for what I know is right and just. Help me not to rely too heavily on politically and financially powerful people, especially when their views and values clash with my own.

DEVOTIONAL PRACTICE

Places can be deceptive. At one time in history, a church or cathedral was a place of refuge for a person pursued by the authorities. You could always "seek sanctuary" in the peace, calm, and cleanliness of a recognized sanctuary. But the custom is not always honored, and in the case of Thomas Becket, an archbishop was not always safe even in his own cathedral.

Conversely, places that appear dirty, violent, and chaotic might be places of grace: a slummy street; a cluttered, vacant lot; a dangerous-looking alley; or a block running through the worst neighborhoods of a city. These can be places where the Spirit is alive and well and nurturing the people who live or work there.

As a devotional practice ask the Spirit to make its workings known to you when you pass places that seem "unsanctified." Ask for the faith to believe that the Spirit works in strange ways, even in these unlikely places. Offer a prayer for the people whose lives are vulnerable and threatened there that they might be receptive to the strength and grace of the Spirit.

ST. THOMAS MORE

"Dreamer of Utopia."

1478–1535

JUNE 22

In 1505 Thomas More married and settled down to the genteel life of a writer, scholar, civil servant, lawyer, husband, and father. He and his wife Jane had four children, and their home became one of the fashionable intellectual salons in Renaissance England. In 1616 he began writing *Utopia*, his fantasy about an imaginary land where reason, harmony, and goodwill ruled and where citizens avoided most of the sufferings and hardships of ordinary society. More also wrote poetry, history, prayers, and devotional books, and he translated Latin classics. It was a good life.

In 1521 More was knighted, and eight years later he became lord chancellor to the King, Henry VIII. It was during this time that Henry's marital frustrations led to the crisis that would split the Church in England. Fearing he would have no heir by his wife, Catherine of Aragon, Henry sought a divorce to marry Anne Boleyn. To be official, the divorce and remarriage would require Rome's blessing. The pope, however, was not compliant.

In 1532 More resigned as lord chancellor in order to separate himself from the political realignments and ethical compromises that were necessary to stay on the king's good side. He retired to his home in Chelsea, relieved that he could devote himself to the scholarly life to which he was more temperamentally suited than the world of royal politics.

When Henry passed the Act of Succession to legalize his offspring by his marriage to Boleyn, More refused to sign because of the oath it contained. He remained silent. In 1534 he was imprisoned in the Tower of London, where the new lord chancellor, Cromwell, asked him to comment on the Act of Supremacy, a law making Henry the head of the Church in England. Again More was silent.

Outraged because he could not get the support of one of the most famous men in Europe (and a former friend), Henry ordered More to be put to death, substituting simple beheading for the usual, and more painful, death by being hanged, drawn, and quartered. On the day of his execution More blessed the executioner, joked with the lieutenant, offered prayers for the people of London, and died claiming that he was still "the king's good servant—but God's first."

PRAYER

Thomas, give me the insight to see how society could be made better by me each day by living out my ideals, even though it is not always easy to do this. Share with me the courage you had to face your king, friends, family, even death rather than compromise what you truly believed.

DEVOTIONAL PRACTICE

Thomas More dreamed of an ideal land free from the corruption and suffering common to human society. He did not, however, let his dreams and ideals blind him to the realities of life. In the spirit of More, seek to balance your ideals with the realities of your life, and use the following ritual to impress upon yourself how delicate the balance can be.

Buy a small, old-fashioned scale, composed of a stand and a crossbar with a dish hanging on each end. Fill one dish with coins and the other with small stones so that they are in balance. Let the coins represent society, and the stones represent the eternal values that inspire you. Each evening reflect on your decisions and actions during the day, and decide whether you upheld the balance. If not, remove a coin or a stone appropriately. Replace it in the morning, with the intention to live with more balance in the coming day.

ST. THOMAS OF VILLANOVA

"An advocate of the poor and the discouraged."

1488–1555

SEPTEMBER 22

Thomas was born in Castille near the town of Villanueva de los Infantes, from which he gets his name, Villanova. Although he was absentminded and suffered from a poor memory all his life, he was a good student, received the highest university degrees, joined the Augustinian friars, and became a priest in 1518. Over the course of his professional life, he was chaplain to Emperor Charles V and the archbishop of Valencia, a post he held for eleven years.

When he became archbishop in 1545, Thomas used the great authority he enjoyed to fund services for the poor, particularly destitute orphans and poor mothers. During his tenure, it is said, no young mother or married woman was without help in the form of food, clothing, shelter, and money. Indeed, several hundred poor people came daily to the diocesan doors to receive a meal, a glass of wine, and a small monetary handout.

An ecclesiastical abuse that Thomas attempted, but failed, to totally reform was the treatment of newly converted Moors, or Moriscos. During the years when the Spanish Inquisition was at its height, great pressure was put on the Moorish population of Spain to become Catholics. Many did so under duress. Others chose to do so, but found Catholic ways so alien to their own cultural heritage that they were unable to observe them. The Inquisition had authority over lapsed and heretical Catholics, so many Moriscos discovered that joining the Catholic religion put them in jeopardy of suffering many of the abuses of the Church's Inquisitors. Thomas created a college for the children of new converts, and set up funds to train priests especially for working with Moorish Catholics.

Although Thomas did not go to the Council of Trent, the convocation called in response to the Protestant Reformation to correct the worst abuses of the Church and institute reforms, he made two sensible suggestions, neither of which was adopted. He argued that bishops should be chosen only from priests who are native to the diocese they will serve, and that there should be no switching of bishops from one diocese to another. Thomas's strong belief was in the intimate relationship between a bishop and his region, his people, and their particular needs and concerns.

In 1555 Thomas suffered heart pains and realized his death was near. In typical fashion, he distributed all his personal money to the poor and gave his belongings to his college, except for his bed, which he bequeathed to the prison to be used by prisoners. He did, however, ask the jailer if he might "borrow" the bed until he died. On September 8, Thomas of Villanova passed away, and the jailer claimed the bed.

PRAYER

Thomas, I need to be more accepting of people who do not always live up to their commitments, just as you took compassion on new converts who found it hard to practice the Catholic faith. Not everyone who falls short is a hypocrite. Show me the ways to practice patience and compassion toward those who fail and toward myself as well when I fail to live up to my commitments.

DEVOTIONAL PRACTICE

People lose money every day—some by spending or investing foolishly, others because they drop it on the ground. When you find a coin on the ground and pick it up, consider it a sign that you should be more charitable toward the poor, who can lose money through no fault of their own, just like the rest of us. Pick up the coin, and resolve to give a contribution of greater worth to charity or a homeless person that very day.

ST. THORFINN

"Poems for the dead."

C. 1285

JANUARY 8

In the 1330s the Cistercian monks near Bruges in Flanders were doing some construction on their abbey when it became necessary to open the tombs in the chapel. One sarcophagus gave off a remarkably sweet odor, and when the stone coffin was opened, it turned out to be the remains of a Norwegian bishop who had died in the monastery over fifty years before. His name was Thorfinn.

The abbot inquired about the bishop, and found an old monk named Walter de Muda who remembered him. In fact, De Muda had written a poem about Thorfinn and hung it in the crypt over the coffin. The monks found the parchment on which the poem was written, and it had not weathered or aged over the half century. Thinking that these omens were too striking to ignore, the abbot asked De Muda to write up his reminiscences about the bishop.

It seems that Thorfinn had been part of the Agreement of Tønsberg, in 1277, in which the Norwegian king, Magnus VI, and the Archbishop of Nidaros worked out privileges for the clergy and monks in that area of Norway. A succeeding king reneged on the agreement and banished the archbishop and two other bishops, one of them Thorfinn.

Thorfinn suffered many hardships during his exile, including shipwreck, and ended up in Flanders, where he lived at the Cistercian monastery. He may have been a Cistercian himself, as there was a Cistercian monastery near Nidaros. Thorfinn made a pilgrimage to Rome at one point, returned to Flanders in poor health, and realized he was dying. He distributed what possessions he had to his mother, brothers, sisters, and a few religious communities that he favored. Since his mother was still alive in an era when people tended to die young, Thorfinn himself might have been a young man when he died.

PRAYER

Thorfinn, your story would have been lost to the world had it not been for the miraculous omens that surrounded your burial in the monastic crypt. Remind me how important it is to remember the deceased, particularly friends and family members who have passed on. They are among the ancestors, the saints, the holy ones in eternity, and I should honor their memories and call upon them when in need.

DEVOTIONAL PRACTICE

In many cultures the ancestors are honored as if they are still among the living. In a way, honoring the saints is a similar practice. But we do not need to limit our devotion to people who died several centuries ago. It is comforting and actually conducive to our well-being to be mindful of the dead we have known in this life.

In the spirit of old Walter de Muda, write a poem for each person in your life who has passed on. You might collect these poems in a special journal or folder. Occasionally, perhaps on the person's birthday or death day, or a day that was important to the two of you, read the poem and spend time communing with the person's spirit, asking for advice and expressing your continuing love.

ST. VALÉRY

"Being on good terms with birds and insects."

D. C. 622

APRIL 1

Valéry was born in the mountains of Auvergne and tended sheep as a small boy. Eager for knowledge, he asked a local tutor to instruct him in the alphabet, and he read and memorized the Psalms. One day on a visit to a monastery with his uncle, he refused to leave. He got his way, and stayed primarily to study. When he got older, he left and wandered around a bit looking for the spiritual teacher who would satisfy his needs. Valéry found him in the great St. Columban, the Irish missionary who established several important monasteries across Europe. Valéry stayed with Columban at Luxeuil until the monks were expelled by the local rulers.

While still a novice at Luxeuil, Valéry was working a section of the monastic gardens during a time when the area was being ravaged by insects. All the vegetables were destroyed except in his plot of land. Columban recognized the hand of God in this and decided to let Valéry make his vows early.

After the monks' expulsion, Valéry and a companion began to preach in the northwestern area of France, but they decided to give it up to be hermits. The call to a life of solitude and contemplation was strong in both of them. They settled near the mouth of the Somme. Soon other hermits began to build their huts in the same area to be near Valéry, and he eventually organized them into a community.

One of the inconveniences of having others around, however, was that Valéry could not always feed the birds peacefully when they came to perch on his shoulder and hand. On many occasions, he would have to tell visitors to leave him and the birds alone. "Let the innocent creatures eat their meal in peace," he would admonish.

Valéry's reputation lived on after he died. Two French towns were named after him: Valéry-sur-Somme and Valéry-en-Caux. Four hundred years later, William the Conqueror, about to embark on his famous invasion of England from the French coast, had Valéry's body dug up and displayed for veneration in the hopes that the saint would bring him a favorable wind. The rest is history, and Valéry became one of the many patron saints of sailors.

PRAYER

Valéry, both birds and insects are part of God's creation, with a right to be here as much as human beings. Yet we cannot always live together in peace. I pray that I may always respect the creatures with whom I share the planet, even though they are not all my favorites.

DEVOTIONAL PRACTICE

Life and death, creation and destruction, are part of the great cycle of life. We all slap mosquitoes, spray ants, and kill flies when we have to. These acts could be done in what we might call a "sacred manner"—namely, by acknowledging the victims as fellow creatures who play an important role in the great web of life. The soil that grows our food is made up of the dead bodies of countless insects and bugs. Many of the birds that bring us so much pleasure feed on insects. Everything is connected.

As a devotional practice, try not to kill insects if at all possible. You can trap a spider under a glass or cup, hold it in with a piece of paper or cardboard, and release it outdoors. When you must take steps to protect yourself from insects, do so with a prayer of respect that acknowledges their role in the universe. When you kill an insect, say, "Little bug, forgive me, but I must send you back to our Creator."

ST. VERONICA

"Carrier of a sacred cloth."

FIRST CENTURY

JULY 12

Veronica was one of the women who accompanied Jesus along the route to Calvary. When she saw him suffering under the weight of the cross, she offered him a cloth to wipe his face. The imprint of his sweat and blood remained on the cloth. Tradition tells us that Veronica kept the cloth because she saw in it the true image of Jesus' face. It has been suggested that the name Veronica is a variation or composite of "ver" (true) and "icon" (image). No matter how accurate the impression on the cloth appeared to be, Veronica knew that it was an imprint of the face of Jesus of Nazareth.

Like so many people in the Gospel stories, Veronica is not very well known, other than that the teachings and healings of Jesus changed her life. Indeed, the really remarkable "impression" left by the man from Galilee is not on a cloth but on the minds, hearts, and souls of the people who met him. Jesus' continuing ability to impress his values and grace upon the lives of generations who lived after him is testimony to the divine and eternal truths he represents. Love, forgiveness, compassion, and service can make a lasting impression on all those we meet when we too embody them in our daily lives.

PRAYER

Veronica, show me the way to carry the image of Jesus with me in my daily life. Help me to demonstrate the same compassion you showed on the way to Calvary when you wiped Jesus' face with a cloth.

Buy a small cloth, such as a handkerchief, and bless it as a token of your commitment to live the values that Jesus taught. Then take the cloth and press it against the face on a statue or painting of Jesus to get a spiritual (not literal) impression. As you hold it there for a few moments, make a dedication to the spirit of St. Veronica that you will treasure this cloth and honor it in special ways because it has the impression of Jesus' face on it. Carry the cloth, or use it on an altar or shrine as a testimony that you will live out the eternal values of the Gospel.

ST. VINCENT DE PAUL

"The courses of human suffering."

C. 1580–1660

SEPTEMBER 27

Vincent de Paul was attracted to the comfortable life. He grew up in a large family that maintained a small farm, where Vincent, his parents, three brothers, and two sisters worked hard. Privileged to go to school, Vincent was ordained at age twenty in 1600, and he saw before him a life of comfort and ease. He planned to have assignments, friends, and activities that would give him a place of honor as a priest in Catholic France.

But in 1605 he went to Marseilles to claim a legacy that had been left to him, and on the return he was captured by pirates and sold into slavery in Algeria. Within two years he escaped and returned to France. The experience, however, moved him deeply, and although he continued to enjoy the plush life of a priest, he was destined to cast his lot with unfortunate and displaced people.

In 1609 de Paul was chaplain to Queen Margaret of Valois and enjoyed an income from a small abbey. In 1613 he became tutor in the house of Count de Gondi who was the general supervisor of galley slaves. That same year he devoted a great deal of his ministry to the slaves, and by 1619 he was chaplain to slaves waiting to be shipped to foreign countries. His life of comfort and luxury had acquired a hard edge. Moved by the human suffering he encountered in his work, he founded a congregation, known as the Vincentians and Lazarists, to care for the spiritual lives of French peasants.

From then on, de Paul was involved in ministries to the disadvantaged, sick, and homeless. He set up organizations to care for the poor, established hospitals and orphanages, ransomed slaves from north Africa, and founded relief organizations to get food and supplies to disaster areas. He also established seminaries to train priests to carry on this work. In 1633 de Paul and Louise de Marillac founded the Sisters of Charity, an order of nuns engaged in the same type of ministries. Throughout his busy life, de Paul found time to write on spiritual topics and to continue to move in royal and aristocratic circles. Indeed, much of the funding for his projects came from wealthy benefactors. Yet in his heart he was still a peasant, although privileged to live and work in ways that most men and women from the rural countryside could never dream of.

De Paul died peacefully in his chair at age eighty. Today the Vincent de Paul Societies around the world continue his work of caring for the poor and suffering. He is the patron of all charitable work.

PRAYER

Vincent, I pray that when I enjoy the good things of life, I will not let them blind me to the misery and suffering of others. I ask that there always be time and energy in my life to do good works for the less fortunate.

DEVOTIONAL PRACTICE

An obvious devotional practice to honor the spirit and work of Vincent de Paul is to contribute used clothing to the Vincent de Paul Societies that have offices in most major cities or to a similar charity if there is none where you live. But to reap more spiritual energy from your contribution, both for yourself and the individuals who will receive your clothing, do the following:

Gather the articles of clothing you intend to contribute and wear them one more time. Be mindful while wearing them that you are giving them away. As in saying good-bye to an old friend, be respectful and loving toward the clothing. And as you wear the clothing, offer prayers, blessings, and good wishes for the men or women who will wear them next.

ST. VINCENT PALLOTTI

"Be holy in the world."

1795–1850

JANUARY 22

Vincent Pallotti, a priest working in Rome in the first half of the nineteenth century, had set up a school to train agriculturalists in the new methods of farming and livestock production. Pallotti's own father was a grocer, and even though Vincent's first priestly assignment was an academic position at the University of Rome, his heart seems to have been with the working-class people like his family and the neighbors he had grown up with. In time he devoted himself solely to an active pastoral mission among working people, especially to provide them with classes and training programs.

Pallotti's programs included, in addition to agricultural training, classes for market gardeners, joiners, shoemakers, tailors, and coachmen. Not only did he want working people to know the latest methods in their trade and the most effective means of managing their financial resources, he also wanted people to take pride in what they did. He once wrote to a teacher who was thinking of joining the Trappists: "You are not cut out for the silence and austerities of Trappists and hermits. Be holy in the world, in your social relationships, in your work and your leisure, in your teaching. . . . Holiness is simply to do God's will, always and everywhere."

In 1835 Pallotti's work became formally institutionalized in the Society of Catholic Apostolate, an organization whose members included priests, nuns, and laypeople. Inspired by Pallotti, the Catholic Apostolate became involved in education, working with the poor, preaching, and always, as he wisely pointed out, bringing a sense of the sacred into one's daily work whatever that might be.

"Catholic Action," as it came to be known, calls for its members, whether religious or lay, to make a difference in the world.

Pallotti spent his career helping the poor, often giving them his own clothing so that he came home partly naked, and often taking risks to help people reform their lives. On one occasion, he dressed as an old woman to gain admittance to the sick room of a man who had threatened to shoot the first priest who came near. Pallotti got near and convinced the ailing man to reconcile his life with God. Pallotti's reputation as a confessor, counselor, exorcist, and healer spread throughout Rome, and he was in great demand until he died at age fifty-five. As a colleague said of him, "He did all that he could do; as for what he couldn't do—well, he did that too."

PRAYER

Vincent, give me the vision to find in my daily work the opportunity to praise God and serve his people. In whatever ways I can, I pray that I might inspire others to take pride in what they do, compliment them, and make them feel worthy of God's grace.

DEVOTIONAL PRACTICE

Find some small object or tool that can serve as a symbol of what you do for a living—for example, a pencil, hammer, broom, screwdriver, book, needle, soap, plastic glove. Choose some time to dedicate and bless this symbol in a private but formal manner. For example, bless it with water or incense, put it on an altar for three days, burn a candle beside it. Write a short prayer or poem honoring the object or tool. As you go about your daily work, recall this ritual and be mindful of how the work you do is pleasing to God and a service to others.

ST. VITUS

"Divine performer."

D. C. 300

JUNE 15

Vitus, the only son of a Sicilian senator, became a Christian at age twelve and began to perform miraculous healings. When he healed the withered hand of a local judge, the Sicilian governor called him before the authorities to discover where his miraculous powers were coming from. Vitus replied that he was filled with the Holy Spirit, whereupon an attempt was made to get him to renounce his new faith. No arguments or threats, however, would persuade the young boy to reject what he believed. Since it did not seem safe to remain living in Sicily where he was under suspicion from non-Christian authorities, Vitus and two companions—Modestus, his tutor, and Crescentia, his servant—fled to Rome. On the way, an eagle brought food to them.

Things were hardly better in Rome. Vitus cast an evil spirit out of the emperor Diocletian's son, which brought him a great deal of notoriety. He became something of a celebrity and was expected to sacrifice to the Roman gods. Vitus refused, saying that his power did not come from those gods. Authorities then assumed that his power was sorcery, coming from some evil spirit, so he was imprisoned and tortured. Boiling oil failed to harm him, and a wild lion went tame in his presence. Then as the attempts to torture him continued, a storm arose, accompanied by earthquakes. Local temples shook and collapsed. The emperor felt he was being overcome by the shenanigans of a child. In the confusion, Vitus and his companions were led away by an angel, but eventually they were captured in another town and martyred.

Traditions of honoring Vitus go back into the earliest centuries, and over time he has become the patron saint of dancers, comedians, actors, epileptics, and people afflicted with chorea, also called St. Vitus' dance. He is also a protector against storms.

PRAYER

Vitus, I can imagine that you enjoyed your healing "performances" and found them fun. You became the patron saint of actors and probably had a natural talent as a child to entertain others when you displayed the gifts God gave you. Help me to take enjoyment in the talents I have and not be shy about them.

DEVOTIONAL PRACTICE

In the spirit of St. Vitus, the patron of dancers and actors, express your gratitude for whatever talents God has given you by dancing. You can use some music that you enjoy, or make your own beat and rhythm with a small frame drum or rattle. Find a time when you are alone (so you need not feel self-conscious), and dance your gratitude by letting the music or the sounds of the drum or rattle move your body. Feel in the movements of your body the same kind of energy that you bring when you use your talents and skills, whatever they may be. Enjoy the dancing, just as you enjoy your other talents.

ST. WILLIAM OF YORK

"Nothing seems to go right . . . or easy."

D. 1154

JUNE 8

The career of William of York had so many twists and turns, rises and falls that it is somewhat amazing that he succeeded to sainthood. His father, a count, was treasurer to King Henry I, and his mother was the half sister of King Stephen, so William was born into the ruling families of England. After studies and ordination, he became treasurer of the church in York, and in 1140 he was elected archbishop. That's when his troubles began.

Members of the powerful Cistercian and Augustinian orders opposed William's election, accusing him of simony, sexual misconduct, and being too much under the influence of the king. The archbishop of Canterbury denied him consecration as bishop, and so the case went to Rome, where the pope decided in William's favor. A papal legate was sent with the pallium, the official vestment that signified William's authority. Then through his own procrastination, William failed to make the preparations to formally receive the legate. While William tarried, the pope died, and the legate went back to Rome.

The next pope, Eugene III, a Cistercian, sided with the opposition and suspended William. Outraged, William's followers attacked Fountains Abbey, where Murdac, a friend of the pope's, was abbot. They burned the farms and physically mutilated the archdeacon. In retaliation, the pope deposed William altogether and supported Murdac, the abused abbot, as the next archbishop of York.

William quietly retired to Winchester, where for the next six years he lived a life of penance and asceticism, in contrast to the luxuries that he had enjoyed as an influential churchman. In 1153, Pope Eugenius and Murdac died, and the new pope reappointed William as archbishop. The following year, he triumphantly returned to York, but his troubles were not over. So many people turned out to welcome him that the bridge on which they were standing collapsed, throwing his supporters into the river. None were harmed. William forgave the factions that had opposed him over the years and promised to make amends for the destruction caused by his followers at Fountains Abbey, but one month after his installation as bishop, he took ill and died.

PRAYER

William, your career as a churchman proves how God can throw obstacles in front of us, testing our resolve and patience. Help me when things always seem to go wrong to stay optimistic and to believe that what happens is God's will. I pray that I will learn from my adversities and grow spiritually even when setbacks and misfortunes challenge my faith.

DEVOTIONAL PRACTICE

Sometimes we don't keep our luck in perspective, often thinking we have more bad luck than good. At the end of a day when things really seemed to go wrong, take a few minutes to tally the day's events. Make two columns, listing in one the things that went wrong, in the other the things that went well. You might discover that there were more things in the second column than in the first. But even if not, try to look at quality rather than quantity. Sometimes, in retrospect, the few, small things that went well on a bad day actually carry more importance, meaning, and grace because they were islands of sanity or humor when everything else seemed to be crashing down around you.

ST. WULFSTAN

"But for the grace of God."

C. 1008–1095

JANUARY 19

When William the Conqueror came to power in England in 1066, he brought with him a Norman-French entourage of knights, nobles, bishops, clerics, workers, and servants. Never again would English culture be primarily Anglo-Saxon and Celtic. The new Norman influence would be seen in food, language, clothing, religion, government, and many nooks and crannies of English culture. Wulfstan of Worcester was the only Anglo-Saxon bishop allowed to remain in office when William replaced all the others with Normans.

Wulfstan stood out from other churchmen in many ways. A bishop's place in medieval society was among the noble and aristocratic elements. In fact, bishops owned extensive property and estates, and commanded armies. When Wulfstan gave a feast, his steward would invite the rich and powerful, who would arrive and take their places in the grand hall. But then Wulfstan would enter at the head of a crowd of peasants whom he had personally invited. Dukes and nobles were often outraged to sit at the same table with people they considered rabble.

Wulfstan also gave clothes, food, and baths to the poor. He spoke to them in English about the Latin scriptures that they could not read. When he discovered that the children of the poor were not being baptized because parents could not pay the fees to the local priests, he stood before the church doors and baptized the babies of anyone who showed up. Sometimes he stood there from morning until evening, and people came all day long to have their children baptized.

In the port of Bristol, native English who had fallen into debt were being sold as slaves and prostitutes to the Vikings, who were then holding key ports in Ireland. Government policies had failed to curb the nefarious trade, so Wulfstan went personally to Bristol, lived with the people waiting to be shipped off, and preached and ministered to them. Eventually, his efforts paid off, and the slave trade was abolished in Bristol.

Wulfstan was bishop for thirty-two years, then died of an illness in Worcester, the city he had helped to make a more decent place to live.

PRAYER

Wulfstan, I pray that I will always find a place in my heart, and in my life, to assist those who are less fortunate than I am. I also ask that I realize that "but for the grace of God," my life could have brought me to the same circumstances.

DEVOTIONAL PRACTICE

One gets the impression that "respectable" people always felt a bit uncomfortable around Wulfstan because they never knew what he would say or do next to challenge their so-called respectable ways. His mind and heart understood the less fortunate members of society. It is important to be able to identify with people whose lives are much harder than our own.

As a meditational exercise, choose a type of person you consider less fortunate than yourself—such as a homeless person, a prostitute, a petty thief, a deadbeat dad, an alcoholic, a drug pusher, a drug-addicted teenager. On a piece of paper list the twenty-four hours of the day. Then put yourself into that person's shoes and visualize walking through the day. Write next to each hour what you imagine the person would be doing then. It doesn't matter how accurate you are. The important thing is to gather a sense of rapport with another human being as he or she rises in the morning, dresses, bathes or doesn't bathe, eats or doesn't eat three times a day, talks to others, encounters the seasons and weather, goes to sleep, dreams, and so forth. When you finish accounting for each hour, write a prayer or blessing at the bottom of the page for the people caught in the daily life you have just described.

CALENDAR OF SAINTS' DAYS

JANUARY

  2: BASIL THE GREAT

  3: GENEVIEVE
    JOSEPH MARY TOMMASI

  4: ELIZABETH ANN SETON

  5: JOHN NEPOMUCENE NEUMANN

  8: THORFINN

10: PETER ORSEOLO

11: ETHNE AND FEDELM

15: ITA

17: ANTHONY OF EGYPT

19: WULFSTAN

20: SEBASTIAN

21: AGNES

22: VINCENT PALLOTTI

24: FRANCIS DE SALES

25: PAUL OF TARSUS
    PHILIP THE APOSTLE

28: CANAIRE
    THOMAS AQUINAS

30: HYACINTHA MARISCOTTI
    MUCIAN MARY WIAUX

31: JOHN BOSCO
    MAEDOC

FEBRUARY

1: BRIGID
   HENRY MORSE

2: CATHERINE DE RICCI
   JOAN DE LESTONNAC

3: BLAISE
   IA OF CORNWALL

4: JOHN DE BRITTO

6: DOROTHY

7: APOLLONIA

16: GILBERT OF SEMPRINGHAM

22: MARGARET OF CORTONA

27: ANNE LINE

MARCH

1: DAVID

3: NON OF WALES

7: PERPETUA AND FELICITA

10: JOHN OGILVIE

12: MAXIMILIAN

16: ABRAHAM KIDUNAIA

17: PATRICK

19: JOSEPH

20: CUTHBERT

21: ENDA

APRIL

1: VALÉRY

2: FRANCIS OF PAOLA
MARGARET CLITHEROW
MARY OF EGYPT

3: AGAPE, CHIONIA, AND IRENE

4: BENEDICT THE MOOR
ISIDORE OF SEVILLE

7: AYBERT
JOHN BAPTIST DE LA SALLE

10: PATERNUS

14: ARDALION

16: BERNADETTE
DROGO
MAGNUS OF ORKNEY

17: STEPHEN HARDING

21: ANSELM OF CANTERBURY
CONRAD OF PARZHAM

26: STEPHEN OF PERM

29: CATHERINE OF SIENA

MAY

1: RICHARD PAMPURI

10: ANTONINO OF FLORENCE
SOLANGE

12: DOMINIC OF THE CAUSEWAY

13: JULIAN OF NORWICH

14: BONIFACE OF TARSUS
HALWARD

16: BRENDAN

25: BEDE THE VENERABLE

30: JOAN OF ARC

31: MARY, THE MOTHER OF JESUS
MECHTILDIS OF EDELSTETTEN

JUNE

3: CHARLES LWANGA
KEVIN

4: FRANCIS CARACCIOLO

5: BONIFACE OF GERMANY

8: WILLIAM OF YORK

9: COLUMBA

12: PAULA FRASSINETTI

13: ANTHONY OF PADUA

15: VITUS

16: LUTGARDIS

17: ALBERT CHMIELOWSKI

22: JOHN FISHER
THOMAS MORE

24: JOHN THE BAPTIST

29: PETER THE APOSTLE

JULY

1: JOHN GUALBERT

3: THOMAS THE APOSTLE

5: ATHANASIUS OF ATHOS

6: MARIA GORETTI

12: VERONICA

14: CAMILLUS DE LELLIS

15: BONAVENTURE

22: MARY MAGDALEN
PHILIP EVANS

23: BRIDGET OF SWEDEN

24: CHRISTINA THE ASTONISHING

25: JAMES THE GREATER THE APOSTLE

29: MARTHA

31: IGNATIUS LOYOLA

AUGUST

1: PETER JULIAN EYMARD

4: JOHN VIANNEY

8: DOMINIC

10: LAWRENCE OF ROME

11: ATTRACTA
CLARE

14: MAXIMILIAN KOLBE

18: HELEN

19: JOHN EUDES

20: BERNARD OF CLAIRVAUX

23: ROSE OF LIMA

25: LOUIS, KING OF FRANCE

26: ELIZABETH BICHIER DES ANGES

27: MONICA

28: AUGUSTINE OF HIPPO
MOSES THE BLACK

30: MARGARET WARD

31: AIDAN

SEPTEMBER

1: FIACRE

3: GREGORY THE GREAT

4: IDA OF HERZFELD
MARINUS
ROSE OF VITERBO

7: ANASTASIUS THE FULLER

9: CIARAN
PETER CLAVER

10: NICHOLAS OF TOLENTINO

12: GUY OF ANDERLECHT

13: JOHN CHRYSOSTOM

14: NOTBURGA OF RATTENBURG

15: CATHERINE OF GENOA

17: HILDEGARD OF BINGEN
ROBERT BELLARMINE

18: JOHN MASSIAS
JOSEPH OF CUPERTINO

19: EMILY DE RODAT

20: EUSTACE

21: MATTHEW THE APOSTLE

22: THOMAS OF VILLANOVA

23: ADAMNAN

25: FINDBARR OF CORK

26: COSMAS AND DAMIAN
THERESE COUDERC

27: VINCENT DE PAUL

29: RHIPSIME

30: JEROME

OCTOBER

1: TERESA OF LISIEUX

4: FRANCIS OF ASSISI

6: MARY FRANCES

7: OSITH

8: THAIS

13: EDWARD THE CONFESSOR

15: TERESA OF AVILA

16: GALL
MARGARET MARY ALACOQUE

18: LUKE

20: BERTILLA BOSCARDIN

21: HILARION

22: PHILIP OF HERACLEA

28: JUDE THE APOSTLE

NOVEMBER

2: MARCIAN

3: MALACHY
MARTIN DE PORRES

4: CHARLES BORROMEO

6: ILLTUD OF WALES

9: BENEN

11: MARTIN OF TOURS

12: JOSAPHAT

13: FRANCES XAVIER CABRINI

14: LAWRENCE O'TOOLE

15: ALBERT THE GREAT

16: MARGARET OF SCOTLAND

17: HILD
HUGH OF LINCOLN
PHILIPPINE DUCHESNE
ROQUE GONZÁLEZ

18: ODO OF CLUNY

22: CECILIA

23: COLUMBAN

28: CATHERINE LABOURÉ

30: ANDREW THE APOSTLE

DECEMBER

ABOUT THE AUTHOR

Tom Cowan attended a Jesuit seminary and received a Ph.D. in history from St. Louis University. He has been a student and teacher of religions and mysticism since the 1960s. He frequently lectures and conducts workshops nationwide on various aspects of spirituality, Celtic shamanism, dreamwork, and creativity. The author or coauthor of over twenty-five books, he lives in Highland, New York.